BIBLE AND LITERATURE
SERIES

Editor
David M. Gunn

TRADITIONAL SAYINGS IN THE OLD TESTAMENT

A Contextual Study

CAROLE R. FONTAINE

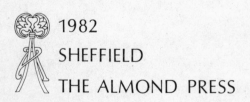
1982
SHEFFIELD
THE ALMOND PRESS

BIBLE AND LITERATURE SERIES, 5

Copyright © 1982 The Almond Press

British Library Cataloguing in Publication Data:

Fontaine, Carole R.
  Traditional sayings in the Old Testament.—
  (Bible and literature series, ISSN 0260-4493; 5)
  1. Bible. O.T.—Criticism and interpretation
  I. Title   II. Series
  221.6'6   BS1115

  ISBN 0-907459-08-0
  ISBN 0-907459-09-9 Pbk

Published by
The Almond Press
P.O. Box 208
Sheffield S10 5DW
England

Printed in Great Britain
by Redwood Burn Limited
Trowbridge, Wiltshire
1982

CONTENTS

APPENDIXES

LIST OF FIGURES

LIST OF TABLES

FOREWARD

Close attention to the internal dynamics of a text, as any literary critic knows, reveals a good deal of information about individual artistry, intentionality and interpretative moves. The value of such study for the understanding of a text has long been accepted as applicable to the study of Sacred Scripture. Growing interest in interdisciplinary approaches, such as those offered by folklore, structuralism, transformational-generative linguistics and semiotics, has added to the library of "methods" available for the refinement of textual study. In this realm, it is possible to bring greater precision to the study of comparative materials (often lacking in the past, as eager scholars swept from one corpus of literature to another, sometimes without sufficient attention to varying cultural contexts), as well as to broaden the range of questions asked of the biblical text itself. Within the fields of folklore and genre studies, methodological approaches which allow for more systematic investigation of the social dimensions of a text - its basic underlying structures, its social intent, its performance and its success in achieving its goal - have given new hope to the beleaguered form critic of wisdom literature in the Hebrew Bible, since it is here that the sharp lack of precise information concerning the life setting (Sitz im Leben) of wisdom forms has impeded a full understanding of the function of wisdom within ancient Israel. While the most "basic" genre of wisdom, the saying, has always been recognized as serving a social function, whether in the Jerusalem court or the "tribes" of Israel, little progress has been made in assessing the actual ways in which a saying might be employed in a social context. The wisdom sayings found collected in the book of Proverbs offer very little scope for such study, since they are simply that - a collection without clear contexts of use. Hence, this study turns to the use of sayings outside the corpus of wisdom literature in order to gain some insight into the function of the saying - wisdom's ambassador-at-large in the "real world" - in Israelite culture. Through the study of models of "proverb performance", that is, the way in which a saying is selected from a given stock of proverbs, applied to a given context and the "rules" by which it is interpreted by its hearers, we begin to see a vital, traditional wisdom which is operant in society at a variety of levels and not simply in the elitist bureaucracies of the court sages and scribes. The functional goal of such traditional wisdom is the restoration of order in society (according to that society's construal of "order") through the use of verbal behaviors rather than physically destructive ones. This biblical model for "conflict resolution" by means of negotiation rather than aggression has an important message for today's world.

This study originally appeared as a dissertation under the direction of Rev. Roland E. Murphy, O. Carm. His patience, insight and sensitivity are, in large measure, responsible for the scope and flexibility of this research, while any defects in execution belong solely to its author. Acknowledgements should also go the members of my doctoral committee (Drs. Lloyd Bailey, Eric Meyers, Harry Partin, and Orval Wintermute) for their helpful comments. Special thanks is also due to Professor Brevard S. Childs at Yale Divinity School, who first introduced me to Israelite wisdom. My colleagues and friends from North Carolina, who are now well-versed in the intricacies of proverb performance, regardless of their interest in the topic, also deserve thanks for their patience and lively interest, especially Rev. Michael Norman Dunbar, James T. Faucette, Cheryl Rubinstein, Cathy Severns, and Claudia Camp. I should also like to thank Dr. David Gunn for his interest and encouragement in this research, as well as my husband Dr. Craig W. Fontaine, for his long-suffering goodwill and most especially, for his word processor. My colleague William C. Robinson, Jr. and my research assistant, Ms. Marcy Bailey-Adams, deserve special thanks for their stimulating comments, suggestions and help with the revisions of my original work.

This work is dedicated to all who seek the way of wisdom and peace in a restless world.

Carole R. Fontaine

Newton Centre, MA
1981

INTRODUCTION

The goal of this study is to present an analysis of the form, style, content, and contextual use of a representative number of traditional sayings which occur in the Old Testament outside the corpus of wisdom literature. Although such sayings are treated in commentaries on the individual books in which they appear, they have never been analyzed from the perspective of their use in context, or their relation to the themes found in the sayings in the wisdom literature. The identification of these traditional sayings will rest on the results of previous wisdom scholarship, but a working definition of the traditional saying will be proposed which reflects both considerations from Old Testament studies and also from paroemiology and folklore, where interest in the use of sayings in society has produced a number of studies which are helpful to the study of the Old Testament saying. Chapter I presents the consensus of Old Testament scholarship on the sayings found in the so-called "historical" and prophetic books. In Chapter II, a survey of paroemiological and folklore studies on the definition, structural study, analysis of form, content, context and function of the proverb and traditional saying is undertaken, stressing those aspects which are of most interest and importance to the understanding of the function of the traditional saying in ancient Israel.

Special attention will be given to the "folk ideas," that is, the unexamined presuppositions of a culture, which underlie the meaning and use of the traditional saying in context, and a comparison will be made between the messages found in the traditional sayings used in context and parallels found in the wisdom sayings, and other ancient Near Eastern materials. Chapter III presents a detailed exegesis of selected passages where "proverb performance" takes place (that is, where there is the purposeful transmission of a traditional saying in an interaction), using models drawn from Old Testament wisdom studies and folklore studies. The passages examined in detail are Jg. 8:2, 8:21; 1 Sam. 16:7; 24:14 (v.13 in English), and 1 Kg. 20:11. Chapter IV attempts to draw conclusions about the patterns of use found in the contextual studies, and suggests a "structure" of proverb performance in the Old Testament. The Appendixes contain analysis charts, a glossary of terms and symbols used in the analysis of proverb performance, and an excursus on proverb performance in the prophetic literature of the Old Testament.

Chapter I

A SURVEY OF SCHOLARLY OPINION ON
THE TRADITIONAL SAYING IN THE OLD TESTAMENT

Old Testament research on the traditional sayings found outside the wisdom literature in the Old Testament has generally been conducted by those scholars whose interest centered, at least in part, around wisdom literature, since the development of the wisdom saying is a topic which naturally leads to a discussion of possible "popular" precursors. The term "traditional saying" has been adopted arbitrarily here to refer to those sayings found outside the wisdom corpus in the Hebrew Bible. They have been given a variety of designations, such as "folk saying," "folk proverb," "popular proverb," "popular saying" and so on.[1] For our purposes in this present chapter, we will follow the descriptive lines set up by previous form critical research: the traditional saying will exhibit fewer signs of "artistic" or literary shaping (i.e., parallel bicola, etc.) than those sayings found in the wisdom books, and authorship is presumed to be "anonymous" although the saying must have achieved currency among the "folk" or given group to become part of its standard proverbial stock.

The "wisdom" interests of those who have studied the traditional saying have, in many respects, determined the methodology used to discuss the sayings, and other considerations, such as use in context, have frequently received less attention than deserved. Research has been hampered, too, by the particular fluidity of application inherent in any saying which achieves currency, and this has remained problematical for studies of both the traditional saying and the wisdom saying. We will begin our discussion of the Old Testament scholarship on the saying by considering the work of Otto Eissfeldt, whose pioneering study on the "māshāl" has served as the point of departure for later works on many of the aspects of the saying, both popular and learned.

2

Chapter I: A Survey of Scholarly Opinion

1. Otto Eissfeldt

Eissfeldt's form critical work on the saying presents a logical starting point for any discussion of the saying, since his attempts to discuss the genre designation of "māshāl" encompassed both the popular saying ("folk proverb") and the wisdom saying. Recognizing that this designation actually covers a wide number of forms in the Old Testament, Eissfeldt attempted to discuss the various meanings of the root, and discover a basic meaning which might have given rise to the various forms found in the Old Testament under the name of "māshāl."[2] For him, the most basic meaning of the root centers around the concept of similarity or similitude (gleichen, gleich sein),[3] and he proceeds to develop a schematization for the development of Old Testament forms from this fundamental understanding (see Fig. 1). Most important for the purpose of this study, Eissfeldt distinguishes between two types of saying found as "mᵉshālîm": the folk proverb (Volkssprichwort), and the wisdom saying (Weisheitsspruch) which arises out of the circle of the wise.[4] While he nowhere addresses himself to the task of giving an exact definition for the folk proverb, Eissfeldt says of the form that it is "known and understood by the folk, who transmit it from generation to generation, without anyone knowing who its author might be ...."[5] This is in contrast to the artistic saying which is authored by the wise. One may infer from this that the following features are operative in Eissfeldt's understanding of the folk proverb: (1) it is current among the folk, often with a long history of transmission; (2) it is comprehensible to the folk; and (3) it is anonymous. In contrast, the wisdom saying ("ein rechter Maschal") reveals itself "through the depth of the thought, and also, the external form of the māshāl is not superficial: [it is] a fixed (feste) form, for which parallelism is customary."[6]

Eissfeldt distinquishes four groups of popular or folk proverbs in the Old Testament, which constitute part of a "proverbial idiom" (sprichwörtlicher Redensarten).[7] The first group is formed by those sayings which are explicitly referred to as "māshāl" in the text; the second consists of those sayings which are introduced by the formula "and therefore they say" or similar introductory words. Eissfeldt further augments his list of folk proverbs by adding those passages which "sound like proverbs," although he recognizes that there is a good deal of subjectivity involved in the

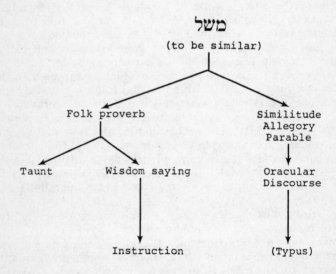

FIGURE 1: Eissfeldt's Development of the Forms of the
"Māshāl" from the Basic Concept of "Similitude"

SOURCE: Otto Eissfeldt, Der Maschal im Alten Testament
(1913), p.43

4

Chapter I: A Survey of Scholarly Opinion

I   Sayings designated as "māshāl" in the text

    1 Sam. 10:12 (19:24)
    1 Sam. 24:13 [14]
    Ezek. 12:22
    Ezek. 18:2 (Jer. 31:29)

II   Sayings introduced by "and therefore they say" or similar formula

Gen. 10:9	Ezek. 9:9
2 Sam. 5:8	Ezek. 18:25,29; 33:17,20
2 Sam. 20:18	Ezek. 33:10
Is. 40:27	Ezek. 37:11
Zeph. 1:12	

III   Passages which "sound like proverbs"

Gen. 16:12	Is. 22:13
Jg. 8:2	Is. 37:3 (66:9; Hos. 13:3)
Jg. 8:21	Jer. 8:20
Jg. 14:18	Jer. 8:22
1 Sam. 16:7	Jer. 12:13
1 Sam. 24:14	Jer. 23:28
(2 Sam. 9:8; 16:9)	Jer. 51:58 (Hab. 2:13)
1 Kg. 18:21	Hos. 8:7
1 Kg. 20:11	

IV   Wisdom sayings which originated as folk proverbs (Volkssprichwort)

Pr. 10:6 (10:11)	Pr. 16:31
Pr. 10:91	Pr. 17:28
Pr. 10:15 (18:11)	Pr. 19:12 (20:2)
Pr. 11:2	Pr. 27:1
Pr. 11:13 (20:19)	Pr. 27:17
Pr. 11:16	Pr. 28:2
Pr. 11:21 (16:5)	Sir. 2:5
Pr. 12:14	Sir. 13:1
Pr. 13:24	Sir. 13:17
Pr. 14:31 (17:5)	Sir. 27:26
Pr. 16:18 (18:12)	(Pr. 26:27; Ecc. 10:8)

TABLE 1: Eissfeldt's Listing of Folk Proverbs Outside Wisdom Literature and Those Incorporated Into the Book of Proverbs

SOURCE: Otto Eissfeldt, Der Maschal im Alten Testament (1913), pp.45-46

selection of such passages. Finally, and perhaps most controversial of all of his classifications, Eissfeldt distinguishes a number of sayings from wisdom materials which he feels originated as old folk proverbs which were later expanded by means of a second line to bring them into the standard form of the wisdom saying (see Table 1).[8]

The presuppositions which underlie the formation of these groups of sayings are open to question, as later scholars, especially H.-J. Hermisson, have pointed out. Neither the designation in the text of a particular saying as a "māshāl," nor the appearance of an introductory formula can be considered sufficient grounds alone for concluding that one is dealing with a <u>folk</u> proverb, with all its implications concerning origins. Eissfeldt himself was aware that designating certain passages as folk proverbs on the basis of their proverbial sound puts the scholar on rather "shaky ground," and it might be added that this is especially true where such determinations are made in a language which is not the scholar's native tongue. The premise which forms the basis for the identification of a folk saying in the wisdom materials - that is, that the "one-line" saying is the evolutionary precursor of the "two-limbed" wisdom saying - is certainly open to debate.[9]

In his discussion of the form, style, and content of the folk proverbs, Eissfeldt observes that they are written mostly in prose, and exhibit little in the way of parallelism.[10] There is no fixed rhythm in the oldest examples of the popular saying, although one may find a type of "intended rhythm" expressed here and there. Further, the occasional examples of alliteration or end rhyme found in the folk proverb should caution the scholar against pushing too vigorously the assignment of these sayings to the category of prose.[11]

In terms of style, Eissfeldt finds the folk proverbs to be short, expressed straightforwardly in clear style. Most often, the message is conveyed through a picture or example which provides an illustration for the hearer. These pictures are drawn from a variety of spheres: animal and plant life (Gen. 16:12, Jer. 23:28, etc.), family life (Is. 37:3), and the military (1 Kg. 20:11). Since there are few examples of the amplified comparisons so common to the wisdom saying, the folk proverb achieves its vividness and conveys its message through the use of the concrete picture which produces the same form (Gestalt) before the eyes of the hearer.[12]

In regard to the content of the folk proverbs, Eissfeldt speaks of the "universal truths of life" which are conveyed by the pictures built up as examples in the saying, without becoming more specific as to what types of common experiential truths are most apt to find expression in the folk saying which are proverbial forms of expression (sprichwörtliche Redensarten), such as Gen. 10:9, Jg. 8:2, and 1 Sam. 24:15, and those which are sayings (Aussprüche) in the proper sense, such as Pr. 11:2, 1 Sam. 24:14, and Jg. 8:21.[13] This distinction, however, is not properly one of content, but rather one of form.

Many supported Eissfeldt's conclusions about the prehistory of the wisdom sayings in the Book of Proverbs, and assumed that the one-line folk proverb was the earlier form which gave rise to the more sophisticated two-line wisdom saying.[14] Recently, however, Eissfeldt's theories about the development of the wisdom saying[15] from the simpler folk saying have come under attack from a variety of critics. Critical examination of Egyptian wisdom materials have undermined the "simple-to-complex" theory of the formation of wisdom genres in general, and H.-J. Hermisson rejects the notion of the popular character of Eissfeldt's list of folk proverbs as it applies to their supposed origin, and finds little evidence of folk proverbs incorporated into the Book of Proverbs.[16] It is to the work of these critics that we now turn.

2. H.-J. Hermisson and André Jolles

In his critique of Eissfeldt's study Hermisson has been heavily influenced by the work of German literary critic André Jolles, whose ground-breaking work on oral and literary forms continues to be a starting place for most modern discussions of genre.[17] In his work, Einfache Formen, Jolles undertakes the ambitious task of differentiating and describing nine archetypal "simple forms" from which all larger literary works are constructed.[18] Starting with a concept of the creative power of language, Jolles conceives of each simple form as the product of a particular type of intellectual orientation (Geistesbeschäftigung). These different ways of perceiving the experience of the world give rise to characteristic genres (through certain "verbal gestures" (Sprachgebärden). Thus, each intellectual orientation finds expression in a "realized simple form" (Gegenwärtige Einfache Form), but the ideal "simple form" typical of each intellectual orientation is capable of being actualized in a variety of ways through a range of different verbal gestures which might be made.[19]

While Jolles' concept of the verbal gesture is often obscure, his method of analysis allows one to distinguish between the ideal generic form which may be actualized, and the way it is actualized in the realized form. Further, his discussion of the function of oral and literary forms in evoking new perceptions of the world in those who have not had similar experiences is a sensitive analysis of the creative power of linguistic expression.[20] Unfortunately, he fails to make explicit his rationale for using different methodologies to discuss the various simple forms (compare, for example, his treatment of "Mythe" which is analyzed in terms of its function, and his discussion of "Sage," which is analyzed in terms of its content), nor does he sufficiently address the possibility of a multiplicity of intellectual orientations existing and overlapping within one person or group, in which case the actualization of any given form would take place by a far more complex process than that which he has outlined.

Jolles takes up his discussion of proverb (Sprichwort) after a critical look at Friedrich Seiler's conception of the saying as an elevated form which circulates among the folk and exhibits a "didactic intention."[21] Currency among the folk becomes one of the chief characteristics of the proverb for Seiler, and although he recognizes that this does not necessarily imply that any given saying must be known by all the folk, Seiler's view of the proverb essentially follows the Neo-Romantic position of the origin of the saying "in den Tiefen der Volksseele."[22] Jolles chooses to stress the point that a saying is never created by a whole people, but rather by an individual. He takes violent exception to the characterization of the saying as primarily didactic,[23] and proceeds to apply his own method of analysis to the study of the saying.

For Jolles, the saying (Spruch) is the simple form which, if actualized in a certain way, produces the proverb (Sprichwort) as its realized simple form. The intellectual orientation which expresses itself in the saying is one in which the diversity of the world is perceived in all its particularity, but is drawn together and juxtaposed, thus providing a way to order experience without degenerating into generalization, abstraction, or particularization.[24] The saying, which draws together the experience of the world into a cohesive, related perception, exhibits a fundamental "compressive" power.[25]

Given his conception of the intellectual processes at work in the actualization of the saying into the proverb, Jolles finds the much cited "didactic character of the saying to be a secondary characteristic." He comments, in opposition to Seiler's statements:

> The Saying (Spruch) is not didactic; it has not didactic character; of itself it has no didactic tendency. We do not mean to say that we do not learn from experience, but rather that in the world of which we are speaking, experience is not conceived as something from which we are supposed to learn. The didactic is typically a beginning, something that serves as a basis for further building - experience, in the form in which the saying captures it, is a conclusion. Experience looks backward, it has a resigned character. The same thing is true of its actualization in the proverb (Sprichwort), which is not a beginning, but a conclusion, a countersignature, and by which it preserves its character as experience.[26]

While Jolles is correct in his recognition that didacticism is not the defining characteristic in the <u>creation</u> of the saying, his failure to differentiate between the processes at work in the formation of saying and its later use, as in a didactic setting, must qualify his observations on the nature of the experience embodied in the proverb. This experience may well represent a "conclusion" to the creator of the proverb, but in a didactic situation the same proverb represents a beginning for the student who hears it. It may well be that the creative, generative process which draws a "conclusion" from diverse experience and embodies it in a saying is the same process which makes the proverb so ideal in didactic settings, since the proverb allows the hearer to appropriate the conclusion without having participated in the actual experience. Further, one might make a case for the statement that the actualization of experience in a proverb, and the proverb itself, is never simply descriptive or observational, for by the very juxtaposition of elements or formulation of conclusions, one has made a kind of judgment as to the relative validity of the concepts involved.[27]

Jolles' faithful attention to such features as style and syntax, which are often dismissed as ornamental rather than constitutive features of the saying, stems from his appreciation of Wilhelm Grimm's statements about "a truth... which, breaking through in a flash, finds a higher expression of itself."[28] The compressed style and syntax, the use of figurative language and poetic devices, and above all, the recognition that a proverb loses its power when paraphrased all lead Jolles to the conclusion that the way in which the saying is actualized into a proverb is not an accidental feature of expression.[29] Rather, ."..the language of the proverb (Sprichwort) is such, that all its separate parts, in their meaning, syntax and stylistic combinations, in their audible movement, stand in defense against each generalization and abstraction."[30]

H.-J. Hermisson has drawn heavily upon Jolles' understanding of the intellectual orientation which underlies the formation of the proverb, especially with regard to the evaluation of the importance of the didactic aspect to the nature of the saying.[31] His major interest falls within the area of investigation of the origin of the sayings found in the Book of Proverbs, and in relation to this, he evaluates Eissfeldt's thesis that many of the sayings originated as or developed from folk proverbs. He accepts the usual formal distinction made between the types of materials in the collection of sayings in the book of Proverbs (i.e., sayings or statement [Aussage] and admonition [Mahnwort]). Then Hermisson observes that "the criteria for a proverb are ... to be sure, negative: it should not be didactic; positive: it should bring a conclusion out of the sum of experience or simply establish a state of affairs, an 'order,' without having given thereby an indication of what a person should or should not do."[32] For this reason, Hermisson is able to rule out the possible origin among the folk for many of the sayings in the Book of Proverbs, since those which are frankly didactic, according to his thinking, must have originated in a wisdom "school" setting.[33]

Hermisson critiques Eissfeldt's categories of folk proverbs and in each case, finds the criteria employed for selection to be less than conclusive. Hermisson is properly skeptical concerning Eissfeldt's acceptance of the textual designation of a statement as a "māshāl" or the appearance of an introductory formula as sufficient grounds for concluding that a passage is indeed a true folk proverb.[34] Concerning those passages which Eissfeldt has concluded to be folk proverbs on the basis of their "proverbial sound," Hermisson insists that closer examination of a passage in its larger context often reveals ample justification for dismissing the saying as a genuine folk proverb.[35] Indeed, he concludes that only the sayings in Jg. 8:21 and 1 Sam. 16:7 exhibit the form of a genuine (echt) proverb, and even here, he still finds cause to doubt their origin among the folk.[36] Hermisson recognizes that his definition of a folk proverb, which combines Jolles' understanding of the nature of a proverb with the necessary origin of the saying among the ever elusive "folk," is hardly identical with Eissfeldt's, of whom he says, "the fleetness of a coined phrase is sufficient for him, and when he thus conceives a proverb in its basic meaning as 'a much spoken word,' his selection in general may be permitted to be justified."[37]

Hermisson is at his most trenchant in his discussion of Eissfeldt's position that many of the sayings in the book of Proverbs originated as folk proverbs. He calls into question Eissfeldt's premise that sayings whose first lines are identical (or similar), but whose second lines differ, must have originated as one-line folk proverbs which were later expanded. Further, he feels that the content of the saying proposed by Eissfeldt does not necessarily demand an origin among the folk, since wisdom sayings consistently exhibit broad interests in a variety of phenomena. Those sayings which exhibit didactic interests are automatically precluded from folk origins by Hermisson's very definition of the (folk)-proverbs, along with any sayings in the book of Proverbs which show Egyptian influence. The form of the sayings under discussion also shows a much closer affinity to that of the artistic saying than to the short, terse, non-parallel, and prosaic style of the folk proverb, nor does the appearance of the wisdom saying in Israel necessarily mean that the folk proverb would have been engulfed by the wisdom form. Finally, in a marvelously tautological argument, Hermisson contends that since so few "genuine" proverbs (by his definition) actually exist in the Old Testament, it would be highly unlikely to discover so many incorporated into the Book of Proverbs.[38]

While Hermisson has performed a valuable service in calling into question many of Eissfeldt's presuppositions concerning the existence of folk proverbs in the Book of Proverbs and the necessary evolutionary development of the artistic saying from a shorter, simpler form, his treatment of many of the passages outside of the wisdom collections fails to do justice to the material, since his own goals and assumptions had already determined the outcome of his research. Although his recognition that the "folk" character of a saying may actually apply more properly to the sphere of its use rather than its origin[39] is valid, his desire to locate the "Sitz im Leben" of the sayings found in Proverbs in the "wisdom schools" and his narrow evaluation of the "folk" as they existed in Israel have caused him to overlook the implications of his statement with regard to the use of both wisdom sayings and folk proverbs outside wisdom circles. While it is certainly true that most wisdom literature may have originated in a scholarly circle with specific (didactic) goals,[40] the fact that many sayings, whatever their origin, are found in the Old Testament ascribed to persons outside a wisdom circle, engaged in the process of daily life, is significant indeed, since it allows one to posit a broader base than the Solomonic court and schools alone for the phenomenon of wisdom as a whole. The sayings found outside the wisdom literature need have no direct, organic link to the development and formation of the artistic wisdom saying in order to provide some indication of how wisdom, as a way of encapsulating and reflecting on tradition, may have functioned outside the rarefied atmosphere of the academy.

At many points, Hermisson's arguments fail because his goals have prevented him from pursuing a line of thought further. A saying which makes use of agricultural images or motifs does not necessarily have to originate among the folk; the sages were equally capable of observing the natural world around them, and coining a proverb which reflected such knowledge.[41] Surely it is reasonable to assume, then, that the folk may have been similarly interested in the various aspects of their world which had little relation to their everyday existence; one need not posit a court school as the sole of origin of royal or "king" sayings.[42] Hermisson's presuppositions concerning the nature and concerns of the "folk" have seriously impaired his evaluations of the supposed origins of some materials under discussion, as Gerstenberger has properly pointed out.[43] Hermisson's evaluation of the folk as essentially nomads-turned-peasant[44] is probably much too narrow to encompass the reality of the concept. Gerstenberger, interested as he is in maintaining the viability of the clan as a source for the wisdom traditions, argues that the "urban" elements of Israel's population would also have been part of the overall makeup of the "folk."[45] At any rate, Hermisson's characterization of this "peasant folk" in terms of the degree of sophistication of expression and variety of interests to be expected from such a group strongly reflects Western Civilization's typical, post-Enlightenment evaluation of such groups, and for that reason, should be evaluated in the light of modern, anthropological research on societies which are other than literate.[46] Further, it is far from certain that <u>content</u> alone can ever provide a clearcut and unassailable indication of origin, and since Hermisson has not been so obliging as to provide any positive criteria for the identification of the folk proverb,[47] one must conclude that the debate over the existence of folk proverbs in the Old Testament is far from over.

It should be noted that Hermisson's insistence on the "school" setting as the major, and perhaps only, Sitz im Leben of wisdom has recently been criticized for a number of reasons. Erhard Gerstenberger has argued persuasively for the recognition of "clan" wisdom (Sippenweisheit) as an important element for any understanding of the wisdom movement as a whole,[48] and R. N. Whybray's study on the possible existence of the "school" setting in Israel has cast some doubt on the usual analogies drawn from Mesopotamia and Egypt.[49] On the basis of these arguments and others, James Crenshaw tends to favor the existence of folk proverbs and the view of clan wisdom as a major sociological setting for the wisdom movement. He thinks "one can move beyond the literary stage of proverbial composition to an oral period when the astute observer of human behaviour and natural events coined brief maxims that represented the distillate of his knowledge."[50] R. E. Murphy has pointed out in respect to the quest for the "original" Sitz im Leben of the wisdom saying that the general validity of a saying endows it with a flexibility which allows it to cross life settings and still remain relevant - hence, most attempts to provide a detailed or exclusive Sitz im Leben or reconstruct specific prehistory must remain "highly conjectural."[51]

3. Other Discussions of the Saying in the Old Testament

Georg Fohrer, in his revision and enlargement of Ernst Sellin's Introduction to the Old Testament, follows Eissfeldt's schematization of the development of the artistic wisdom saying from the popular or folk proverb.[52] His definition of the popular proverb stresses the "prosaic" quality of its style, universality of content, and occasional attachment to a specific historical context.[53] Once more, a problematic[54] feature of the proverb emerges, as Fohrer comments that such sayings are "immediately evident to the ear."[55] Ultimately, forms which incorporated rhythm come to prevail, rather than the older prose sayings, and the wisdom aphorism represents the final "literary" development from the folk proverb.[56] Fohrer touches fleetingly on some aspects of the use to which a saying may be put,[57] and one may conclude that this fluidity stems not only from the general "truth" encapsulated within a saying, but also from its quality as a māshāl, "a statement having the power to create a new reality or gain recognition for an experience of the people or the wise and present it as a valid reality."[58] Fohrer also mentions Is. 3:10-11; 32:6-8; 40:18-20; 41:7; 44:9-20; 46:5-8 as "sayings of wisdom instructors" which exist outside the wisdom literature, and refers to Is. 28:23-29 and Am 3:3-6 as "rhetorical forms borrowed from wisdom."[59]

Aage Bentzen's Introduction to the Old Testament also reflects some of the general assumptions of Eissfeldt's work, but stress is laid on the discontinuity between the "popular" saying and the "artistic" wisdom sentence.[60] The popular sayings "have no poetical form, neither parallelism nor rhythm, and most of them have no religious character," and in the creation of the wisdom sentence, "the art of poetry has, to a high degree altered the original popular proverb in respect of its form."[61] Some popular material is probably preserved among the wisdom materials in altered form as a result of the activity of the sages, but Bentzen doubts that the traditional saying can be the true origin of the form and style of the wisdom sentence, since the features so typical to the wisdom sentence seem to be lacking in the popular materials,[62] in his estimation.

William McKane gives little attention to the discussion of the popular proverb, since his particular perspectives on the meaning of māshāl, definition of the proverb, and form critical studies of the "Instruction" genre have scant connection with the form and function of the popular proverb in Israel.[63] McKane discusses the passages 1 Sam. 10:11, 19:24, Gen. 10:9, 1 Sam. 24:14, Ezek. 16:44, 1 Kg. 20:11, Jer. 31:29, Ezek. 18:2, Ezek. 12:22, Luke 4:23, which he refers to as popular proverbs, with an eye to explicating the sayings in the light of his understanding of the term "māshāl," as "model" or "paradigm."[64] For this reason, McKane's treatment of popular proverb adds little to the discussion from the perspective of form, content and use, although his recognition of the "paradigmatic" character of proverbs has implications for understanding the "why" and "how" of proverb use.[65] It might be worthwhile here to note McKane's definition of the proverb, which stresses certain aspects of the proverb not usually found in other Old Testament discussions of the form.

I have developed an exact definition of "proverb" in

which the emphasis is laid on representative potential and openness to interpretation. The "proverb," in virtue of its concreteness, sometimes in virtue of the organization of imagery, has a representative capacity which can be intuited by future interpreters. The paradox of the "proverb" is that it acquires immortality because of its particularity; that because of its lack of explicitness, its allusiveness or even opaqueness, it does not become an antique, but awaits continually the situation to illumine which it was coined. Among the sentences of the book of Proverbs there are not many such "proverbs.".. [66]

Since McKane has chosen to stress a sort of "hermeneutical openness" as the paramount feature of the proverb, he is consistent in his evaluation that much in the Book of Proverbs cannot be designated as proverbs as such, due to the strong didactic tone found in many of the wisdom "Gattungen." [67] McKane then proceeds to divide the wisdom sentences in the book of Proverbs into three classes: Class A, which contains "Old Wisdom" materials, and concentrates on teaching the individual the mastery of life; Class B, which focuses more on the concerns of the community; and Class C, which derives from "Yahwistic piety," and which McKane feels to be a reinterpretation of earlier materials. [68]

Gerhard von Rad, in his sensitive and stunning work on Israel's wisdom traditions, devotes most of his attention to the intellectual and artistic processes at work in the formation and use of the wisdom saying, and discusses the "folk" saying only in its relation to the wisdom form. [69] Based on Hermisson's work, von Rad moves away from Eissfeldt's traditional position on the development of the wisdom saying or aphorism, although he allows that is is possible that "this or that popular proverb has also found its way into the collection." [70] His thoughtful analysis of the literary and symbolic content of the single-line wisdom saying leads him to conclude that the developmental straightjacket of "small-to-large" evolution of literary units is misleading for other wisdom forms as well, since "The single line often enough makes higher claims and demands a greater degree of intellectual participation than a developed didactic poem. The single line is, as a rule, much more dense and affords more room for maneuver from the point of view of meaning and application than the didactic poem, the content of which is much less ambiguous as to its meaning."[71] Von Rad reflects the influence of Jolles in his understanding of the sentences as essentially neutral rather than didactic,[72] but regards such "gnomic apperception" as a "rudimentary expression of man's search for knowledge."[73] These encapsulations of human experience retain a certain flexibility, however - they leave themselves open to interpretation and adaptation, and such phenomena may be observed in the history of transmission of the sentences.[74] As always, von Rad displays his own particular sensitivity in the discussion of the essential coherence of form and content in relation to the processes of formation and use, stressing that "the process of becoming aware of the perception and of giving linguistic expression to it in word and form are one and the same act .... The frequency of paronomasia in these proverbs, of assonance and alliteration, still shows us something of the magical incantatory function possessed by the resonance of the word."[75] With regard to the folk proverb, he comments, "If the popular proverb already reveals a tendency to linguistic refinement in that it happily exists in elevated language, then the literary proverb which comes from the schools differs from it by an essentially still stronger cultivation both of language and of content."[76] With respect to the use of proverbial wisdom in society, von Rad suggests that such material, by virtue of the ready presentation of knowledge made possible by the fortunate bonding of form and content, may have played a greater role in the management of daily life than the more formal, cultic guides for conduct.[77]

Roland E. Murphy, in his discussions of form critical studies on the Book of Proverbs, has properly commented on the speculative nature of Eissfeldt's premises about the development of the wisdom saying.[78] Not only could the two-line parallel wisdom saying be just as "primitive" as a form as the one-line sentence, but the one-line saying could easily be an "incipit" or fragment of an earlier longer form,[79] nor is there any reason why the two forms must be regarded as mutually exclusive early forms. Murphy recognizes Hermisson's emphasis on the "folk" character of the proverb in reference to use rather than origin as a useful distinction, but refrains from endorsing Hermisson's dogmatic assertions about the nonexistence of folk proverbs in the Old Testament and Israel in general, since "one cannot deny the existence of sharp metaphor and turns of speech that would have existed among the common people."[80] The sentences found in the Book of Proverbs reflect the literary shaping of the sages, and while some popular wisdom probably did find its way into the wisdom collections, there is simply not enough evidence available to reconstruct a prehistory of any given saying.[81] While a "school" setting seems to be a reasonable one to posit as the place in life of wisdom literature, it can hardly be considered the only life setting, nor can one "claim that all the sayings in Proverbs must have originated in the school .... The folk saying - which in many cases may be as "literary" as the artistic saying - is best understood as originating in one of the manifold sociological settings, such as parental advice, instructions by elders, the inherited wisdom of local gurus."[82] Murphy follows the general distinction between those sentences which are essentially neutral observations and those with didactic intent, and stresses the "limited" quality of the saying in general, which, because of its abbreviated form, cannot adequately reflect the "details and exceptions" of which the sages were no doubt aware.[83] The limited, and often ambivalent nature of the saying often leads to reinterpretation.[84]

Claus Westermann has used some comparative anthropological materials from tribal societies to shed light on the process of transmission of proverbs as it may have taken place in ancient Israel.[85] Westermann believes that the proverb (Sprichwort) per se developed out of a pre-political, pre-historical period in the history of Israel, when transmission was primarily oral.[86] Such proverbs would have arisen from a specific context to which they spoke, and their message, often framed in terms of comparisons, was essentially open to verification. The proverb assumes a certain degree of equality on the part of user and hearer, since the hearer is called upon to affirm the message of the proverb. Westermann sees this in sharp contrast to the admonition (Mahnwort), where a superior addresses an inferior, and thus, concludes that the earliest proverbs were primarily in the form of indicative sayings, often making use of comparisons and images drawn from daily life.

For Westermann, the occurrence of a proverb in a collection clearly represents a secondary stage of transmission, when the "wisdom" contained in a given saying has been evaluated and consciously preserved.[87] The book of Proverbs, with its mixed content of admonitions, introductions, abstract sayings developed around a single theme (such as the righteous and the wicked), and sayings exhibiting parallelism, which Westermann apparently feels to be an artistic, poetic development from the earlier simple saying, reflects a later stage of intellectual activity and conscious evaluation of earlier materials which is removed from the less sophisticated tribal period out of which the earlier saying (Aussagespruch) developed.[88] Given that proverbs have been found throughout the world among primitive peoples, it is not necessary to posit direct Egyptian and Mesopotamian influence to explain the existence of proverbs in ancient Israel; rather, it is logical, on the basis of comparative materials, to assume that such materials existed in Israel during the tribal period.[89] This stream of traditional materials, originally transmitted orally and aimed at least in part toward the education of group members, would have joined other sources (the court school, foreign influence) at a later period in the history of transmission.[90]

Westermann supports von Rad's schematization of the development of wisdom in Israel, from an early, tribal period through "royal" cultivation of earlier wisdom materials and the composition of new forms to fit new purposes (such as the education of court officials and scribes), up to a final stage when a "theologization" of wisdom took place.[91] While it is not possible to endorse Westermann's conclusions without reservations about the development of artistic forms from earlier popular forms, or the distinct difference in life settings for indicative and volative forms, he has performed a valuable service to the field concerning the origin of Israel's wisdom traditions by his use of comparative materials. His recognition that experiental wisdom encapsulated in proverbs which tell "the way it is" and thus provide the raw materials from which decisions are made is almost certain to have existed within the tribal society eliminated the need to explain how wisdom could have appeared on the scene as a totally new phenomenon during the Solomonic period. Also, his evaluation of the high place occupied by proverbs in societies which are other than literate, as "a speech form which defines the whole life (Dasein), ... (whose) scope of usage encompasses areas such as law, education and others, which have not yet developed separate speech forms"[92] shows a sensitive attention to the importance of the genre in the daily life of a community.

R. B. Y. Scott, in his discussions of the various motifs to be found in Old Testament wisdom literature, and his attempts to give an overarching picture of the development of wisdom in ancient Israel, has given a great deal of attention to the study of folk proverb, especially in connection with its appearance in the Book of Proverbs.[93] Scott thinks the passages recognized by most Old Testament scholars as folk sayings are evidence of a strong tradition of popular wisdom in Israel, and he follows Eissfeldt in his general remarks about the development of "literary" sayings from some popular sources by means of expanded parallelism.[94] For Scott, the distinction between the popular proverb and the literary wisdom sentence is clearly discernible in a number of ways: the wisdom sentence often gives way to "complacent and unreflective moralizing," whereas the popular proverb concerns itself with observational and picturesque content drawn from daily life;[95] in formal terms, the wisdom saying exhibits a good deal of regularity in its use of the parallel couplet, while the folk saying is short and compact, often marked by stylistic devices of assonance, alliteration, etc.;[96] and while the "authority" of the wisdom saying derives from the status of its author as a "learned religious teacher," that of the traditional saying stems from "the social authority of general consent or of the obvious truism."[97] Further, the strong didactic quality of the wisdom sentence makes its message self-evident, but the terse and pointed quality which Scott finds so characteristic of the popular saying often renders the folk proverb virtually unintelligible apart from the context of its use.[98]

Given this understanding of the differences in content, form, authority, and life setting (the school vs. society at large) which exist between the folk and wisdom saying, Scott outlines two categories among the "secular" sayings in the book of Proverbs which he believes to have been derived from a popular proverbial corpus: "(1) Folk sayings (or literary couplets based on folk sayings) which are more suitable to exchanges between adults meeting 'in the gate' than to authoritarian instruction of youth in home or school; and (2) Folk sayings or their derivatives which seek to impress on the hearers the moral standards and values of home and community, but without any indication that these are grounded in an unseen order of reality."[99] Examples of the first category are Pr. 11:16, 11:22, 16:26a, 18:23, 19:7a, 19:4a, 22:13, 19:13b and 15:30b,[100] with the possible inclusion of 10:15a, 13:8,23, 14:4a,20, 15:15, 18:22a, 19:6b, 20:25, 21:9 and parallels, 25:20, 27:10c, 18:19a and 29:5,24a. The second group is represented by 11:2a, 13:24a, 17:1, 17:13, 17:14a, 20:29, and 27:5, and possibly by 16:18, 17:6, 18:3a, 9, 19, 24, 29:11a,

17, 19a, 29, and 25:27a. It should be noted that Scott has formulated these categories in response to McKane's divisions of types of sayings in the book of Proverbs, and wishes to argue for more precise distinctions among the non-religious or secular sayings on the basis of probable life setting, form and content. Further, Scott is not unaware of the problems involved in ascribing a specific date or origin to any given proverb, since the sages were perfectly capable of framing their thought in "popular" form,[101] nor does he subscribe to the view that popular, traditional wisdom would have ceased to exist with the growth of the literary and court-associated wisdom movement.[102]

In his analysis of the folk proverbs from the ancient Near East, Scott maintains that there are indeed a number of popular proverbs extant within the Old Testament, which may be identified both through formal characteristics and content. Such sayings are the product of a "folk wisdom" which "appears spontaneously in traditional societies,"[103] and Scott finds it reasonable to assume that this popular wisdom would have been a contributing source for the wisdom tradition.[104] Using comparative materials from Mesopotamian and Egyptian wisdom literature and proverb collections, Scott identifies what he terms "proverb idioms" or characteristic "idea patterns" (which) provide a kind of instinctive classification of the experiences of life..."[105] In Scott's terminology, the main categories of these idioms are:

(1) identity, equivalence, or invariable association
(2) contrast, non-identity, paradox
(3) similarity, analogy, typology
(4) contrary to order, futile, absurd
(5) proverbs which classify and characterize persons, actions or situations
(6) value, lack of value, relative value, proportion or degree
(7) cause and consequence[106]

The proverb idioms are generally conveyed through the use of pictures and generalizations drawn from the observation of life, and idioms commonly operate with the conceptual framework of "order."

While Scott has advanced the study of the folk proverb by opening up a general discussion of the folk proverb on the basis of its own features rather than solely on its relation to the wisdom saying, it must be concluded that Scott's work is more suggestive than explanatory. It is by no means clear from his discussion of "proverb idiom" how he relates the idea conveyed by a saying to the image which conveys it, or whether he would maintain that such idea patterns underlie the wisdom sentence as well as the colloquial saying. It is difficult as well to discern distinctive features of a saying which would cause Scott to classify it as "equivalence" (1) rather than "analogy" (3). Similar questions might be raised for the other categories which he has proposed - for example, proverbs "which classify and characterize persons, actions, or situations" (5) might actually belong to one of his other classifications, depending on the message they convey. In this respect, we find that Scott classes Gen. 19:9, "Like Nimrod, a mighty hunter before the Lord," under "typology" (3) rather than under "equivalence" (1) or "characterization" (5). In general, his description of the classes of proverb idioms suffers from the confusion of stylistic features with formal structural elements, and considerations of content.

Scott's overall treatment of the distinctions between the wisdom saying and the folk saying, although justified in many of its particulars (such as his comments on form), reflects a strong bias against the prevailing theory that the "school" provides the setting for wisdom sayings. Scott does not seem to have taken into account the variety of presuppositions upon which Eissfeldt's position concerning the incorporation of folk proverbs into the book of Proverbs rests, nor does he reply to the problems with this approach raised by Hermisson. While he has raised interesting points here and there about the possible use of the folk proverb in society and the importance of context for understanding both content and use, he fails to discuss these aspects of the folk saying an any great length.

James Crenshaw, in his reviews of the state of form critical studies in wisdom, has presented a well-balanced picture of the debate over the relation of the folk proverb to the wisdom saying.[107] Crenshaw, although aware of the problems with Eissfeldt's work, avoids the extreme position of Hermisson on the existence of folk proverbs in the Old Testament.[108] For Crenshaw, the popular proverb is "the simplest form of the Sprichwort," and he accepts the general stylistic and formal comments on the nature of the folk proverb made by other scholars.[109] He says of the folk saying that "By nature secular and non-didactic, these popular proverbs were occasionally enlisted in the service of morality and consequently assumed a religious tenor."[110] With respect to the application of the description "māshāl" applied to both folk sayings and wisdom sentences, Crenshaw outlines several literary types to which the term is commonly applied.

Based in part on the work of R. B. Y. Scott and E. Gerstenberger, Crenshaw argues for a multiplicity of sources for the wisdom tradition as a whole. In his view, Hermisson's characterization of the life setting of wisdom as almost exclusively that of the school cannot be supported for a number of reasons. Whybray's work highlights some of the problems with the court and temple school analogies drawn from Israel's neighbours,[111] and Crenshaw feels that the life setting of education within the home and clan cannot be easily dismissed as one of the loci of wisdom.[112] In this respect, he agrees with R. E. Murphy concerning the difficulty in pinpointing a specific life setting, and concludes that "the precise origin of any passage is open to question."[113]

Crenshaw endorses the view that the proverb is to be understood as "an elementary quest for order, comparisons, and contrasts," a position which is currently popular with most wisdom scholars.[114] The didactic aspect of the proverb is seen by Crenshaw as a secondary feature, and he defines the proverb in the following way:

> The proverb is bilinear and registers a conclusion based on experience; as such it must be self-confirming, commending itself to empirical validation or to disconfirmation. Since the saying is a result of the collective experience of mankind, it has a retropsective character, and because of its nature as an observation of how things are, it lacks the imperative. Hence any didactic intent is secondary to the proverb, and the style is succinct, epigrammatic, and highly metaphorical. However, even the literary proverb may be set within a didactic context, as in the case of the folk proverb. This pedagogic function of the aphorism was abetted by the addition of motivation clauses, which led to a disintegration of the form of the proverb, as well as by the attaching of consequences of conduct. Certain stylistic features give evidence of serious reflection in the service of teaching ...[115]

It is not difficult to see that Crenshaw has been influenced in his thinking by Jolles' understanding of the proverb, but his choice of wording is often unfortunate. It is not clear whether, when he speaks of the proverb as bilinear, he is referring to the folk proverb or the wisdom saying, since the folk proverb is generally accepted as lacking the bilinear form more common to the wisdom saying. It may be that Crenshaw hesitates to draw the distinctions of "nature" between the (folk) proverb and the artistic wisdom saying which have been made by such scholars as Hermisson, and is attempting a more synthetic treatment of the constitutive features of the proverb in general. At any rate, his discussion here, as elsewhere, would benefit from a more careful choice of vocabulary, or more explicit statement of presuppositions.

Applications of a number of current folklorist approaches to proverb study have recently made their appearance in Old Testament and Near Eastern studies, even as anthropological and folklore studies of performance, enactment and transmission have been used to enrich Biblical scholarship's theories of "oral tradition" and oral literature.[116] Angel Marzal has used theories of proverb performance, along with George Milner's structural descriptions of the saying to identify and exegete proverbial passages in the Mari letters.[117] Bendt Alster has also adapted structural and contextual studies to help elucidate the overall structure, and specific meanings of Sumerian proverbs as they occur in collections, the instruction genre, and other literary forms.[118] Alster has also used paroemiological considerations to aid in the identification of proverbs, concluding that a phrase must exhibit "bound" form (i.e., show a fixed-phrase, which is compact and short), and embody common knowledge which is capable of multiple applications.[119] Alster concludes that "It is obvious that if a text cites a proverb, then it is not enough to translate the words. The text has not been understood unless the idea which the proverb expresses has been analyzed and related to the context in which it is placed."[120]

In the realm of Old Testament studies, Glendon Bryce has used structural analysis to study the "Better-than" saying (tôb-Spruch) in the wisdom literature, and feels that the recognition of the binary oppositions inherent in such sayings may be used to "develop some insight into the moral givens of a culture, and to suggest specific interests of collectors or possibly even the Sitz im Leben of specific collections."[121] Robert Gordis' work on the variety of uses of quotations in biblical and rabbinic literature moves into the realm of "performance meaning" and has done much to shed light on some difficult passages in Job and Ecc.[122] Gordis argues for the use of such stylistic features as parallelism,

23

"realism" and "idiomatic brevity" as criteria for the identification of proverbial passages, along with the typical "out of context" appearance of such statements.[123]

Summary and Unresolved Questions

We have seen that the discussion of the nature, form and content of the folk proverb as it occurs in the Old Testament has been conducted, for the most part, with respect to its relation to the more artistic and stylized wisdom saying. Since Eissfeldt's work on the "māshāl" was first undertaken, the folk saying has been taken as the "proto-form" of the wisdom saying, and hence, much of the following study in this area centered on arguments over which features could or could not have given birth to the parallel couplet utilized by the sages. Few scholars today accept Eissfeldt's conclusions without some serious reservations, though not many are willing to follow Hermisson's conclusions and banish the folk saying entirely from the pages of the Old Testament. Current discussions of the nature of the saying and its relation to wisdom forms are beginning to recognize and re-examine the presuppositions regarding evolutionary development of the wisdom saying from the popular saying, the type of content to be expected from such a group as the "wise" or the "folk," and so on. Although the research done on the popular proverb still tends to concentrate on aspects or origin, with the consequent result that other features of the folk proverb are given only cursory treatment, it is still possible to state the "consensus" of opinion on the Old Testament folk proverb in the following way:

Form:
Short, predominantly written in prose, but exhibiting stylistic features (assonance, end rhyme, rudimentary rhythm, etc.) which "elevate" the saying's style and allow it to be distinguished from ordinary prose. (Crenshaw, Eissfeldt, Fohrer, von Rad, Scott.)

Content:
Drawn primarily from the spheres of daily life, occupations, and natural environment. While the proverb per se is not essentially didactic in content, its messages seem to operate within the realm of order, norms or observations of "the way it is." The content must be comprehensible to the society or folk at large, and simple comparisons seem to make up the bulk of the content. The content shows the universal truths of life which are open to confirmation by the individual, and are

able to be applied to a variety of contexts. (Alster, Crenshaw, Eissfeldt, Fohrer, Hermisson, Murphy, Scott, Westermann.)

Authority:
The authority of the folk proverb derives primarily from experience which confirms the content. For this reason, it is likely that the guides provided by the saying for right conduct played an important role in the life of the tribe, since the "truth" embodied in the saying was available for easy appropriation, and might be validated by the confirmation of experience. (Crenshaw, von Rad, Scott, Westermann.)

Relation to the wisdom saying:
It is not possible to state categorically that the wisdom saying developed from the "earlier" folk proverb, since the "folk" character is more a statement concerning use/currency than origin. Similarly it is not possible to deny that some of the materials in the Book of Proverbs may have originated in folk materials. The appearance of such materials in collections must be viewed in their transmission, which reflects evaluation and conscious preservation. Undoubtedly, such a folk tradition of saying and popular wisdom must be seen as a contributing source to the wisdom traditions of ancient Israel. (Crenshaw, Hermisson, Murphy, Scott, Westermann.)

Use in literary context; use in society:
Because of the succinct and often oblique style of the folk saying, a context of use is often needed to understand its message. Structural studies may be useful for developing ways to identify sayings in a literary context. More attention must be given to how and why a saying is used when it is found in a literary context. Comparative studies which show vigorous traditions of proverb use in primitive or tribal societies provide insights into what sort of popular wisdom traditions may have existed in ancient Israel at a similar period of cultural development. (Alster, Bryce, Gordis, Marzal, Scott, Westermann.)

A number of questions new to previous wisdom research might be raised concerning the nature and use of the folk proverb found in the Old Testament. While it is probably impossible to make definite statements about the date of origin or life in which such sayings arose, analysis of the sayings as a group may allow one to draw general conclusions about the type of content found and the ideas and images which make up that content. This, in turn, will allow a comparison to be made between what is found in the folk proverb as compared to the content of the wisdom saying, and while this may not yield any precise results concerning the development of the wisdom saying, it will provide a basis for the discussion of the similarities and differences between the two groups. Further, a study of the way in which the message of a saying is manipulated when it appears in a given context will provide insights into the function and use of the saying (in its literary setting and in society as well), and this will allow a comparison of function with the general goals of wisdom instruction and sayings. The following areas, then, of Old Testament research on the (folk) proverb should be studied:

1. Attempts should be made to clarify and more precisely define the nature of the saying, and the terminology used to refer to the saying should reflect the results of such inquiry.

2. Study of use in context should be undertaken to clarify ambiguous passages, and discern the function of a saying in literary and broader cultural settings.

3. Old Testament research on the saying or proverb has tended to de-emphasize the didactic aspects or the saying in favor of stressing an observational, neutral character. Further, the premise has been that the saying operates in a sphere of "order" and norms. Attention to the saying as it is used in a given context should help in the effort to evaluate these basic presuppositions, which are, for the most part, philosophical rather than literary or "biblical."

4. More recent research has tended to use comparative anthropological materials, along with types of analyses drawn from structural and folklore studies. Study should be undertaken to discover whether these investigations may be used further to discuss the nature, content, and use of sayings in context as they occur in the Old Testament.

Scholars in the fields of folklore and paroemiology have long dealt with the problems involved in attempting to define the proverb, popular or learned, and to establish patterns of use in context. The proverb is recognized as a distinct and pervasive genre of oral literature, and for this reason, a great deal of anthropological and literary research has been done which can be of benefit to any discussion of the folk saying in the Old Testament. Comparative study of the saying will also act as a "corrective" to some Old Testament research in this area, which tends to be dominated by "wisdom" concerns which may actually interfere with the development of an adequate understanding of the folk saying. We will turn, then, to paroemiology and folklore studies on the saying, giving special attention to definition, form, content, use and function.

Chapter II

PAROEMIOLOGY AND FOLKLORE STUDIES
ON THE PROVERB AND SAYING

Interest in the nature and use of the proverb or saying is nearly as old as the genre itself, since the persuasive and paradoxical qualities of these forms of expression have long been noted. Thus, the Egyptian sage might observe that "speech is more difficult than any craft,"[1] and among the goals of wisdom study stated by the Old Testament teacher of wisdom is that one should learn "to understand a proverb and a figure, the words of the wise and their riddles" (Pr. 1:6). The philosophers of ancient Greece used and discussed the nature of proverbs and sayings, and Aristotle said of the maxim (which he differentiates from the proverb proper as a "general statement") that, "Even trite and common maxims should be used, if they can serve; since, just because they are common, they seem right, on the supposition that all the world is agreed about them."[2]

During the Middle Ages interest in the proverb continued, since, as was the case in ancient times, the proverb served as the "content" as well as the "copy-book" lesson for those who would be educated.[3] As early as 1593, Elizabethan rhetoricians were emphasizing aspects of the use and function of proverbs and sayings in discussion of the form, as may be seen from Henry Peacham's entry under "Paroemia" in his second edition of The Garden of Eloquence.

Amongst all the excellent forms of speech there are none other more briefe, more significant, more evident or more excellent, than apt proverbs: for what figure of speech is more fit to teach, more forcible to persuade, more wise to forewarn, more sharpe to reprove, more strong to confirme or more piercing to imprint? Briefly, they are most profitable, and most pleasant, and may well be called, the Summaries of maners, or, the Images of human life: for in them there is contained a generall doctrine of direction, and particular rules for all duties in all persons.[4]

Today, interest in the proverb and saying is growing as never before for a variety of reasons, although for some time it has been felt that interest in this particular genre has been dying. The traditional paroemiological approaches to the study of the proverb continue, as exemplified by the work of Archer Taylor, Marjorie Kimmerle and others, but the growing discipline of folklore has offered new insights and methods into such research and has given new interest to the study of the genre. New questions are being asked about the content of proverbs and sayings found in collections, as new methods of analysis are developed, and proverb scholars such as Wolfgang Mieder and others, are beginning to turn to the study of proverbs and sayings which occur in literature. The recognition of the proverb and saying as a widespread form of oral literature, which because of its brevity, is apt to be accurately recorded when it is found outside collections preserved in written sources has been helpful in the attempt to "recover" the folklore of groups which now depend primarily on written rather than oral transmission. Structural studies of the genre are also growing, since the structural study of the shortest units of folklore may ultimately provide insights into folklore as a larger phenomenon, as well as presenting a validation of the methodology. The advantages offered by structural studies for cross-cultural study of the genre have generated new excitement as folklorists attempt to uncover and compare the various "world views" which form the raw material from which proverbs are fashioned. "Contextual" folklore studies are similarly interested in the study of the form, since an understanding of how proverbs "work" in interactions provides valuable insights into the way cultural conditioning intersects individual needs and desires in a context of use.

All of these approaches to the study of the definition, form, content, style, use and function of the proverb offer fresh perspectives for the understanding of the genre as it is found in the Old Testament. Paroemiology is that "branch" of folklore studies which collects and collates proverbs, analyzes local and international variants and makes some attempt at tracing the cross-cultural diffusion of proverbs. Paroemiological research provides insights into the diff-iculties of defining the genre and understanding of its fundamental nature; folklore studies seek to explore use and function of the forms in traditional societies and relate these to the function of oral literature as a whole. After a discussion of the meaning of the term "folk" as it is used by paroemiologists and folklorists, we will survey the work done in both fields in view of its possible applications to Old Testament study.

Before discussing the work done on proverbs in the field of folklore, it might be helpful to survey the variety of meanings which scholars in that field ascribe to the term "folk". Although one can point to certain early authors whose works dealt with subjects which would today be described as "folk"-lore,[5] the work "folklore" did not appear until the mid-nineteenth century, some thirty years after the appearance of the works of the Grimm brothers. The cultural loading with which the term was invested came in part from the growth of nationalism and romanticism, and reflected an underlying evolutionary belief that societies proceeded from the least civilized (primitive, preliterate, or savage) to the most civilized (literate, industrialized). On this "time-line" of civilization, the folk were conceived of as occupying a middle ground between primitive and industrialized societies, and they were often defined by "the illiterate in a literate society."[6] In the most narrow sense, the folk were identified with the European peasantry, and although this usage broadened gradually, the folk continued to be defined as their supposed contrast to the elite, urbanized, literate group upon whose cultural and spiritual boundaries they were thought to live.

This typical definition of the folk as a "dependent" body whose identity was shaped by a relationship to a superior group caused a number of problems for those engaged in the study of non-Western societies. Since the folk could only exist in relation to a more "civilized" literate group, scholars were forced into the position of asserting that such groups as primitive, tribal societies, as well as groups in urban societies had no folk-lore. Groups which fell at either end of the continuum could not possess folk-lore, because they had no folk. The defining feature of the folk - illiteracy - made dealing with the verbal art of societies which were other than literate but which existed independently of a literate society virtually impossible, since the conceptual framework of the early folklorists could not accommodate such groups. Finally, because the study of folklore grew up partly in response to the European search for national origins, urbanized groups tended to be overlooked as possible constituents of the folk, since the folk was implicitly designated as "rural" or "peasant" in contrast to the civilized urban elite.[7] Folklorist Alan Dundes has schematized the nineteenth century understanding of the folk in the following way:

Savage or Primitive	Folk or Peasant	Civilized or Elite
Pre- or Non-literate	Illiterate	Literate
	Rural	Urban
	Lower stratum	Upper stratum

Figure 2:   19th Century Understanding of the "Folk."
SOURCE: Alan Dundes, "Who Are the Folk?", in Frontiers of Folklore, ed. William R. Bascom (1977), p. 20.

The modern study of folklore more or less has come to accept the nineteenth century understanding of the folk as inadequate for a number of reasons. New awareness of the ethnocentricity inherent in such terms as "non-literate" or "non-Western" has caused many to attempt to sharpen terminology and redefine much-used concepts. Further, the wealth of information collected from unbiased field studies has undermined to a great extent previous notions that primitive or "folk" cultures are necessarily unsophisticated; nor can literacy be used as an adequate yardstick of cultural or artistic achievement for societies which are not "literate" in the Western understanding of the word. The recognition of numerous genres of oral literature which exist on a worldwide basis, even among groups who, by definition, should not possess folklore, has forced many to give a new definition to the term "folk." In particular, students of North and South American cultures ("primitive" groups with no elite) and Marxist folklorists (dealing with industrialized, urban groups which are literate) have led the way in redefining the folk as an operational term. Dundes gives the following definition:

The term "folk" can refer to any group of people whatsoever who share at least one common factor. It does not matter what the linking factor is - it could be a common occupation, language, or religion - but what is important is that a group formed for whatever reason will have some traditions which it calls its own. In theory a group must consist of at least two persons, but generally most groups consist of many individuals. A member of the group may not know all other members, but he will probably know the common core of traditions belonging to the group, traditions which help the group

31

have a sense of group identity. With this flexible definition of folk, a group could be as large as a nation or as small as a family.[8]

Dundes goes on to stress that a folk group need not be familial or national in character, but may be geographical, occupational, religious, ethnic or racial.[9] No one member of a folk group need know all the items of the group repertoire of folklore, or know all the other members of the group, but every member will possess a knowledge of some or most of the common lore.[10]

Such a definition of the folk is preferable for a variety of reasons: it avoids Western stereotypes of non-Western societies; it allows the folklorist to move away from the concept of the rural, lower-class, illiterate peasant as the sole possessor of folklore; and it provides the student of literature and anthropologist alike with a model for dealing with the verbal art of "primitive" and "urban" groups who had previously been consigned to the limbo of the Unclassified. Although this broader definition has much to recommend it, it must be noted that not all folklorists would agree with Dundes' reinterpretation of "folk," and that, in general, older works will use the term in its nineteenth century sense (i.e., "peasant"). However, it is important to recognize that the fields of folklore and anthropology are beginning to reflect upon their origins and move away from presuppositions which reflect cultural bias rather than empirically verifiable fact.

PAROEMIOLOGY

1. Definition of the Proverb and Traditional Saying

Turning to studies on folklore and paroemiology, we find a good deal of discussion in the area of defining and naming the proverb. Descriptive attempts to analyze the proverb or traditional saying approach the task from a variety of perspectives: (1) formal definitions based on styles and content; (2) functional definitions; and (3) structural analyses which aim to "get beyond" definition on the basis of surface features or function.[11] Although there is, as yet, no effective consensus on which types of analysis can be said to define the proverb most efficiently, all approaches stress the value of studying the traditional saying, the smallest unit of folklore, both for the insights into this fixed-phrase genre itself and also because of the broader implications which may be drawn for the study of oral literature as a whole.[12]

Chapter II : Paroemiology and Folklore Studies

No survey of the literature on the traditional saying would be complete without Archer Taylor's oft-quoted introduction to his work The Proverb. At the outset, Taylor tells us:

> The definition of a proverb is too difficult to repay the undertaking; and should we fortunately combine in a single definition all the essential elements and give each the proper emphasis, we should not even then have a touch-stone. An incommunicable quality tells us this sentence is proverbial and that one is not. Hence no definition will enable us to identify positively a sentence as proverbial .... Let us be content with recognizing that a proverb is a saying current among the folk.[13]

As his discussion continues, he treats the problem of individual or communal origin, recognizing that the creation of a saying must be, initially, an individual event, but that the currency which makes a saying "traditional" ultimately depends on acceptance by the folk. Further, for the sake of analysis, Taylor makes no distinction between metaphorical sayings (proverbs) and non-metaphorical sayings (maxims, apothegms), beyond the statement that the occurrence of metaphor in a saying gives it broader applications in its usage.[14]

Similar traditional types of definition of the proverb attempt to combine aspects of proverb styles and content to arrive at a basic description of the phenomenon. For A. H. Krappe, the traditional saying "represents in its essential form, some homely truth expressed in a concise and terse manner so as to recommend itself to a more or less extended circle ... the two essential features of the proverb are therefore its didacticism for the content, and its conciseness for the form."[15] Like Taylor, Krappe supports the individual, if anonymous, authorship of the traditional saying, draws no great distinction between the metaphorical and non-metaphorical sayings, and points to features of proverb style (mnemotechnical devices, etc.) as functional in fixing this genre in the popular mind and, thus, facilitating recall and use.[16]

Bengt Holbek, a Scandinavian folklorist, moves toward the functionalist definition of this genre. He feels that the style of proverbs is a "logical consequence of their function."[17] The proper function of a proverb is to draw an analogy between actual or hypothesized situations and a "body of traditional wisdom."[18] Thus, form effectively follows function, and he accepts co-worker Iver Kjaer's definition of proverbs as "anonymous traditional sayings about human life (directly or metaphorically), with the addition that they assume the form of complete sentences."[19] Drawing his conclusions about proverb style from his study of the Danish stock of proverbs (which he nonetheless feels to be generally valid for all traditional sayings), he concludes that the style, since it must enable one to draw the correspondence between traditional wisdom and events in real life, must be (1) "as general, perspicuous, and straight-forward as possible" to facilitate such applications, and (2) "in order to preserve the proverbs the illiterate mind may ... make use of certain mnemonic devices (such as rhythm, alliteration, and the like), which at the same time serve to embellish the proverbs, thereby elevating them above the ordinary speech."[20] With these considerations of proverb style, he believes he has found Taylor's "touch-stone" for proverb definition and identification.[21]

Some of the pitfalls of attempting to define and classify proverbs or traditional sayings on the basis of style may be seen in M. Kimmerle's scheme for identifying and classifying sayings which use "syntax for the basis of form, and the names of concrete objects for the basis of subject matter."[22] Concentration on the "surface" features of the sayings leads Kimmerle to class "If it rained duck soup, he'd be there with a fork" under the heading of "Food," when, in actuality, it has more in common with "If it rained five-dollar gold pieces, he'd be there with boxing gloves on," which is found under the classification "Games, Dances, Musical Instruments."[23] Both sayings reflect a similar intrinsic relationship between the hypothetical situations posed, which has little to do either with the colorful images used or the specific concrete objects mentioned. It is interesting to note here that not only is the message of the sayings fundamentally the same, but both are also constructed along the same "architectural formula," "if ..., then ...."[24] Further, it is not clear that a discussion of these sayings in terms of their function (in a conversation, for example) would adequately define their essential qualities.[25]

2. Structural Studies of the Proverb and Traditional Saying

Recent studies in folklore have attempted to extend structural analysis to the realm of paroemiology.[26] Alan Dundes has attempted to distinguish between the various features inherent in every proverb as: (1) the proverb "image," based on the literal or "textural" level of the proverb; (2) the proverb "message," the ultimate meaning of the proverb as illustrated by the image: and (3) the "architectural formula" upon which the image is constructed and the message conveyed.[27] It is his belief that it is the architectural formula which should undergo structural analysis since the image and message appear to be relatively independent of the compositional, "architectural" formula.[28]

Dundes' final statements on the structural definition of the traditional saying derive in part from his analysis of the relationship between the proverb and the riddle.[29] Dundes has described the "minimum" proverb or riddle as consisting of "one descriptive element, that is to say, one unit composed of one topic and one comment."[30] In a proverb, the topic is explicit and known to both speaker and hearer, whereas in the riddle, the referent of the descriptive comment must be "guessed," but often it is the context of "performance" of the text which determines whether the item is functioning as a proverb (known referent) or riddle (unknown referent).[31]

Given Dundes' minimum structural model for the saying (one topic and one comment forming the descriptive element), it becomes impossible to have a proverb which consists of a single word.[32] Further, sayings which consist of a single descriptive element (one topic, one comment, e.g., "Revenge is sweet") are always identificational rather than oppositional, or contrastive. With the addition of another descriptive element to the minimum proverb, it becomes possible to construct oppositional or contrastive sayings (e.g., "Warm hands, cold heart"), as well as the "multi-descriptive element" identificational proverbs (i.e., "Where there's a will, there's a way").[33] In his discussion of the subtypes of identificational and contrastive sayings, Dundes identifies the simple equational proverb ($A = B$), with its basic transformations ("He who is A is B"; "Where there's A, there's B"; cause $\rightarrow$ effect, etc.).[34] A similar transformation of the equational, identificational proverb exhibits "a series of two or more descriptive elements ... often linked by a repetition of either the topic or comment: "Many men, many minds."[35] Dundes feels such sayings may be rewritten in the typical equational form without alteration of the meaning, a proof of the structural equivalency of the transformation.[36] Finally, he mentions a group of sayings, similar to the equational proverbs and their transformations, but which are "more coordinate or conjunctional than equational," such as "Live and learn."[37]

Oppositional or contrastive proverbs exhibit the same pattern of a basic formula and its transformations. The simplest oppositional sayings would be built along the formula of A ≠ B (i.e., "Beggars can't be choosers"), and exhibit such transformations as A is greater/less than B (which would include the "Better-than" sayings).[38] Other forms of the oppositional proverb include those where negation is not confined to the verbal statement (where A or B may appear as negative), sayings where normal cause and effect is denied or reversed, and sayings where antithetical contradictions occur (i.e., "A straight stick is crooked in the water").[39] The use of oppositional word pairs to create contrastive proverbs is discussed, as well as the occurence of sayings which exhibit "complementary distribution" or include both contrastive and identificational features, and call for more sophisticated analyses to determine the relationship between the descriptive elements.[40] Ultimately, Dundes is able to conclude on the basis of such structural analysis that "all proverbs are potentially propositions which compare and/or contrast."[41]

The advantages of employing, at least in part, Dundes' approach to the definition and analysis of the traditional saying are many. Such analysis facilitates the study of the saying on the basis of the relationships existing between the elements of the proverb, and is helpful in that it can account for both the "minimum" proverb such as "Time is money," as well as the more common, multi-descriptive element saying. Further, the use of the terms "topic" and "comment" provides the paroemiologist with concepts for the study of proverbs which are free from the dependence on syntax and style which often hinders the study of sayings in a foreign language, and it offers the first step toward a "cross-culturally valid definition of the proverb."[42] The schemata presented are also able to deal effectively with both the metaphorical and the non-metaphorical saying, the "folk" saying and the "learned" proverb.[43] Finally, and of perhaps the most interest to the study of folklore, the use of structural analysis in the study of proverbs may be taken as a "test case" to determine the general validity of such methodology in the study of folklore.[44]

Finnish folklorist Matti Kuusi has attempted to employ structural analysis in his proverb studies in order to find an internationally valid "type-system" for proverbs and which might be used in the evaluation of proverb collections.[45]

Working from his dissatisfaction with Russian proverb scholar Grigory Permyakov's[46] attempt to systematize the entire body of proverbs and proverb collections, Kuusi has taken exception to systems of analysis which deal with the surface structure and linguistic features of proverbs which do not readily translate into viable techniques of study for proverbial traditions of other cultures. While admitting that "structural analysis is not a skeleton key to all the locked doors of paroemiology," he finds that it shows "the relations of binary opposition to be the most coherent principle (within proverbs). Every proverb can be interpreted as a selection between two alternative responses."[47] His type system, organized around his perception of the saying as an embodiment of binary oppositions, proposes by a letter code to allow one scholar to communicate to another exactly what type of proverb is being discussed without both having to know the original language of the saying in order to discuss the "Baukern" ("kernel" - see Appendix A)) of the proverb, and its relation to other proverbs.[48]

Recently a less successful attempt to define the nature of the proverb, ostensibly along structural lines, has been made by George B. Milner.[49] Milner defines the proverb as a traditional saying with a quadripartite structure. Each saying consists, then, of a "head" and a "tail" which may be either positive or negative, depending on the values assigned to the two quarters which make up each half of the saying.[50] There are a number of problems in following Milner's scheme, chief among them the unsettled feeling that one has actually said very little about the structure or meaning of the saying after one has subjected it to Milner's scheme of investigation. In fact, due to the necessity of assigning positive or negative values to each quarter of the saying, the analysis actually works from a rather subjective base, and content takes precedent over form for Milner's purposes.[51]

Another use of structural analysis to clarify the nature of the proverb has been made by Nigel Barley in his work on the proverb and the maxim. In hopes of clarifying the differences between the proverb and the maxim, Barley has used a structural approach to define the literal, non-metaphorical statement (the maxim) and the metaphorical saying (the proverb). He finds that "the distinction between proverb and maxim is not absolute difference of type but rather one of level."[52] There is no structural difference between the two, even though the maxim is expressed in general terms which may be taken literally, whereas the proverb according

37

to his definition deals in metaphor, and "is always capable of being paraphrased by a maxim."[53] However, the "relevance restrictions" are explicit because of its literal, generalized form, and thus its application may be somewhat limited (i.e., "Once a thief, always a thief"). The proverb, though, because of its metaphorical, particularized form, has its relevance restriction "listed in its lexical entry" in that it functions as a "paradigmatic unit," and is susceptible to wider interpretation and application.[54] It is the internal logical relationships between the given terms of the proverb and maxim which constitute the "context-free core" (i.e., kernel) of the saying, and allows it to be understood and analyzed in the absence of contextual referents.[55]

It is in the paradigmatic nature of the proverb (and to a lesser extent, the maxim), with its inherent relevance restrictions, that Barley finds the "essential nature" of the proverb, which is laid bare through structural analysis.[56] The logical relationships within the proverb serve as "portable paradigms," whose "fundamental role" is "as a device for mapping one field of experience on to another."[57] Thus, Barley defines the proverb as "a standard statement of moral or categorical imperatives in fixed metaphorical paradigmatic form. It deals with fundamental logical relationships," and comments that "the proverb and maxim ensure that there is no such thing as a totally new situation by the establishing of relationships between events and categories. They can also be regarded as mechanisms by which the mind builds up larger-scale "bits," a switch from building with bricks to building with prefabricated units."[58] In his understanding of the structure and function of proverbs and maxims, Barley moves into the realm of the "functional" approach to folklore about which more will be said.

Recent emphasis on the "structure" of traditional sayings might lead one to expect the neglect of content for the sake of form. However, one finds that some folklore studies assert, almost aggressively, that it is only when form and structure are understood that content can be properly evaluated and interpreted.[59] It may be appropriate here to discuss the consensus of proverb scholarship on the matter of the "content" of sayings.

3. Content of Proverbs and Traditional Sayings

It is in the consideration of the "content" of traditional sayings that most folklorists seem to be in agreement, regardless of their approach to the nature and use of the proverb. Obviously, the content - that is, the proverb message conveyed by the image - is that portion of the saying which is most accessible to study, for it is this which confronts us upon reading or hearing the text of the item. Even when the message is unclear because it springs from a society where unfamiliar, culturally conditioned values obtain, the image is usually clearly presented and understandable.

On the most basic level, it is agreed that the images found in traditional sayings reflect the daily life and attitudes of the "folk." "Clearly enough, the imagery of proverbs springs from the common objects of everyday experience at its simplest level ...."[60] A saying which made use of little-known symbols or vocabulary would be less likely to remain current within a community than those which address their hearers in a familiar tongue. For this reason, the images of proverb are "homey"; they "smack of the soil and the folk," because their subject matter is "drawn from the interest and the world of the common man."[61] Hence, one finds a greater occurrence of the use of domestic animals as referents instead of wild, common items drawn from the household, agricultural community, or trades, or the concerns of a specific folk subgroup in which the saying is current.[62] It is this investigation of the content, as well as the use of traditional sayings, which leads Taylor to conclude that "At all times proverbs have meant more to the folk than to the learned."[63]

Discussion of the content of proverbs must not rest with a mere documentation of the types of elements used to construct the proverb image, since the "message" of the sayings conveys expressive content as well, and may be relatively independent of the image used.[64] If the content of traditional sayings consisted solely in the image, it seems doubtful that folk communities would have bothered to "record" such mundane items as "Barking dogs seldom bite," in its repertoire of "traditional wisdom."[65] Clearly, the expressive content of the traditional sayings includes more than that which is found in a literal reading of the proverb image.

The content of the traditional saying may well seem to be "crystallized similes from ordinary life,"[66] but it is in those relationships which obtain between the given terms of the proverb that the "message" is to be found.[67] Further, it is the perception of these relationships inherent within the saying that allows the proverb to be applied, "metaphorically" as it were, to other situations which have little or nothing to do with the basic terms of the proverb image.[68] For example, the saying "Once bitten, twice shy," though it may have originally reflected on the wary behavior of someone who had been bitten by an animal or insect, is really discussing the relationship between previous unpleasant experiences and subsequent behavior in situations which appear similar to the unpleasant one. Thus it may be reasonably applied to any relevant situation, although the possibility of actually being "bitten" may not occur in the context of use. This logical relationship between the terms of the proverb (in the example above, the relationship between "before" and "after") constitute Barley's "context-free core," or kernel, of the proverb,[69] or Jason's "abstraction idea" which is "the binding element in the relation between the proverb and society: the idea mediates between the multitude of particular contexts in social life and their poetic symbolization in the proverb."[70] The wide applicability of the relationships explicated in the proverb message accounts not only for the long life of many traditional sayings (that is, their message is not exhausted by a single application), but also points to the factors which influence and determine the nature of proverb use. As folklorist Roger Abrahams so aptly summarizes,

> In a proverb the elements of the description have an inevitable and organic relationship; they make sense together, and they cohere in an active way. To put it another way, the combination of elements of description sets up an image or idea in an immediately meaningful and dynamic Gestalt. The clarity of this pattern in combination with the felicity of phrasing of the proverb provides a tone of appropriateness and more weight enabling it to function as a guide for future action.[71]

The recognition that the message of a proverb may be applied "metaphorically" to a number of contexts is an important aspect of how a proverb functions, and may well be a contributing factor in the stress on metaphorical features found in so many studies on the proverb. It is immediately apparent that the saying which is more metaphorical is more easily applied than the saying (maxim) which may only be taken literally.[72] Indeed, Aristotle defined proverbs as "Metaphors from species to species,"[73] and students of the proverb today still stress this feature of the traditional saying as being, perhaps, one of its more important elements.[74] While the incorporation of a metaphor into the composition of a proverb may make it more easily remembered because it creates a vivid image, confers pleasure on the hearer/reader who has unraveled the meaning of the metaphor, and allows for greater succinctness,[75] the importance of the metaphor in the proverb probably lies in the fact that the form is especially well-suited for its function: the metaphorical proverb allows its user to move easily from message to application, and provides its user with protection from those who might disagree by means of the "indirection" of its language.[76]

Given that the content of traditional sayings consists, at its most basic level, of the presentation of logical relationships between its terms, and that users and hearers of the proverb relate this content to other situations via metaphor, it may be fruitful to consider the process of "categorization" at work in both the formation and application of a proverb.[77] When a proverb presents an insight into a relationship between its various terms, regardless of whether the correspondence is one of equivalents or dissimilarity, a statement has been made which "orders" the perception of experience. The categories which a traditional saying sets up or relates its message to need not be universally valid ones in order to function meaningfully. (For example, "Once a thief, always a thief" may not always be true.) The process of establishing a category serves to allow individuals to create order out of a myriad of experiences which might otherwise remain chaotic and resist assimilation, for "the learning and utilization of categories represents one of the most elementary and general forms of cognition by which man adjusts to his environment."[78] Once a category has been learned, it becomes a tool which functions to allow persons to react to new situations on the basis of past experience, by relating phenomena to the already existing structure of category systems.[79] When the categories of "fool" and "wise man" have been learned, the appropriate response to representatives of each category is possible (i.e., one should ignore the fool's talk, but listen to the advice of the wise).[80]

Three important considerations should be mentioned when discussing systems of categories. First, the formation of categories which relate meaningfully to one's experience of the world is fundmentally a human activity. Order is imposed, rather than discerned, as Bruner comments: " Science and common-sense inquiry alike do not discover the ways in which events are grouped in the world; they invent ways of grouping."[81] Whether or not such groupings are intrinsically valid may not be nearly so important a question as the inquiry into the benefits which recognizing such categories may confer upon society. For example, the recent switch of "soybean" from the category of "Feed" to the category of "Food" may bring considerable benefits, but the essence of the soybean has not changed.

Secondly, it is important to recognize that, while the process by which all individuals form categories is the same, the nature of the categories formed will be tied up irrevocably with the culture out of which the individual comes. Operational categories of Western European society differ widely from those of other cultures, and obviously, those portions of the proverbial stock which explicate a society's functional categories will mirror such variations. Bruner sums up:

> The categories in terms of which man sorts out and responds to the world around him reflect deeply the culture into which he is born .... In a sense, his personal history comes to reflect the traditions and the thought ways of his culture, for the events that make it up are filtered through the categorical systems he has learned.[82]

Finally, it must be pointed out that the categories of which a person or society makes use need not be explicit to be functional. Such categories often operate at a sub-conscious level, as basic premises which may remain unquestioned and unsystematized. In much writing outside the realm of folklore studies, it is common to find such premises or working categories referred to as "myths," an appellation which could scarcely be said to have found favor with folklorists and anthropologists. Dundes has proposed the term "folk ideas" for such unselfconscious postulates, and says of their occurrence in folklore genres:

> By "folk ideas" I mean traditional notions that a group of people have about the nature of man, of the world, and of man's life in the world. Folk ideas would not constitute a genre of folklore but rather would be expressed in a great variety of different genres. Proverbs would almost certainly represent the expression of one or more folk ideas, but the same folk ideas might also appear in folktales .... However, in so far as folk

ideas are unstated premises which underlie the thought and action of a given group of people, they are not likely to appear consistently in any fixed-phrased form.[83]

Such an understanding of the relation of proverbs to the formation of categories, and the folk ideas which underlie such categories may aid in the analysis of the content of a traditional saying. Consider, for example, the operational category of "time" (and its associated concepts) which often finds its way into the proverbial stock of a culture. The Swahili proverb "Haraka, haraka, haina baraka" ("Haste, haste, brings no blessing") encapsulates a cultural perspective much like that of the ancient wisdom concept of the "right time." When found in context in a modern play, the saying is used by a parent to dissuade his mate from seeking an early marriage for their child.[84] "Haste" in such a matter is quite out of place in a culture where time moves slowly and momentous events in life are savored and drawn out as long as possible. The message in the context of use is "slow down and enjoy!" - quite a different message than that which a Westerner might supply, coming from a culture where "Haste makes waste" and "Time is money." Even glossing the Swahili context with a Western proverb which has the same contextual and proverb referents, "Marry in haste, repent at leisure," fails to bring the proper understanding of the situation, since its message reflects different categories of cultural presuppositions.

A considerable group of folklorists who have undertaken the study of the traditional saying have not been satisfied to confine their inquiries to questions of style and content. For them, one of the most decisive features of the proverb lies in the functions which it may serve in a given culture. The investigation of the function of the saying is closely related to considerations of the function of folklore in general, and attempts are made to relate the data from fieldwork studies to a theoretical framework which encompasses all the genres of folklore. Proverbs are a favorite topic of study for the scholars who take the functional approach to folklore, and it is to these studies on the function and context of traditional sayings that we now turn.

FOLKLORE STUDIES

1. Function and Context of Proverbs
   and Traditional Sayings

Recognition of the importance of the function of folklore

is by no means a new or revolutionary concept, even though functional considerations have often been eclipsed by historical and comparative approaches to folklore. Scholars like A. I. Hallowell and B. Malinowski repeatedly emphasised the necessity of investigating the social context and functions of folklore genres, expecially myth, within society. Only with such study could anthropologists and folklorists begin to understand the hitherto unexplored relation of folklore to culture.[85] Further, only when function and context are considered as an integral feature of folklore can any item or genre be understood properly, since study of function provides valuable insights into the essence of the phenomenon.[86] Such studies caused Malinowski to conclude that myth is no "idle tale," but rather "a vital ingredient of human civilization" which functions as "a warrant, a charter, and often even a practical guide" for numerous facets of a culture.[87]

Folklorist William Bascom has delineated four functions of folklore within society: it acts as (1) a projective system which provides psychological release, (2) a validation of culture, (3) a vehicle for education, and (4) a means of social control.[88] In Bascom's view, this perception of folklore as a projective system which "reveals man's frustrations and attempts to escape in fantasy from repressions imposed upon him by society" furnishes the folklorist with a framework in which to understand the often bizarre inversions of a culture's "everyday" life found in so many of the genres.[89] "Amusement" can no longer be regarded as the sole function of folklore, although it is obviously an important feature. Likewise, the validation of a culture's institutions, rituals and customs provided by items of folklore is a major function often overlooked when folklore is regarded primarily as a form of literary expression or verbal art.

The function of folklore in the realm of education in societies which are other than literate is a significant one, not only because various forms transmit culturally accepted rules of conduct but also because the actual information found in folklore may be greatly valued for its own sake.[90] Finally, an important role of folklore lies in its ability to maintain social control by approving those who conform and censuring those who do not. Thus, folklore may become "an internalized check on behavior" in societies where it is "employed to control, influence, or direct the activities of others from the time the first lullaby is sung, or ogre tale is told to them."[91]

Chapter II : Paroemiology and Folklore Studies

Although Bascom alludes to proverbs as fulfilling all of the functions described above, he places the most emphasis on the roles of education and social control,[92] although others have cited the function of proverbs as culture-validating and providing psychological release by easing tensions as equally important.[93] Those who study proverbs are much intrigued by the notion of "cultural ambiguity" to which, in Bascom's theoretical model, the function of folklore is addressed. When a situation arises in which there is a need to resolve the ambiguity of making one's way "correctly" through life, or offer an evaluation of another's actions it is here that a proverb is most likely to be used. Says Bascom of African proverbs:

> Because of the high regard in which they are held and because they are considered as especially appropriate to adult life, African proverbs are highly effective in exercising social control. Because they express the morals or ethics of the group, they are convenient standards of appraising behavior in terms of the approved norms. Because they are pungently, wittily and sententiously stated, they are ideally suited for commenting on the behavior of others. They are used to express social approval or disapproval; praise for those who conform to accepted social conventions and criticism or ridicule of those who deviate; warning, defiance, or derision of a rival or enemy and advice, counsel, or warning to a friend when either contemplates action which may lead to social friction, open hostilities, or direct punishment by society.[94]

Such an understanding of the function of proverbs in society is scarcely foreign to those who have approached the subject from a more traditional perspective, although it has led some to emphasize the "moral" or didactic content and function above all else. Krappe stresses the pedagogic features of the proverb as the single most crucial identifying element in this genre.[95] Similarly, Taylor comments on the function of the saying,

> As a guide to life's problems, the proverb summarizes a situation, passes a judgment, or offers a course of action. It is a consolation in difficulties large and small, and a guide when a choice must be made. It expresses morality suited to the common man. It is cautious and conservative in recommending the middle way: "Virtus in medio, Nequid nimis."[96]

45

Traditional Sayings in the Old Testament

A number of studies exist which present the proverb stock of a given group, and most address the topic of the function of the proverbs within the group, although with varying degrees of success. Tribal and so-called primitive societies, in particular, have been the subject of much study with regard to the function and context of proverb use, since such groups often have a vigorous tradition of proverb use and may show less "cultural contamination" of their working proverbial stock. Herzog, in his study of the Jabo proverbs of Liberia, refers to a number of functions which traditional sayings serve among the population he observed: presentation of a method of "coping" with the novel situation in the light of tradition; classification and evaluation of actions under legal consideration; resolution of social tensions and personal dissatisfaction or confusion; and the "intellectual function ... of subsuming the particular under the general."[97] John Messenger, Jr.'s work on the legal use of Anang proverbs in Nigeria, along with Raymond Firth's study of Maori proverbs, recognizes functions similar to those outlined by Herzog.[98] The role of proverbs in legal proceedings is not confined to African Societies. Much of the Anglo-Saxon corpus of sayings, as well as European proverbs, appear to have played a part in legal settings, "common law" etc. (e.g., "Possession, is nine-points of the law," "Fair exchange is no robbery").[99]

More recently, studies of proverb use have begun to stress the inclusion of context situations of use along with the text of the proverb. This attention to "contextual" features of proverb performance gives research such as Dundes' and Arewa's treatment of the educational use of the Yoruba proverb an added dimension of meaning, for they have shown that much of a proverb's meaning derives from its context of use (e.g., who says what to whom under what circumstances).[100] Their approach to the study of proverb use draws heavily on the concept of folklore as communication and the "ethnography of speaking" approach:

One needs to ask not only for proverbs, and for what counts as a proverb, but also for information as to the other components of the situations in which proverbs are used. What are the rules governing who can use proverbs, or particular proverbs, and to whom? Upon what occasions? In what places? With what other persons present or absent? Using what channel (e.g., speech, drumming, etc.)? Do restrictions or prescriptions as to the use of proverbs or a proverb have to do with particular topics? With the specific relationship between

speaker and addressee? What exactly are the contributing contextual factors which make the use of
proverbs, or of a particular proverb, possible or not
possible, appropriate or inappropriate?[101]

The interactions between function and context of use has
led to new methods for describing and discriminating between
the various fixed-phrase genres. More and more, folklorists
are turning their attention to context as a key to unlock the
doors to understanding function, form, structure, meaning,
and even general social interaction.[102]

For Eleanor A. Forster, context and function come
together in a decisive way to allow the field worker and
folklorist to make a genre distinction between proverbs and
superstitions.[103] It is only through an analysis of the
context of use that one is able to determine such distinctions,
and each proverb or traditional saying may be seen, in
Forster's view, to have three levels of context in any event of
proverb performance.[104] These levels are: (A) the situation
which it refers to; (B) an inner context when it is spoken, and
(C) a milieu context of the environmental perspective.[105]
Context A, is "literal context" which refers directly to the
proverb metaphor, i.e., the proverb message as conveyed by
the image. Context B or the "micro-context" consists of the
situation which elicits the proverb and in which the proverb is
used (spoken or written). The "macro-context" or context C
refers to the broader cultural matrix whose ideas are
embodied in both the literal metaphor of the proverb and the
user's application of the metaphor in a specific situation. The
"macro-context," since it is the area in which one finds the
"folk ideas," or commonly held presuppositions of a culture,
may be the area which is, ultimately, of most interest to the
cultural historian or exegete, but the ideas embodied here
may only be approached through the detailed analysis of the
other contextual levels, as "contextualist" Roger Abrahams
points out: "the recording of contextual data is absolutely
central to the understanding both of expressive style of
specific groups and of the ways in which proverbs (and other
genres of traditional expression) are related to the value
structure of the community and the daily workings out of
institutional life."[106]

Heda Jason had used the aspect of proverb function in
society to develop a hypothetical model of proverb
formations, which moves from particular instances to
symbolization of the "abstraction idea" in the proverb

47

metaphor, and then back to particular, individual situations to which the proverb is applied.[107] Over time, or under different circumstances of use, the proverb metaphor may give rise to an abstraction idea which may differ from that which led to the formation of the proverb ("Abstraction idea B"). Jason concludes that the "message" of the proverb found in the metaphor is related to the general function of oral literature "as a connective element between the value system and the social system, suggesting certain attitudes towards the society's values and its problematic points."[108] An important feature of proverb use in society is found in the fact that both the problem and its resolution are expressed metaphorically, and such "indirection" affords protection to the proverb user, since a variety of interpretations are usually possible. Similarly, the status of the proverb as a "traditionally sanctioned vehicle to express one's thoughts and intentions" also works to shield the user from unpleasant repercussions or misunderstandings.[109] In conclusion, Jason points to three aspects concerning the relations of proverbs to society:

(1)   the use of the proverb by members of the society (traditional vehicle of expression);

(2)   the way in which the proverb addresses the listener (intent to teach; advise);

(3)   the message the proverb carries and confers upon the listener (the function of the proverb: resolves problematical situations.)[110]

Barbara Kirshenblatt-Gimblett has applied the new emphasis on the context of proverb use to the theories of "proverb meaning": if proverbs are said to express absolute or general truths, how can one effectively account for contradictory proverbs ("Look before you leap"; "He who hesitates is lost")? Kirshenblatt-Gimblett concludes that proverbs express "relative" truth, and that a "proverb's meaning, rather than being autonomous of the proverb's use as we are led to believe by proverb collections, is indeed contextually specified."[111] In part, the relativity of the proverb's message results from several sources of "multiple meaning," such as "(1) syntactic ambiguity ...; (2) lexical ambiguity ... and (3) "key" (kinetic features of proverb performance, tone of voice, physical setting, etc.)."[112] Determining the proverb's "base meaning" (i.e., the message, or kernel relationship conveyed by the image) is the first step in any analysis, but ultimately what is being discussed in

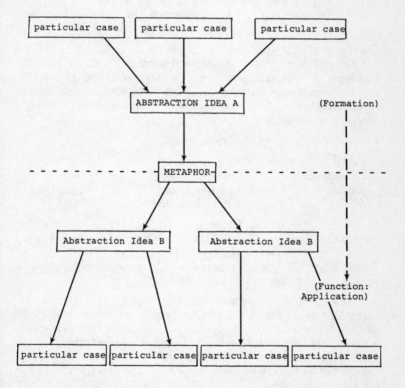

FIGURE 3: Heda Jason's Model of Interaction Between Proverb Formation and Function

SOURCE: Heda Jason, "Proverbs in Society: the Problem of Meaning and Function," Prov 17 (1971), p.620

proverb use is "proverb performance meaning" which is conditioned by the following factors:

(1)   proverbs express relative rather than absolute truth;

(2)   a proverb's meaning and "truth" are conditioned by the context;

(3)   a proverb that fits semantically may not be socially appropriate in terms of what the participants in the situation wish to accomplish;

(4)   a person tends to select a proverb on the basis of what the situation requires rather than simply or solely becuase of either a given proverb's semantic fit or its "truth" in some abstract sense;

(5)   situations can be evaluated in more than one way.[113]

Documentations of various contextual uses of a single proverb are presented in order to illustrate the considerations involved in evaluati14ong proverb performance, and the author moves towards an "enactment theory" of proverb use in her final evaluation of the components of proverb performance meaning (see Figure 4).

Proverb Performance Meaning =

| Participants' Evaluation of Situation | + | Participants' Understanding of Proverb's Base Meaning | + | Interactional Strategy of Proverb User |

Figure 4:   Proverb Performance Meaning
SOURCE: Barbara Kirshenblatt-Gimblett, "Toward a Theory of Proverb Meaning," Proverbium 22 (1973): 826.
Note that all the components which make up proverb performance meaning are variable.

Attention to context and function forms the basis for the investigation of the messages of Swahili proverbs in a study done by Carolyn A. Parker, working with both field situations and literary use of proverbs. Parker has defined the proverb as "a message coded by tradition and transmitted to evaluate and/or affect human behavior."[114] She focuses on the proverb as a "learned" element of culture, "traditional" in that its surface form remains fairly stable, and "purposive" in that its function is to convey a message which comments on ambiguous situations in every day life.[115] Her emphasis on the proverb as "code" incorporates the idea of the proverb metaphor as central to the <u>form</u> of the proverb, and its application to a context by analogy as the crucial aspect of its <u>function</u>.

> The definition places stress on the primary feature of proverbs: code. Proverbs are not only metaphors, they are applied metaphors which point out a parallel between two situations: that to which they refer and that in which they occur. It is the culture with its special constructions of reality which serves as the codebook for both the content and context of its proverbs. Moreover, the present definition places stress on the primary function of a proverb: message transmission. Relative length of text, relative truth, degree of morality and wisdom are arbitrary considerations .... A proverb is a phenomenon with a purpose and this purpose is relative to behavior which is significant within its cultural context because it challenges or reaffirms notions of what proper behavior should be.[116]

Thus, Parker follows Taylor and Barley in distinguishing between the proverb and the saying as metaphorical and non-metaphorical, respectively. The application of a statement to its literal referents (i.e., saying "Look before you leap" to a broad-jumper) would not constitute proverb performance, whereas the application of the same statement to a different set of contextual referents would (i.e., saying "Look before you leap" to someone pondering an important decision).

Parker attempts to clarify the relationship between the proverb's role of evaluation and the attempt to affect behavior, through an analysis of the transmission of the proverb's message. Three roles in proverb performance are identified: object, source, and receiver. The "object" in a context is the one(s) who, through behavior planned or completed, has elicited the proverb; the "source" is the actual proverb user who "sends" the message; and the "receiver," logically enough, is the one(s) who hears/reads the message.[117] When the object and receiver are the same, the intent of the proverb performance is to <u>affect</u> behavior; when the three roles are filled by different persons, the proverb is "purely evaluative" (see Figure 5).[118]

Parker makes use of Forster's "levels of context" (literal, micro-, and macro-context), and illustrates the interplay between the three from her fieldwork. She concludes on the basis of her own contextual studies that the essential

Evaluative Proverb Performance:

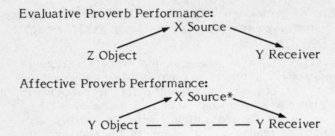

*Source is generally of superior or equivalent status relative to the object/receiver.

Figure 5: Types of Proverb Performance in Swahili Society
SOURCE: Carolyn Ann Parker, "Aspects of a Theory of Proverbs: Contexts and Messages in Swahili," (1973), p. 139.

function of the proverb in actual use in interactions in Swahili society (i.e., in the micro-context) is primarily that of evaluation. She believes that the other functions of folklore outlined by Bascom may be found superimposed over this primary function, but that, regardless of the variations found in proverb meaning or in the intent of the proverb user, this basic function - evaluation - remains the same on the level of the micro-context.[119]

One of the most comprehensive treatments of the proverb genre from the "contextualist" perspective is to be found in the writings of folklorist Roger Abrahams. Based on his studies of a variety of what he calls "conversational genres," Abrahams has stressed the need to speak of the "rhetorical theory" of folklore, which recognizes not only the item of the genre but also its performance which attempts to affect the hearing (reading) audience.[120]

> Folklore, being traditional activity, argues traditionally; it uses arguments and persuasive techniques developed in the past to cope with recurrences of social problem situations ....

> Each item of traditional expression articulates conflict in some way; it also provides some manner of temporary resolutions .... The controlling power of folklore, the carrying out of its rhetorical intent, resides in the ability of the item and the performer to establish a sense of identity between a "real" situation and its artificial embodiment.[121]

Thus, Abrahams has incorporated the notions of context (performance) into Bascom's understanding of folklore as a projective system which resolves the conflicts of a society, while conferring the positive pleasures found in amusement, social interaction, dissolution (at least temporarily) of tension, and intellectual stimulation.[122]

Proverbs, for Abrahams, fall into the classification of "formal conventions" of conversational genres, along with superstitions, taunts, curses, and prayers.[123] Because of their metaphorical "cloak, they are less aggressive in appearance than the curse or taunt, although, obviously, some aggressive intent remains since the function of the proverb is to affect social interaction,"[124] and they are especially well suited for their function, because of their appearance of objectivity, traditional sanction, and wit.

Proverbs implement their "rhetorical strategy" in contextual use by giving a "traditional name" to recurrent situations, and presenting a method of coping which has been used in the past. Abrahams suggested that the proverb's effect in "clarifying" the situation may stem in part from the balance between its elements, especially noticeable when the composition is binary. He identifies four types of proverbs as the most common: "positive equivalence (Time is money); negative equivalence (Money isn't everything); positive causational (Haste makes waste); and negative causational (Two wrongs don't make a right)."[125] Finally, a proper strategy for the solution of problems may be proposed after the situation has been correctly categorized, in the light of tradition, and "one can fruitfully use the occurrences of proverbs in context as an index to the places where the social structure of the community is weakest and needs the greatest amount of control."[126] In "active" use when referring to present events, proverbs are used to present a "strategy" or plan of action to affect events; in "passive use" when referring to past events, proverbs present an evaluation or model for understanding what has occurred, along with shaping orientation toward similar events in the future.[127] Although the proverb is perfectly susceptible to analysis when contextual information is absent, such documentation is necessary to understand the dynamics of proverb use, particularly in conversation, when proverb strategy (that is, the attempt to affect or evaluate) fails if the referents are not clearly indicated.[128]

2. Proverb Collections and Proverbs in Literary Sources

It is to be expected that the growing emphasis on the context of folklore and the interpretation of the function of folklore genres should have its influence on the direction of current studies. On all fronts in folklore studies, the challenge is being raised to move beyond simple identification and classification as the sole end of research in folklore.[129] In the realm of paroemiology, the simple proverb collection, while it may well represent the first step in research into the nature and use of proverbs, is no longer a sufficient source for the types of investigation which are being proposed. Indeed, one leading paroemiologist has gone so far as to state that "the proverb in a collection is dead."[130] Although the image and message of the saying in a collection may be accessible to analysis, the dimension of the use is lost. Full contextual data may be supplied with current and future studies which are conducted in the field, but what is to be done about the "context" of use of proverbs which come down to us from an earlier time? In order to deal with these features of proverb study, however tentatively, the folklorist and paroemiologist alike must turn to such written or literary sources as are available from earlier periods.

Recognizing that the dynamic concept of fieldwork which is so dear to the hearts of folklorists of the contextual and functional schools developed only at the beginning of the 19th century, Richard Dorson has proposed a typology of folklore found in printed sources.[131] Noting that a printed source is one "in which folk traditions have found lodging more or less accidentally and casually,"[132] Dorson moves along a continuum of sources which range from "close-to-oral" (collections with verbatim reportage) to "remote-from-oral" (literature based on folklore).[133] Dorson states that the shortest genres have the best chance of being recorded without alteration (a heartening observation for paroemiologists!), and points out that "printed and oral texts do not necessarily compete with each other, but may act in conjunction, in mutually stimulating camaraderie."[134] Literature is an especially rich source for folklore, but careful attention must be given both to the author's "intent" in the use of folklore which may alter the genre, and to the place the work occupies on the folklore-to-literature continuum.[135]

Archer Taylor also addressed the problem of the study of proverbs as they occur in literature, pointing out that use varies widely from genre to genre.[136] Satire, historical song, sermons, writing of rhetorical intent, and literature which aims at a flavor of "local color" are all apt to make more use of proverbs than such genres as lyrical and epic poetry or narrative, although works of the latter type should not automatically be dismissed from consideration.[137] Further, changes in the use of proverb literature do and have occurred over time, so that attention must be paid to the historical circumstances in which the work was composed.

Paroemiologist Wolfgang Mieder has addressed the problems of literary proverb studies, based on the conviction that "the proverbs of earlier times can only be found by scanning written works,"[138] and proposes that such study should move beyond identification to deal with questions of context, function, and creative use of folk genres by an author.[139] He, too, stresses that type of literary genre is an important factor in the occurrence and use made of proverbs, although his evaluation of the likelihood of proverb use in prose narrative is more positive than that of Taylor. Drama, which is of special interest because of its portrayal of conversation, and "regional" works which aim at depicting the life and culture of a given group, and "represent the true language of the folk as it was and still is" are especially suitable for study.[140] Mieder also supports the investigation of proverb occurrence in those genres of literature which have been thought traditionally to have little or no incidence of proverb use such as lyrical poetry.[141] The occurrence of proverbs in modern "popular" literature (i.e., paperback novels) and advertising bears witness to one of the essential features of the proverb, "namely its adaptability to any situation."[142] Concerning the function of proverb use in literary works, Meider concludes:

> Just as the number of proverbs might differ from one work to another, so might the function of the proverbs be of a varied kind. Often proverbs function as mere expressions of popular wisdom, as explanation, advice, warning, rationalization, etc. It all depends in what context the proverb is used. Since the context in which the proverb is used is not always a serious one, proverbs can lose their underlying didactic tendency very quickly to be fitted into a humorous, ironic, or even satirical situation. The author will find particular functions for

the proverbs and it is up to the investigator to find out the most frequent and striking usages of the proverbs in the literary work and the age that it represents .... Each age, each author, each work and each situation will force a new function onto the proverb .... It lives only when used, and as a mirror of life it can function in an infinite number of ways. Asking for the function of the proverb in a literary work is the breath of life of such an investigation. The answers obtained show how the proverb lives and how it can be an important part of an author's style.[143]

Based on his extensive work on Chaucer's Canterbury Tales, literary critic and proverb scholar Bartlett Jere Whiting has addressed the question of how to tell whether an author using a proverb in a literary work has used a "real" (i.e., extant) proverb or invented one to fit his purposes. In particular, he has developed five criteria to aid such assessments:

(1) citation of the proverb before the time of the author;
(2) citation of the proverb after the author's time, but in a work judged unlikely to have been influenced by that author;
(3) indication by the author that a proverb is being cited, which the critic may choose to believe;
(4) stylistic violation of the context by the proverb (as in Canterbury Tales, D 655-658);
(5) recognition that paroemiologists are generally able to detect an author's attempt to "counterfeit" a proverb.[144]

Concerning the function of proverbs in literary genres, Whiting points out that their use is not solely for didactic purposes, and refers to early English drama, where they enliven the dialogue in the comic scenes in an effort, perhaps, to give it realism."[145]

Turning to contemporary African literature, one finds a good example of how "unwritten traditions pass into literary form,"[146] as such authors as Chinua Achebe, Ebrahim N. Hussein, Suleiman Omar Said Baalawy, and others provide a rich literary context for the sayings of their peoples in plays, novels, and short stories.[147] Reflecting the vigorous oral tradition of societies which still make daily use of proverbs, the vernacular literature uses proverbs in "dialogue, in the course of narrative as moral commentary by the narrator, or

56

as rhetorical devices in poetry,"[148] and even "single words or phrases" can be evocative of the current proverbial stock of the culture.[149] Although such societies offer ample opportunity to study proverbs in fieldwork situations, anthropologists and folklorists alike do not hesitate to make critical use of the literary sources available for study when fieldwork is impracticable.[150]

Peter Seitel has used the novels of Chinua Achebe to study some aspects of proverb use among the Ibo of Eastern Nigeria. Defining proverbs as "short, traditional, 'out-of-context' statements used to further some social end,"[151] Seitel's investigation centers around "contextual" considerations of proverb use raised by Dundes and Arewa's "ethnography of speech approach."[152] The author outlines his goals as follows:

> Given that a person has memorized a certain number of proverb texts, by application of what set of rules does he speak them in a culturally appropriate manner and by what criteria does he judge the correctness of another's usage? Alternately stated, the goal of the method presented is to delineate the culturally shared system which enables a person to use proverbs in a socially acceptable manner.[153]

Seitel's methodological presuppositions concerning the use of literary sources to investigate aspects of proverb use rests on the assumption that when a novel has been shown through comparison with other ethnographic data on the same society, to portray accurately the features of day-to-day life such as marriage customs, social organization, etc., then one may assume that the portrayal of proverb use found in the work will similarly reflect a "truthful" picture of proverb performance within the culture.[154] Obviously, the use of literary sources contains inherent limitations as a method for contextual study: informants are not available for comment on the "correctness" of the proverb performance or various different interpretations of the proverb which might also be appropriate to the context; only a limited number of proverbs will occur in a literary work, and those are there fundamentally to serve the author's purpose; proverbs dealing with animals, although very frequent in the Ibo culture, seldom seem to show up in literary settings; and the "out-of-context" features (both in terms of violation of syntax and normal word combinations) of a proverb's occurrence in a literary context seems to be blurred by the use of an English translation.[155] Still, the literary source which meets the presupposed standard of verisimilitude offers a valuable area for proverb study, since the "context" of use is described, and open to analysis.

Seitel has outlined a model of the various components involved in any event of "proverb performance," which he calls the Interaction Situation, the Proverb Situation, and the Context Situation (see Figure 6). The Interaction Situation describes the actual event of proverb use, and includes such considerations as the social occasion (private conversation, meeting of elders, etc.), age and sex of the hearer and proverb user, social status, kinship categories, and so on. Along with these facets of the Interaction Situation, the intention of the proverb user is added, since the literary work generally makes clear the "strategy" of the event of proverb performance. Added to the description of the Interaction Situation are the features of the "Proverb Situation"[156] and the "Context Situation," that is, the situation or events which the proverb user correlates with the situation obtaining in the proverb. In Section I., the Interaction Situation of this model, "X" stands for the proverb user (Parker's "Source") and "Y" represents the hearer to whom the proverb is addressed ("Receiver"); $\nleftrightarrow$ indicates the relationship between them (such as age, sex, equality of rank, education, intent of the proverb user). These factors constitute the Interaction Situation. In Section II, the Proverb Situation, "A" and "B" represent the given terms found in the proverb image and $\sim$ stands for the logical relationship between them, often some sort of "verbal idea" (such as causation, identification, contrast). In Section III, the Context Situation, "C" and "D" stand for the "hidden terms" to which the elements of the Proverb Situation (the "given" terms "A" and "B" in the proverb image) are being related metaphorically by the proverb user. The relationship between the elements of the Context Situation "C" and "D" is indicated by $\sim$, and the dotted lines indicate the correspondence felt by the proverb user to exist between the Proverb Situation and the Context Situation. No correspondence may in fact exist, but it is the speaker's contention that it does. The entire diagram might be paraphrased as representing a situation in which "X says to Y, 'A is to ($\sim$) B (the Proverb Situation) as (: :) C is to ($\sim$) D' (the Context Situation)."

Of particular interest is Seitel's finding that when the correspondence between A and C is one between the proverb's given term and Speaker X in some situation (in

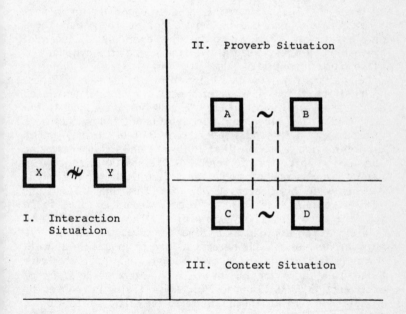

FIGURE 6: Social and Metaphorical Relationships in Proverb Use
SOURCE: Peter Seitel, "Proverbs: A Social Use of Metaphor," in: Folklore Genres (1976), p.129

other words, whenever C equals X), the correspondence is generally a positive one. In contrast, whenever C refers to hearer Y, a third person not present, or a remote situation upon which speaker X is commenting, the correspondence between A and C is generally construed as a negative one. On the basis of the analysis of the sample, which is admittedly a small one, Seitel contends that whenever a proverb is used to apply to the person employing it, is is used positively; when the proverb applies to a second or third person, it is used negatively. Further, Seitel feels that two primary "strategies" emerge, by which proverb use attempts to resolve the conflicts felt in the interaction situation: "First, he (the proverb user) may propose to defeat one side of the contradiction, giving victory to the other .... Second, he may propose that the contradiction which he perceives in a situation and which the intended hearer also perceives is in fact the natural state of the world and must be endured."[157] These strategies hold true for the incidences of proverb use analyzed by Seitel, and he feels that these may ultimately be seen to be the dominant fratures of proverb use in cross-cultural examinations of the dynamics of proverb use in context.

Let us illustrate how this diagram might be used to discuss an incidence of "proverb performance" in a biblical text, such as Job 34, where the second "Elihu" poem begins. As the dramatic setting which continues here is defined by the prose introduction to the Elihu speeches in 32:1-6, we may set up the Interaction Situation (I) as follows. Elihu (X) is addressing Job and his three "comforters" (Y); the relationship between them (⧸⧸) is one of perceived inferiority, since Elihu is younger than his hearers (32:4, 6f.). This implies that his counsel contains less "wisdom" since wisdom is to be found with the aged (Jb. 12:12,20; 15:10; 32:7). However, it is also clear from the context that Elihu perceives the relationship between himself and his hearers as one of inequality as well, since his hearers, by their previous arguments, have shown themselves to be lacking in wisdom despite their years of experience (32:2ff). Elihu, in 34:3, uses a saying introduced by a causal "kî," to justify his claim to the critical attention of his hearers.[158]

The Proverb Situation (II) deals with the message of the saying "The ear tests words (A) as the palate tastes food (B)." The relationship between the two images presented (~) is one of equivalence in the area of discrimination; that is, the hearer is able to judge the fitness of an argument on its intrinsic merits, even as the taster judges food on its taste. The implication here is also that the hearer/taster is able to experience and judge an objective stimulus by means of human faculties which all possess.

The Context Situation (III) is clear from Elihu's appeal: "Hear my words, you wise men, and give ear to me, you who know; for the ear tests words as the palate tastes food. Let us choose what is right; let us determine among ourselves what is good." Elihu requests that his audience "test" his argument on its own merit (C), rather than evaluate it on the basis of peripheral features, such as the youth (and hence, the implied inexperience) of its proponent. If his audience does this, then Elihu believes that they too will affirm "what is good" in his position, on its own claims, even as the palate is able to judge the taste of food (D). Thus, we might fill in the diagram, as in Figure 7.

A paraphrase of this interaction might be, Elihu says to Job and his comforters (as well as the later hearers/readers of the text!), "Even as the palate judges food on the basis of its taste (instrinsic quality knowable to humans through common faculties), so should you evaluate my position on the basis of its own merits, rather than discounting it because of my youth."[159] Elihu uses the saying here with reference to future evaluations to be made by his hearers; his purpose is to affect the subsequent attitude of his audience. The hearers in the Context Situation (C) are to be identified with the addressees, Job and his friends, in the Interaction Situation (Y). Since Elihu is exhorting his hearers to make use of their rational faculties and give his a fair hearing, and in light of his earlier unflattering statements about the arguments of both Job and his friends,[160] we may take this correspondence between the referents of the Interaction Situation and the Context Situation (Y = C) as a relatively negative one, from the source Elihu's perspective. Elihu perceives the "wisdom" of his audience as inadequate, as shown by their arguments, and by quoting a saying he makes use of traditional arguments to advance his own position without openly offending his hearers.

The conflicting cultural presuppositions which underlie the interaction between Elihu and his audience, and provide the reason for proverb performance in such an interaction become more clear through the analysis provided by our model. On the one hand, we find the general assumptions about the relative status and wisdom attributed to age and youth;[161] on the other, we find the appeal that such

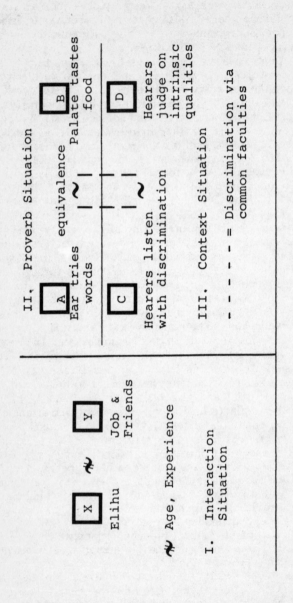

FIGURE 7: Proverb Performance in Job 34

stereotypes be disregarded in favor of judgments made on the merit of an argument itself rather than on the importance of its author. This latter approach is in keeping with a major current in the wisdom tradition, that wisdom is more properly seen as coming from the Lord rather than any human attribute (Jb. 32:8; Pr. 16:1, etc.).

CONCLUSIONS AND DIRECTIONS
For the Study of the Traditional Saying
Drawn from Folklore and Anthropological Studies

A survey of the literature on the proverb - its nature, function, and contextual use - shows that many of the problems under consideration by form critics of Old Testament wisdom literature are likewise of interest to proverb scholars and folklorists. Despite the unresolved problems found in areas such as that of proverb definition, it is still possible to discover valuable insights into the nature and use of the proverb from folklore and paroemiological research which may be applied to the study of the saying in the Old Testament. For our purposes, it might be helpful to consider these conclusions under three major headings: the definition and nature of the saying; methodological approaches to the analysis of the saying; and consideration of life-setting of proverb use.

1. Definition and Nature of the Traditional Saying

The lack of an adequate, cross-culturally valid definition of the traditional saying continues to be troublesome, in spite of recent attempts to redefine the saying along structural or functional lines, and we continue to find a lack of standardization in the use of terminology. Traditional definitions which deal primarily with style and content are clearly inadequate, since they do not readily translate into terms which are applicable to study of non-European proverbs. Emphasis on metaphor as the basis of the proverb is similarly unsuitable, because it leaves no room to deal effectively with sayings which are not metaphorical but which have, nonetheless, achieved currency in a society as proverbs. Structural definitions which center around "topic-comment" units, architectural formulae, or quad-ripartite structures do not distinguish the proverb clearly enough from concise prose statements "constructed" along similar lines, and general stylistic considerations are apt to be lost. Functional or contextual definitions suffer from analogous drawbacks, since other folklore genres could conceivably serve the same function as a proverb in a given context. Attempts to classify proverbs as sayings which deal with "ultimate truths" or didactic content fail because, as has been made clear in contextual studies, proverb meaning depends a great deal upon the context of use, and is scarcely as rigid as traditional discussions of the proverb would have us believe.

For our purposes, we will define the traditional saying as a statement, current among the folk, which is concise, syntactically complete, consisting of at least one topic and comment which may or may not be metaphorical, but which exhibits a logical relationship between its terms. Further, the saying may be marked by stylistic features (mnemonics, rhythm, alliteration, assonance, etc.) or be constructed along recognizable frames ("Better A than B ...," etc.) which distinguish it from other genres (or folk idioms). The referents which form the image are most likely to be drawn from the experience of common, "everyday" life, but the meaning (message) of the saying may vary from context to context, and any "truth claim" for that message must be considered "relative" rather than "absolute." The transmission of the saying, however achieved, is <u>always</u> purposeful, but specific details of contextual use may be necessary to determine the purpose in any given situation.

It might be argued that the definition proposed above does little to improve on previous attempts which missed the mark by being too vague, too broad, or too specific. While it is true that our proposed definition is rather bulky, it combines several literary and anthropological approaches to the proverb so that major considerations such as currency, style, content, meaning, function and context are at least mentioned, even if their relative importance in the makeup of a "proverb" cannot be assessed. Since our ultimate goal is the investigation of the traditional saying as it appears in contexts <u>outside</u> of the wisdom books and proverb collections therein, little will be said concerning the origin of the sayings or the debate over the development of the artistic wisdom saying from the folk saying. Regardless of the origin of a saying, it may be contended that where is appears portrayed in conversation, as an item of folk speech, in arguments, and so on, it constitutes a saying which might have been affirmed by the folk, even if not originated by them. At any rate, debates over the origin of a saying have little relevance to the study of its use in the context. In order to avoid confusion, however, we will use the term "traditional" rather than "folk" to apply to the saying, since "folk" carries the implications of supposed origin as it is used by Old Testament scholars. Further, we will accept Barley's distinction in terminology to differentiate between metaphorical sayings (proverb) and non-metaphorical sayings (maxim) within the broad category of traditional sayings. Taking into account the differences felt by Old Testament form critics to exist between the traditional saying and the stylized two-line wisdom saying, we will accept this distinction in our terminology, and use "wisdom saying" to refer to those sayings in the wisdom materials which bear the marks of literary polish and exhibit a two-line parallel form.

Two final points might be raised here where insights from folklore and paroemiological studies may aid the beleaguered form critic. First, the emphasis found in folklore and paroemiology on the "incommunicable quality" (Taylor, Whiting) which helps identify a saying confirms, at least in part, the assertions of Old Testament wisdom scholars that certain passages "sound like" proverbs (Eissfeldt, Fohrer). While such "intuitive" features should never stand alone as criteria for identification of a saying, they still constitute a recognizable, if vague starting point for the discussion of a text. Second, paroemiological research confirms that the "elevated style" in which traditional and learned sayings are generally couched is no mere happy accident, but rather a fairly consistent feature of the genre. Whether such heightened style is best understood as a literary device to facilitate learning and recall (Krappe, Holbek) or as an expression of a distinctive way of perceiving and reflecting upon reality (Jolles, von Rad), the researcher must not discard considerations of style as ornamental to the form, and these features should not be overlooked when discussing the definition and identification of sayings.

2. Methodological Approaches to the Analysis of the Traditional Saying

Many of the emphases found in "structural" approaches to the study of the traditional saying offer a fresh perspective for the analysis of the genre. A "minimal" saying must contain at least one topic and one comment. This presents useful criteria for the identification of saying, and recognition that such a saying must meet the requirement of complete, if abbreviated, syntax provides an immediate objective basis upon which to distinguish the saying from the proverbial phrase or comparison. Thus, we are provided with the "lowest common denominator" of features which must be present before we may designate any passage as a saying: complete syntax and one topic-comment unit.

The further breakdown of the traditional saying into the components of image, message, and architectural formula provides a useful model for detailed study of the literary and culturally conditioned aspects of the saying. The adoption of such terms also presents an advantage in that it allows one to deal with a variety of sayings - metaphorical, non-metaphorical, those with parallelism and those without, artistic or "folk" sayings - on a level which cuts across such secondary considerations and facilitates specific comparisons of different types of sayings on the basis of meaning and structure. More importantly, the recognition that different images and formulae may be employed to convey the same message will allow more systematic comparisons to be drawn between traditional sayings and those found in the wisdom books proper. For example, the same message - that specific human actions proceed from a corresponding specific human nature - is conveyed by three different types of sayings, 1 Sam. 24:13 ("Out of the wicked comes forth wickedness"), Pr. 15:2 ("The tongue of the wise dispenses knowledge, but the mouths of fools pour out folly"), and Mt. 7:16 ("You will know them by their fruits. Are grapes gathered from thorns, or figs from thistles?"), although the images and architectural formulae employed to convey the message are different.

The division of sayings into the categories of "identificational" ("In an abundance of counselors there is safety," Pr. 11:14b) and "contrastive" ("Better is a man of humble standing who works for himself than one who plays the great man but lacks bread," Pr. 12:9), and their two most basic transformations of positive and negative causation (positive: "He who tills his land will have plenty of bread," Pr. 12:11a; negative: "Riches do not profit in the day of wrath," Pr. 11:4a), is a helpful tool for the study of Old Testament sayings, since this division rests primarily on considerations of message rather than image or form of construction. Identificational and contrastive sayings present a basic evaluation of diverse phenomena and this facilitates the formulation of categories of those things which are "recommended" and "not recommended" - categories which are of tremendous importance to the didactic goals of wisdom instruction. By looking at the sayings outside the wisdom corpus in such groups, it may be possible to explicate their relationship, if any, to the types of identifications and contrasts found in the wisdom sayings.

3. Considerations of the "Life Setting" of Proverb Use

The idea of "proverb performance meaning" and the growing interest in contextual approaches to proverb study in folklore studies may have the most to offer for the investigation of the Old Testament saying. The concept of "life setting" (Sitz im Leben) is a critical one for Old Testament scholarship in general, and while it has been applied to wisdom research and proverb study with respect to the life setting of the <u>origin</u> of sayings, there has been no systematic consideration of the life setting of the <u>use</u> of sayings in social interactions. The notorious adaptability of the saying and the ease with which it may be seen to move from one life setting to another has left its mark on form critical studies of the Old Testament saying, where those investigations were concerned primarily with the life setting in which an item was coined. Beyond the statement of the general didactic nature of many of the sayings in the Old Testament, or discussions of which of the referents of certain proverb images were more likely to point to an origin among the people, the court, or wisdom "academy," little of substance has been said. With a shift in focus from origin to context, it becomes possible to speak of a life setting, albeit a "secondary" one, of proverb use. It is here that contextual studies of proverb use may provide models for investigating the use made of sayings outside wisdom collections. While it is true that the "contexts" of proverb performance to be found in the Old Testament are not a fieldworker's transcription of conversations as they occur in "uncontaminated" societies, it is still likely that the portrayal of proverb performance in these pericopes bears some resemblance to the way sayings were actually used, for otherwise the texts would have been unintelligible to their first audiences. It may not be possible to recover an "oral" use of a given saying, but investigation of the non-wisdom context in which it occurs, even at the literary level, will still provide insights into proverb use in general, and help to explicate the function of the saying within the text itself. Seitel's model, which provides a system by which the roles in interaction in proverb performance may be studied, along with the terms found in the proverb image and the correlation set up by the proverb user between the proverb and context situation, is a useful tool because it allows for the clear delineation of the cultural presuppositions underlying both proverbs and proverb use. Recognition of the "strategy" involved in proverb use, along with insights into the variability of proverb meaning according to context, will provide added depth in our understanding of the nature and possible use of the sayings found within the wisdom literature.

The recognition of the logical relationships which are conveyed by a proverb image and reapplied in context situations may aid the study of the cultural "world view" (such as "world order") which forms the backdrop for the traditional wisdom embodied in the folk sayings of the Old Testament. Elucidation of the "folk ideas" expressed in the sayings, along with a discussion of the types of situations in which proverbs are used may provide valuable insights about the "trouble spots" which exist in a culture and call for social control through the vehicle of proverb use. An appreciation of the "purposeful" intent of proverb use should help to show how "didactic" purpose is related to observational information found in the traditional saying, and may shed further light on how wisdom sayings might have been used in didactic settings, beyond the simple statements concerning use in a school setting. Finally, an understanding of the nature of proverb use (i.e., purposeful, evaluative, etc.) may reveal that the folk sayings in the Old Testament have more in common with "didactic" wisdom sayings than was previously supposed, since neither function in an exclusively observational way once the discussion of use in context is introduced.

In terms of more general considerations of the life setting for the use of traditional sayings, we find again that folklore and anthropological studies make a valuable contribution to the Old Testament debate. Comparative materials have shown that tribal societies and societies which are other than literate have deeply rooted, vigorous traditions of "folk wisdom." Such experience and lore is encapsulated in sayings which are available to the members of the group, ready for use in a variety of ways, and open to confirmation and reinterpretation. Given the evidence of numerous studies conducted throughout the world, it would be unreasonable indeed to assume that ancient Israel alone had no tribal or family locus for at least a part of her wisdom traditions (Westermann).

The growing awareness on the part of folklorists and anthropologists of the need to expand the general understanding of the nature of the "folk" as a group also has important implications for the study of the life setting of Israelite wisdom. The limitations imposed on research by regarding the folk as rural peasants who stand over against the urban, civilized elite have already been recognized by some in Old Testament wisdom studies (Audet, Gerstenberger), and continuing attempts to deal with new understanding of folk groups will enhance our understanding of Old Testament society in general, and prevent us from adopting the elite as the exclusive possessors and tradents.

It might be appropriate at this point to give some suggestion of how the group "Israelite folk" might be defined, taking into account the criticisms lodged against most of the current uses of the term "folk." Norman K. Gottwald has recently used sociological methodology to assess the "uniqueness of Israel" with respect to its neighbours, focusing on the formative period of 1250-1050 B.C.E.[162] While it is beyond the scope of this work to explore all of the ramifications of his sociological analyses as it applies to the theological understanding of Yahweh, Gottwald's work presents a basic understanding of those socioeconomic features and their rhetorical symbolization in "theological" statements concerning Yahweh and "his" people found in the biblical text which would allow an Israelite "folk" to be distinguished from its surrounding Canaanite neighbours. In particular, early Israel might well have had reason to see itself as a distinct "folk" based on the following: the social structure of the settlement period was that of "communal egalitarianism," which represented a radical break from stratified, ranked Canaanite society. Hence, Yahweh's "jealousy," in Gottwald's view, stems from the communal exlusivity of worship needed to maintain such a different world view in a hostile cultural environment. The exclusive worship demanded by the God of Israel reflects the "hyperindividuation" of a "high god" deity who becomes sole divine actor and protector of "his" people. Such religious symbolization indicates the intertribal "Israel's" de-termination to hold itself apart from the demeaning sociopolitical organizations of its neighbors, which were sustained and reinforced by their religious ideology. The gods of the statist social systems, whose activities were often interpreted by means of sexual paradigms of divine fertility upon which all human efforts depended, were worshipped by and on behalf of the elite. Normally, the cult placed a tremendous burden on lower ranking citizens to fulfill its economic requirements, while simultaneously reinforcing the social order with religious legitimations and insuring that that order would be less likely to be challenged because of the diversion of human and economic resources from reform to maintenance of a static cult.

In the same vein, Gottwald points to the lack in Israel of a cult of the dead, with its useless expenditures of precious resources, as well as the modest economic demands placed upon the people by the Israelite priesthood when compared to their Canaanite peers, as the concrete expression in religious ideology of the new "praxis" of a sociopolitical community that was an anomaly among its neighbors. Similarly, he understands the early social organization of the military "citizen army" in Israel, and the emphasis on the "people" as the focus of God's concern rather than simply the king or elite classes to be distinctive features of the Israelite "folk" of this period. The demythologization of divine sexuality, seen in the tendency to characterize Yahweh by leadership rather than sexual or agricultural roles, and the prominence of historical encounters of liberation in Israel's earliest "theological" paradigms are also important features of the Israelite folk of this early period. During the course of Israel's history the view of Yahweh as the sole "purposing" reality active in the world would also lend a distinctive poignancy to the people's struggle with questions of theodicy which is less of a theological issue among Israel's polytheistic neighbors.[163] While definitions of the Israelite "folk" of later periods must take into account the effects of the United Monarchy and its subsequent dissolution into the states of Israel and Judah on the group's self-understanding, we still find in Gottwald's research the beginning of a workable model of the Israelite "folk" during one of its most crucial periods in history.[164]

4. Summary

It has been shown that the use of folklore and anthropological approaches in biblical studies is by no means a revolutionary concept,[165] and, if used circumspectly, it may provide valuable methods of analysis and directions for study. Bearing in mind the necessity of maintaining a certain wariness lest illegitimate categories be imposed upon the biblical text, the goal of this research will be to discuss the form, style, content, use and function of a representative number of traditional sayings in the Old Testament which occur outside of the wisdom literature. Primary attention will be given to those sayings which occur with the greatest amount of "contextual" data, and an attempt will be made to discern general patterns of use in context. We will designate as traditional sayings those passages generally recognized as such by biblical scholars, but evaluation and analysis of the text will be made in the light of the perspectives from folklore studies discussed above.

Chapter III

PROVERB PERFORMANCE IN THE OLD TESTAMENT

We have seen from our earlier discussions that studies of the traditional saying outside the Old Testament wisdom literature have failed to deal with many features which were not directly related to the presuppositions dominating the study of wisdom sayings. Most treatments of traditional sayings in the Old Testament have focused on the relation of the traditional saying to the more "artistic" wisdom saying, so that aspects of origin and, secondarily, content have received the most attention. From an opposite perspective, a cursory perusal of the commentaries on the "historical" books where many of the traditional sayings are to be found, nestled in narrative passages, reveals that biblical scholars working on these books are usually content to pass over a saying used in context with only the briefest of comments on its occurrence. Since our survey of folklore studies and paroemiology has raised several new approaches for the study of the traditional saying based upon the recognition that the "message" of a saying is highly dependent upon its context of use, it is clear that such features should be incorporated into any study of the traditional saying in the Old Testament. Finally, the contextual study of "proverb performance" - that is, the purposeful transmission of a saying in a social interaction[1] - offers insights into the folk ideas which underlie both the saying itself and its use, the "authority" which traditional wisdom wields, and the goals and strategy of the use of such "wisdom." With these observations in mind, detailed study of the appearance of the traditional saying in context in the Old Testament may open the way toward understanding the "popular" use of traditional wisdom in ancient society, and allow a comparison of this use with the function and goals of wisdom literature.

A general statement about the validity of our method of investigation may be appropriate here. Folklorists, not unlike their counterparts in biblical studies, are often forced to deal with sources which, because of the manner of their collection (e.g., by casual travelers or collectors with strong cultural bias) lack the clarity, careful documentation, and avoidance of cultural "contamination" which characterizes materials gathered in accordance with the principles of modern fieldwork. They, too, must sift early materials which may have been colored by the attitudes of the 19th century anthropologist or missionary, and handle traditions which can no longer be validated and researched through direct contact with the groups who formulated them. Yet, even with these hindrances, most folklorists staunchly maintain that it is possible, by means of sensitive and circumspect awareness of the problems which exist in the sources, to produce accurate and valuable research.

In working with "literary sources" in which folklore might be isolated, the student of the traditional saying is considerably more fortunate than many who work with other genres. The traditional saying, because it is brief, is one of the genres most apt to be recorded without alteration when it finds its way into narrative. Similarly, the "elevated style" and abbreviated syntax which often violates the normal syntactical rules in operation in narrative, provide ready and fairly reliable means for the identification of a saying in context. The same is true of the content of a saying, which so often seems "out of place" or "out of context" when the saying occurs in use.[2]

The use of the narrative or so-called "historical" books in the Old Testament, then, is a legitimate one for the study of contextual use of sayings. Identification is made easier by the fact that the style and content of a saying generally causes it to stand out from its narrative surroundings. Further, with a narrative context, we are likely to be given more contextual information about the use of the saying in an interaction than might be found in the use of a saying in a "prophetic" context. Also, although the narratives in the Old Testament may have been just as ruthlessly "contaminated" by the additions or revision of a later editor with a specific theological and historical perspective even as the the early works of anthropologists were often overlaid with Western religious or cultural biases, the saying itself will probably have escaped alteration because of it brevity and fixed form. Because many narrative passages ostensibly present a picture of events as they supposedly took place, or, at the very least may be credited with some degree of verisimilitude without which the interaction presented would be unintelligible to early audiences, we are likely to find a more accurate representation of the way sayings were actually used in interactions than might be found in the prophetic use of sayings, since the prophets routinely appropriated and modified a variety of genres to suit their own programmatic needs. Finally, it is quite possible that many of the Old Testament narratives attained a reasonably "fixed" state (whether oral or written) at an early time, so that editorial comment or systematic reworking of a pericope might still leave the central core of a passage intact. Even where the theological or political aims of the narrator or redactor may be responsible for the appearance of a passage (and hence, the saying used within it), our contention is that the saying must be used in a comprehensible way which approximates the way in which such interactions actually occurred in daily life. We cannot, of course, "prove" that a saying which appears in a context of use has not been altered or reinterpreted from its "original" form in order to suit various contextual needs. Indeed, we would suggest that the saying genre is often altered or reinterpreted by users to meet very specific, contextual needs. Since the purpose of our analysis is <u>not</u> to pass judgment on the origin or currency of a saying which appears in context in the Old Testament, but to investigate the <u>way</u> in which traditional sayings are used, regardless of their origin, folk "authenticity," or currency, we need not be deterred by the fact that we may not be dealing with the original, "Ur"-form of a given saying.

Given that the narrative books of the Old Testament are a legitimate source for the investigation of the use of the traditional saying, by what justification does one select certain passages for consideration and omit others? It is possible to delineate several criteria which determine those passages most suitable for contextual study, given that limitations of space preclude detailed study of every passage suspected of containing a traditional saying. The following criteria have been used:

1. The passage is generally acknowledged by previous Old Testament research to contain a traditional saying
2. The saying itself meets our own criteria developed from folklore studies, in that:
a) it has complete syntax
b) it consists of at least one "descriptive" unit (one topic-comment)

c) it exhibits a logical relationship between its terms
d) it shows some type of "elevated style"
We might also look for the following features which aid in
identification:
e) "out-of-context" statement
f) violation of narrative syntax
g) introduction as a saying in context itself
h) parallels to the saying found in Old Testament wisdom
    or ancient Near East literature
3. Full contextual data given with regard to "Source,"
    "Receiver," and motives in the interaction for the use
    of the saying
4. The pericope has at least a minimal claim to
    versimilitude in its portrayal of proverb performance.[3]

The five passages to be treated below have been selected
for consideration because: (a) they fulfill the four
requirements outlined above; and (b) they represent different
types of forms within the broad category of "traditional
saying." The sayings to be discussed are:

Judges 8:2	-	interrogative "Better-than" saying (tôb-Spruch)
Judges 8:21	-	saying (Aussage) without copula
1 Sam. 16:7	-	bilinear wisdom saying
1 Sam. 24:14 [13]	-	saying (Aussage) with copula
1 Kings 20:11	-	vetitive form

By investigating the use of a variety of types of the
traditional saying, it may be possible to discern patterns of
use which are valid across several categories of sayings. This,
in turn, will aid in the formulation of general observations
about the way in which the traditional saying, in its broadest
sense, functions in context and perhaps in society as well.

Discussions of "proverb performance" in each text will
proceed in the following way. After an introduction to the
pericope which will provide background information for the
context situation and an assessment of the reliability of the
source with respect to the preservation of a moderately
accurate model of proverb performance, the specific
pericope to be studied will be discussed and reconstructed,
where necessary. Using Peter Seitel's model[4] of the
aspects of proverb performance, the passage will be discussed
in terms of: I. The Interaction Situation; II. The Proverb
Situation; and III. The Context Situation. The Interaction
Situation (I.) will outline the Source (X) or user of the saying,
the Receiver (Y) or hearer at whom the saying is directed,

and their relationship to each other ($+$). The Proverb Situation (II.) will evaluate the criteria by which the passage is considered to be a saying, and analyze the logical relationship between the referents (i.e., the topic and comment, A and B respectively) of the saying. Structural analysis will be used to discuss the architectural formula, image and message of the saying. Parallels to these elements of the saying from Old Testament wisdom and ancient Near East texts will be presented, and the "folk ideas" upon which the saying is based will be discussed. The Context Situation (III.) will explicate the metaphorical correlation between the referents of the saying (A,B) and the contextual referents (C,D). The folk ideas which form the background for the correlation set up by the Source will be discussed, along with the intent (affective or evaluative) and strategy of the Source in using the saying. It should be noted here that we do not mean to intimate that our explications of the metaphorical relation in each context are the only legitimate interpretations possible. One of the features of both the proverb and proverb performance is the multiplicity of meanings and interpretations which may be assigned to any one item or incident. We are only suggesting one of the many ways in which the interaction may be understood. Following this, comments will be made on various aspects of the contextual use presented. With this program for analysis in mind, we will now proceed to our investigation of <u>proverb performance</u> in the text.

PROVERB PERFORMANCE IN JUDGES 8:2

Introduction

The book of Judges offers a particularly interesting source for the investigation of the use of traditional sayings in society. Many scholars feel that large portions of the narratives reflect a fairly accurate picture of the life and customs of early Israel during the time of "tribal" settlement and consolidation of the territory gained, through whatever means, during the "Conquest."[5] Although few are now willing to speak of the wholesale continuation of Pentateuch sources "J" and "E" in the book of Judges, it seems certain that the oldest portions of the book had attained a relatively fixed form (whether oral or written) early in the history of transmission, so that later redactions tended to center around the "connectives" between the nuclear stories, prologues, epilogues, and the arrangement of the order of the narratives, whereas "historical" order of the events related was subordinated to the programmatic goals of the Deuteronomistic Redactor concerned to alternate a "good" example of leadership with a "bad."[6] On the whole, the stage in Israel's history which is portrayed in Judges is a "period that was, for them, one of revolutionary social change."[7]

The Gideon stories (Chapters 7 and 8) offer one of the best examples in Judges of the use of a number of sources (which have, at points, been joined in a rather clumsy fashion).[8] Gideon, although never specifically designated either "judge" or "savior,"[9] arises as the leader of a number of tribes in response to the "Midianite crisis." With the domestication of the camel at the end of the Late Bronze Age, the incursion of raiding camel nomads from across the Jordan into the settled areas constituted a very real threat to the economic stability of tribal Israel, since both agriculture and trade were affected.[10] Although many despair of fixing any date for the events recounted in the book of Judges, Gideon's activity is thought to precede that of Deborah and Barak (which comes first in the canonical order), and, on the basis of archaeological evidence, is set during the first half of the 12th century B.C.E.[11]

The genre of the narrative kernels in Judges is said to be that of the "historical romance," "heroic tale," or "hero saga"; that is, a narrative of "popular" character which centers around some ideal or "exemplary figure."[12] The Gideon stories, in particular, exhibit a strong "folkloric" character, with their constant references to divination, signs, dreams, and the miraculous.[13] In such a context, we should not be surprised to find a comfortable setting for the traditional saying - indeed, we might expect it, since we are dealing with materials which not only exhibit affinities with folklore, but which also stem from a time of change, conflict and unrest, when traditional sayings are apt to be pressed into service as guides and controls.[14] The Gideon narratives give us two fine examples of "proverb performance," Jg. 8:2, "Is not the gleaning of the grapes of Ephraim better than the vintage of Abiezer?" and Jg. 8:21, "As the man is, so is his strength," which we will now examine in context.

The Pericope: Jg. 7:24-8:3

The relationship of the account of Gideon's raid on the

Midianites (Chapter 7) and the execution of the Midianite leaders, Oreb and Zeeb, by the Ephraimites (Jg. 7:24-8:3) to the similar account in Jg. 8:4-21 has long been discussed among scholars, with little agreement, apart from the fact that we are dealing here with at least two separate sources. Much simplified, the alternatives are as follows: (1) both pericopes are versions of the same raid, from different sources; or (2) the pericopes are versions of separate raids.[15] The latter has been adopted here for the following reasons: (1) in 7:24-8:3, the Midianites are represented as defeated, with their leaders slain; in 8:4-21, we must assume this is not the case, since the men of Succoth and Penuel refuse help to Gideon, presumably because the camel nomads have already escaped unscathed (vv. 6-8); and (2) the motive for the military action in the earlier story is a response to the general Midianite threat, whereas in 8:4-21, Gideon's motive is the execution of blood vengeance for the murder of his brothers on Mt. Tabor. We will leave more precise determinations of the relationship between the pericopes to source and redaction critics, since our primary interest here is proverb performance within the narratives themselves, and both exhibit a self-contained unity in this respect.

Scholars have also noted the similarities of Jg. 7:24-8:3 to the pericope found in Jg. 12:1-7, where the Ephraimites again take issue with another tribe for not being called early enough to take part in military action. It does not seem necessary to postulate a literary dependency of either story upon the other, since the traditional Ephraimite claim to a superior place among the "tribes" of "Israel" may be seen as a backdrop for a number of disputes between Ephraim and the other tribes.[16] Our pericope seems to be related to the source found in Jg. 6:34ff., where the tribe of Abiezer is roused to meet the Midianite threat, while Asher, Zebulun and Naphtali are "on call," rather than to those traditions which speak of a larger "amphictyonic" force led by Gideon.[17]

It seems likely that this narrative relates a belated participation on the part of the Ephraimites after a major encounter between Gideon and his followers, and the Midianite raiders. The picture of how the military action proceeded is relatively clear: Gideon and his men, having routed the majority of the Midianites, pursue them into the south-east, while messages have been sent to the Ephraimites to come north and "head them off at the pass" so that the Midianites cannot escape across the Jordan.[18] There is a

certain etiological interest in the pericope, which attempts
to give a popular etymology for the place names of "Rock of
Oreb" and "Winepress of Zeeb," and it is here, as von Rad
notes, that "the saga ... parts company with historical reality
...."[19] Some commentators feel it likely that the passage
as a whole reflects two versions of the action, one Manassite
(7:23-25) and the other Ephraimite (8:1-3).[20]

> (23) And the men of Israel were called out from Naphtali
> and from Asher and from all Manasseh, and they pursued
> after Midian. (24) And Gideon sent messengers
> throughout all the hill country of Ephraim, saying,
> "Come down against the Midianites and seize the waters
> against them, as far as Beth-barah, and also the Jordan."
> So all the men of Ephraim were called out, and they
> seized the waters as far as Beth-barah, and also the
> Jordan. (25) And they took the two princes of Midian,
> Oreb and Zeeb; they killed Oreb at the *gleaning* of
> Oreb, and Zeeb they killed at the winepress of Zeeb, as
> they pursued Midian; and they brought the heads of Oreb
> and Zeeb to Gideon beyond the Jordan. (8:1) And the men
> of Ephraim said to him, "What is this that you have done
> to us, not to call us, when you went to fight with
> Midian?" And they upbraided him violently. (2) And he
> said to them, "What have I done now in comparison with
> you? Is not the gleaning of the grapes of Ephraim better
> than the vintage of Abiezer? (3) God has given into your
> hands the princes of Midian, Oreb and Zeeb; what have I
> been able to do in comparison with you?" Then their
> anger against him was abated, when he had said this.[21]

I. The Interaction Situation.

The Source (X) of the use of the interrogative traditional
saying in Jg. 8:2 is Gideon; the Receivers (Y) are the angry
Ephraimites, who, after presenting Gideon with the grisly
trophies of ⁺heir success against the Midianites, tax Gideon
with his failure to involve them in the military action sooner.
It is the hostility of the Ephraimites which elicits Gideon's
use of the saying - that is, the Ephraimites are not only the
Receivers of the saying, but the Object as well.[22]

The relationship which obtains between Gideon, the Source
of the saying, and the Ephraimites, the Object and Receivers
of the saying is one of inequality ($\neq$). Although Gideon has
the status which accrues to a successful military leader, the
Ephraimites - at least in their own opinion - clearly occupy
the superior position, as one of the preeminent clans of the

"core" of early Israel.[23] Further, the Ephraimites feel they have been wronged by Gideon's belated inclusion of their forces in the military action.[24] From Gideon's "soft answer" to their angry charges, we may also assume that Gideon recognizes their superior position - at least in direct confrontations with the haughty neighbor to the south. This understanding of the relative status of the participants in the interaction is of great importance for understanding Gideon's use of an interrogative traditional saying in 8:2, when his behavior is challenged.[25]

II. The Proverb Situation.

The interrogative saying in 8:2, "Is not the gleaning of the grapes of Ephraim better than the vintage of Abiezer?" (halô' ṭôb ^{c}ōlelôt ^{j}eprayim mibṣîr ^{ca}bî^{c}ezer), is cited by Eissfeldt as a passage which "sounds like a proverb," although he classes it as one of those sayings which are examples of "proverbial forms of expression," rather than with those which are sayings in the proper sense.[26] Commentators of the book of Judges usually concur, although descriptive terminology used to discuss the saying differs.[27]

The saying is clearly marked as a question, but this need not automatically exclude it from consideration as a saying,[28] since the basic form is obviously that of the "Better-than" saying (ṭôb-Spruch) which was so popular in the wisdom literature of Egypt and Israel.[29] The saying also exhibits complete syntax, a complete topic-comment unit (topic: the gleanings of Ephraim; comment: better than the vintage of Abiezer), and makes use of comparisons drawn from the images of everyday life. However, the saying, as it appears in our pericope, seems "tailor made" for the context in which it is used, rather than exhibiting the "out of context" feature which so often acts as a guide to the identification of a saying, and it is difficult to picture a number of other contexts in which the saying might be applicable even though it is metaphorical,[30] dealing as it does with specific, concrete referents. We must agree here with Hermisson, that this saying is "oriented toward a historical reality," and is thus unlikely to have been current before the events which it encapsulates took place.[31] However, since our interest is in use in context, we need not be deterred by the "suspect" origin of the passage, and, indeed, there is no way to prove either that this saying could not have been current prior to the events related in the pericope, or that it was not coined by a later author with reference to these events. The fact that Gideon perhaps "coined" a saying suitable for his purposes along a frame which was a popular proverbial form of expression may be even more significant for our understanding of the dynamics of proverb use in society. The compulsion to argue in traditional ways apparently remains in force even when no current saying meets the needs of the situation, thus necessitating the coining of a new saying along traditional lines.[32]

The architectural formula used to construct the saying is that of the "Better-than" saying transformed from a statement into an interrogative (Q ṭôb A min B; Is A better than B?). This is a saying of the "contrastive" type, which may be conveniently symbolized as "A B," since the formula makes clear that A (the gleaning of the grapes of Ephraim) is more highly valued than B (the vintage of Abiezer).

The image used by the saying to convey its message is drawn from the world of agriculture; specifically, the terms used as referents are those for the harvest and gleaning of grapes or olives.[33] "Gleaning" (cōlelôt) and "vintage" (bāṣîr), are logical word pairs, and occur together in Is. 24:13, Mic. 7:1 and Jer. 49:9. The terms of the image also refer implicitly to the earlier reference to the Rock (or Gleaning) of Oreb and Winepress of Zeeb in Jg. 7:25.[34]

The message of the saying may be paraphrased, on a semantic level, as "limited (or secondary) effort by the strong is better than the major (or primary) effort of the weak." The paradox of this message is achieved through the use of the qualifying terms, Ephraim and Abiezer, which transform "gleaning," normally a negative term, and "vintage," usually a positive term, into positive and negative terms respectively.[35] Thus the comparison states that the belated, small effort (gleaning, a negative) on the part of the Ephraimites (positive) is worth more than the vintage (positive) of the clan of Abiezer (negative).[36]

Such paradoxes as presented by Gideon's saying are by no means unfamiliar to the authors of the wisdom sayings, as may be seen in the sayings of both Egypt and Israel. In the Teaching of Amenemope, 8:19-20, we read, "Better is a measure (-), which God gives to you (+) than (>) five thousand (+) gained by violence (-)," which may be symbolized by the structural formula "- + > + -".[37] The Israelite sage had observed such paradoxes as well, in a variety of spheres of life:

Better is a little with fear of the Lord
  than great treasure and trouble with it.
      (- + > + -)   Pr. 15:16

Better is open rebuke than hidden love.
  (Heb. word order: - + > + -)   Pr. 27:5

Better off is a poor man who is well and strong in
constitution than a rich man who is severely afflicted in
body.   (- + > + -)   Sir. 30:14[38]

The specific "folk idea" which forms the backdrop for the
saying in Jg. 8:2 is the recognition that even when the strong
do less than the weak, their efforts are apt to be generally
more effective, and hence more highly valued by virtue of
the status of those who performed the acts.[39] The wisdom
sages may have preferred to favor the righteous-but-poor
person over the wicked-but-rich in their ethical
evaluations,[40] but they were not blind to the fact that the
world often viewed the matter differently: "The poor use
entreaties, but the rich answer roughly" (Pr. 18:23); and "The
rich man's wealth is his strong city; the poverty of the poor is
their ruin" (Pr. 10:15); etc.

To summarize our analysis of the saying, then, we obtain
the following information:

Judges 8:2 "Is not the gleaning of the grapes of Ephraim
           better than the vintage of Abiezer?"

Type: Contrastive (A > B)
Topic: gleaning of grapes of Ephraim (A)
Comment: better than the vintage of Abiezer (B)
Architectural Formula: Q better A than B (tôb A min B)
Image: agriculture (grape/olive harvest)
Message: limited effort of the strong is better than the
           major effort of the weak
Parallels: formula - Old Testament and Egyptian "Better-
           than" sayings
           image - agricultural motifs in Pr. 12:11; 14:4;
           20:4,26; 22:8; 24:30-34; 25:13, 14; 26:1,3; 27:18,
           23-27; 28:3,19
           message - Pr. 18:23

III. The Context Situation.

The Source (X) of proverb use in this instance of proverb
performance is Gideon; the Receivers of the proverb are the
Ephraimites (Y), and it is their anger which has prompted the
employment of the saying. The topic and comment of the

saying are given specific correlations by Gideon in 8:3: "the gleaning of the grapes of Ephraim" (A) stands metaphorically for the execution of Oreb and Zeeb by the Ephraimites (C); the "vintage" of Abiezer" (B) is correlated with the activity of Gideon and his men in the pursuit of the Midianite forces (D). The temporal reference in the context situation is to past events; the intent of the use of the saying is here evaluative. A correspondence is set up between the Ephraimites, the Receivers (Y) of the saying in the Interaction Situation, and the referents in the Context Situation. This correspondence is a positive one, which is evident both in the interrogative phrasing of the saying used to apply to the context, the "better-than" frame along which the saying has been constructed, and by Gideon's own "exegesis" of the saying.[41]

A model, then, for the proverb performance in this pericope may be given as in Figure 8.

Gideon's "intent" in using a metaphorical saying, posed as a question, to deal with the recrimination of the Ephraimites is a purposeful one. Arguing traditionally, his clever use of metaphor, diplomatically couched as a negative question which expects a positive answer, "sets up" his angry addressees to assent to his negative evaluation of his own efforts with respect to theirs. On a more pragmatic level Gideon may be simply pointing out that, in terms of accrued honor and booty, the two leaders executed by the Ephraimites are of greater value than the many "common" soldiers routed by himself and his clan. Classical rhetorician Hugh Blair long ago commented on the use of "Interrogations ... the native language of passion," which operate by means of sympathy to manage groups,

> The unfigured, literal use of Interrogation, is, to ask a question; but when men are prompted by passion, whatever they would affirm, or deny, with great vehemence, they naturally put in the form of a question; expressing thereby the strongest confidence of the truth of their own sentiment, and appealing to their hearers for the impossibility of the contrary .... Now, Interrogations ... being natural signs of a moved and agitated mind, always, when they are properly used, dispose us to sympathize with the dispositions of those who use them, and to feel as they feel.[42]

Gideon's reply to the Ephraimites is cast as an interrogative saying,[43] then, for a purpose - the

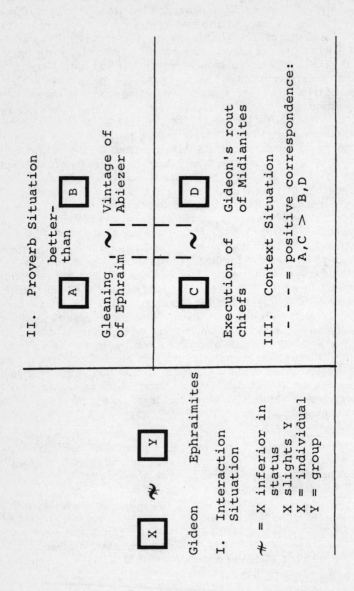

FIGURE 8: Proverb Performance in Judges 8:2

deferential style, as well as the positive content (from the Ephraimites' point of view), serve to manipulate the hostile group without the risk of worsening the situation. By his sagacious use of the indirection afforded by the employment of metaphor and traditional language, Gideon's strategy is successful, and the potentially dangerous situation of rivalry is diffused without further incident, as we are told in 8:3: "... then their anger against him was abated." The use of agricultural images, applied to specific contextual referents, coupled with deft phrasing and pointed interpretation placates the powerful and resolves the conflict. The incidence of proverb performance, which may be paraphrased from our model as "Gideon (X, individual, leader of weak clan) says to the Ephraimites (Y, group, powerful clan slighted by X), "Is not the gleaning of the grapes of Ephraim (A), that is, your execution of Oreb and Zeeb (C) better than the vintage of Abiezer (B), that is, my earlier rout of the raiders?" (D), illustrates the dynamic aspects of traditional wisdom in action in everyday situations.

Comments

Through our analysis of the context in which Gideon's proverbial reply occurs, we have seen that the traditional saying is apt to be found operating in areas of perceived conflict. In this specific pericope, the conflict stems from the problems which customarily arise whenever military force must be gathered for the defence of the "tribes" of Israel (cf. Jg. 5:15-18; 12:1-4). We find that the saying in our pericope is employed between conflicting groups, and it is tempting to infer that there may have existed a common body of "traditional wisdom" upon which one might draw to settle disputes, and which was known and acknowledged by all. The kinds of reflections embodied in this type of traditional lore would have constituted the "building blocks" of a world view shared by a number of groups.[44]

With the figure of Gideon as he appears in our text - diplomatic and calm - we find an excellent example of one who has followed the sages' advice admirably on the subject of the proper conduct in a dispute. The instructions of Egypt and wisdom of Israel had both reflected on the optimum resolution of conflict, and came up with remarkably similar recommendations to the unwilling participant in a quarrel. In the Maxims of Ptahhotep, the wily sage counsels:

> If you find a disputant arguing, one having authority and superior to you, bend down your arms and bow your back; if you disagree with him, he will not side with you. You should make little of the evil speaking by not opposing him in his argument; it means that he will be dubbed an ignoramus when your self-control has matched his prolixity.[45]

Similarly, the Instruction of Amenemope comments that "The strong arm is not (weakened) when it is uncovered, the back is not broken when one bends it; Better is the poor man who speaks sweet words, than the rich man who speaks harshly."[46] The writer of the Satire on the Trades voices the same thought: "If a man reproves you, and you do not know how to oppose his anger, make your reply cautiously in the presence of listeners."[47] The wise men of Israel likewise remarked on the virtues of diplomatic speech in settling strife: Pr. 13:3, "He who guards his mouth preserves his life; he who opens wide his lips comes to ruin"; and Pr. 15:1, "A soft answer turns away wrath, but a harsh word stirs up anger."[48] Gideon, in both his behavior and use of language to gain his ends, provides a fine illustration of the teaching of the wise.[49] One might almost take Pr. 15:23 as an appropriate comment on the proverb performance in our text:

> To make an apt answer is a joy to a man,
> and a word in season, how good it is!

PROVERB PERFORMANCE IN JUDGES 8:21

Introduction

The relationship of the narrative found in Jg. 8:4-21 to the action which precedes it has already been discussed above, where we accepted the interpretation that the accounts in Jg. 7:25-8:3 and 8:4-21 refer to different events.[50] It is clear that the passage in 8:4-21, at any rate, must be set against the background of Midianite raiding, regardless of whether we are to view the action related as a sequel to Chapter 7 or the Ephraimite participation in 7:25-8:3, a doublet to 7:25-8:3, or an independent account of a different event. Gideon, here with the men of his own clan of Abiezer rather than the hosts of "all Israel," crosses into the Transjordan in pursuit of the Midianites who are already far ahead, to judge from the disparaging remarks of the townsfolk of Succoth and Penuel. The primary focus in the narrative is in recounting the pursuit and capture of the Midianite "kings," Zebah and Zalmunna, but it is in verse 18 that we first find the motive for Gideon's tireless pursuit of the raiders: the camel nomads have murdered his brothers.[51] The oldest version of this account doubtless included an introduction which related the slaying of Gideon's brothers at Mt. Tabor by the Midianites, but this is now lost.[52]

Some commentators have been offended by this motive of personal vengeance for Gideon's activity in the Transjordan, as opposed to his role as the leader of the united tribal forces in a defensive action against invaders.[53] However, in our pericope this modern repugnace for revenge must be set aside to view Gideon's action within the cultural milieu of tribal society where the laws of blood vengeance serve not so much as a vehicle to legitimate personal violence but rather as a safeguard for the security of the group as a whole. The solidarity of such a society depends, to a great extent, on the recognition of blood and kinship ties, and the acceptance of the responsibilities which such relations entail.[54] Gideon, as well, is doubly reponsible for the task of avenging the blood of his kin in Judges 8 because the Midianites have not simply slain a member of his clan, but his own full (i.e., uterine) brothers. Consequently, Gideon is obligated to seek reparation at the hands of their killers (v.19). It is likely, too, that the sharp distinctions drawn between the motivation of personal vengeance and that of charismatic leader of God's people following his duty stem more probably from the world of modern interpreters of the text than from that of the narratives of Judges. It is quite likely that the original participants in the action related would not have regarded the two motivations as mutually exclusive, nor are they intrinsically horrified as modern persons are by the execution of this "law of the desert," as the reply (vv. 18, 21) of the captives shows.[55]

After the capture of the Midianite leaders (vv. 10-12), Gideon returns from the Transjordan and settles his grudge against the towns of Succoth and Penuel (vv. 13-17).[56] It is likely that Gideon then returned to his own territory with the captives, since his son Jether, who is present at their execution, in all probability did not take part in the retaliatory raid into the Transjordan, since he was "still a youth" (v. 20).[57] In verses 18-21, we find the specific features of proverb performance, which we will now examine.

18 Then he said to Zebah and Zalmunna, "Where are the men whom you slew at Tabor? They answered, "As you are, so were they, every one of them; they resembled the sons of a king."
19 And he said, "They were my brothers, the sons of my mother; as the Lord lives, if you had saved them alive, I would not slay you."
20 And he said to Jether his first-born, "Rise, and slay them." But the youth did not draw his sword; for he was afraid, because he was still a youth.
21 Then Zebah and Zalmunna said, "Rise yourself, and fall upon us; for as the man is, so is his strength." And Gideon arose, and slew Zebah and Zalmunna; and he took the crescents that were upon the necks of their camels. (RSV)

I. The Interaction Situation.

The Source(s) or users of the traditional saying (X, in the model below) are the Midianite leaders, Zebah and Zalmunna,[58] who are now Gideon's captives, and have, presumably, been brought back across the Transjordan into the territory of Manasseh. The Receiver (Y) or hearer at whom the saying is directed is Gideon, and it is also Gideon whose behavior (in his request that his son slay the captives) has elicited the use of the saying. The relationship between Gideon and the captive leaders ($\mathcal{H}$), although they are basically equal in status as the leaders of their respective groups, is one of basic inequality, since Zebah and Zalmunna are quite literally at Gideon's mercy. Further, the price of the blood-debt for the murder of Gideon's brothers lies between them. However, the Midianites ask for and seem to expect no deviation from the necessity of the execution of blood vengeance; rather, when Gideon questions them concerning the men killed at Tabor,[59] they reply with pride concerning the nobility of bearing of their victims (v. 18). Gideon's answer reveals for the first time the compulsion which drove him to seek out the raiders (i.e., vengeance), and it becomes clear that the murder has put into operation the inexorable series of reprisals which the law of blood vengeance demands (v. 19b, "as the Lord lives, if you had saved them alive, I would not slay you"). It is not the execution itself to which the Midianites object, but rather the manner in which Gideon tries to carry it out which affronts the kings and elicits their use of a traditional saying.

II. The Proverb Situation.

The saying in verse 21, "as the man is, so is his strength": (kā'îš gᵉbûrātô) is cited by Eissfeldt as one of those passages which "sounds like" a proverb, and other scholars have generally acknowledged this to be a saying.[60] It meets the criteria previously posed in Chapter II for the identification of a saying, in that we find complete, if abbreviated, syntax, and a complete topic-comment unit (topic: the might of a man; comment: is like or commensurate with the total man). Although there is no introductory formula which specifies the saying as such, it appears as an "out-of-context" statement which is capable of numerous applications, and which makes use of the basic proverbial style of comparisons. With its brevity and rather deliberate cadence, the saying also meets the more elusive criterion of the possession of "elevated style."[61]

The <u>architectural formula</u> along which the saying has been constructed is one of basic identification ($k^e + B = A$). There is also an instrinsic element of causation as well between the terms of the saying since the totality of the "man" determines any discussion or formulation of specific characteristics, such as "strength" or "military might." Similarly, one might deduce a good deal about the person as a whole from observations of his military prowess and activities. Thus, the relationships between the topic and comment may be conveniently symbolized as "A ← B" ("A is caused by or derived from B"), indicating that the saying is identificational, of the "positive causation" subtype.

The <u>image</u> which the saying uses to convey its message is one drawn from the realm of human characteristics, observable and open to confirmation by all. In this respect, the saying is delightfully impersonal, and thoroughly neutral when lifted out of its contextual setting. Here, we are not told <u>which</u> man's strength or military prowess is like himself - rather, it is <u>any</u> person's strength or might which is being discussed, and from the saying itself, we have no way to deduce the magnitude of such strength. Similarly, if we take "gᵉbûrāh" as referring to military prowess or valor,[62] or as the "might" necessary to exert <u>against</u> a man as an adversary, the saying still gives no clear-cut specifics with which to "fill in" the terms. If such a universal statement seems out of place on the lips of the doomed captives and forces us to search the text for indications of the specific referents in context, we should not hastily emend the text to make the saying "more suitable" in our estimation. Rather, it should be appreciated that it is the way of a saying to speak impersonally of universals, thereby forcing its hearers to involvement, as the mind quickly "breaks the code" and supplies the implied referents which give the saying its meaning in context.

The message of the saying, at its most fundamental level, may be paraphrased as "the whole determines the nature of its parts." At this point, the encapsulation of such an insightful observation in so few words should occasion no surprise to the student of the genre, for this is also the way of the saying. The recognition that the nature of the totality of any entity imparts an indelible stamp on the attributes or constituents of the thing is here applied to the understanding of the nature of persons. The conception of personality found in this saying is one that accords well with the ancient understanding of the nature of persons.[63] The capacities of the body, such as strength, cannot be separated out from the person as a whole, and conversely, the view of the whole person provides a guide as to what capacities one might reasonably expect to find in a given person. This view of human nature stands as one of the "folk ideas" which finds expression in our saying. A related folk idea having to do with the honor due one's status is also implicit within the saying, when "gᵉbûrāh" is given its broader meaning of "power" or "valor." The totality of the man indicates the extent of his valor (and vice versa), and one might also give this the added interpretation that a powerful, valorous man deserves a fitting death. It is this presupposition which motivates the Midianites to question Gideon's choice of executioner.

Parallels, at least in a broad sense, may be cited for this saying. Another traditional saying of the Old Testament found in Ezek. 16:44, "as the mother is, so is her daughter" (kᵉ ʾimmâ bittāh) shows the same architectural formula (kᵉ + B =A), as does Hosea 4:9 and Sir. 10:2. Similarities to both the image and message may be noted in Pr. 27:19, "As in the water face answers to face, so the mind of the man reflects the man." Likewise, the same understanding of the defining relationship between the totality and its parts, or the source and its creations or products, is evident in the message of two Babylonian sayings: "The mother brew is bitter. How is the beer sweet?" and "The wife of a man who cannot talk well is a female slave."[64]

Let us summarize, then, our analysis of the traditional

saying in 8:21 before turning to its use in context.

Judges 8:21 "As the man is, so is his strength"
Type: Identificational (A←B)
Topic: the might of a man (A)
Comment: is as the man is (←B)
Architectural formula: k^e + B = A
Image: human characteristics
Message: the whole determines the nature of its parts; the totality of the person defines the specific capacities; the status or activities of a person determines appropriate actions towards the person
Parallels: Formula - Ezek. 16:44; Hos. 4:9; Sir. 10:2;
             Image - Pr. 27:19;
             Message - Pr. 27:19, and ancient Near East parallels

III. The Context Situation.

A number of characteristic features of "proverb performance" emerge when we consider the context in which our saying appears. The Interaction Situation, as outlined above, is one replete with conflict, but one which is defined to a great extent by the basic necessities of the cultural milieu in which it is set. The conflicts are evident on many levels: the clash between nomadic raiders and settled groups over resources, the obligations of blood vengeance, the differences in capacities and commitment which separate maturity and youth, father and son, and the different perceptions of the status of the various participants in the interaction.

It is obvious from the text that the Midianite leaders feel little regret for the act which has made them the object of Gideon's pursuit. Their reference to their victims is a classic statement of the sort of human insolence that takes its greatest pride in the destruction of what is beautiful and alive: "As you are, so were they, every one of them; they resembled the sons of a king." It may also be inferred from this that they take similar pride in the fact that, if they must indeed be captives, they may find honor in the fact that they are at least the prisoners of the mighty Gideon, whom they compare to his "kingly" brothers.[65] Johannes Pedersen says of the incident:

The two Bedouins do not want to run away from their

deed, on the contrary! They say with pride that they were noble-looking chiefs whom they killed; that honour they are not prepared to forego. They know the cost of it; they have taken their honour from Gideon. They have robbed him of life by taking the lives of his brothers; in that way they have made a breach upon him, while at the same time they themselves have grown. Under other circumstances Gideon might have set them free, but now he cannot let them go, charged with life which they have taken from him. He must take it back, and thus himself become whole once more.[66]

It seems apparent, then, that it is not a desire to escape their "just" fate which causes the chiefs to fall back on the "authoritative" content of a traditional saying to influence Gideon. Rather, it is Gideon's order that his firstborn execute them which elicits the use of the saying, since the death of these "insolent sons of the desert" at the hands of a mere youth was apparently perceived as a insult too shattering even to contemplate.[67] The boy himself is similarly aghast at the thought of carrying out his father's command, whether from realization of his own lack of experience or strength, awe at the status of the intended victims, or the particular clarity of vision sometimes engendered in the young when viewing the carnage so routinely sanctioned by their elders.[68] Various reasons are given by commentators for Gideon's desire to involve the boy in the execution,[69] but whatever the reason, Zebah and Zalmunna respond to Gideon's intent as though it were an insult, and it is this which prompts their statement in 8:21, and provides us with the final features of the Context Situation. Thus, we might reconstruct our model of proverb performance in Judges 8:18-21 as in Figure 9.

The prisoner's use of the traditional saying in the context situation is purposeful, as is evident from the statement which precedes it in 21a: "Rise yourself (ʾattâ) and fall upon us because (kî) 'as the man is, so is his strength.'"[70] The saying appears here presented as the justification for their demand, and in their attempt to influence Gideon's future choice of an executioner after Jether's demurral, their purpose is clearly affective. It is clear from the passage that the desert kings believe that Gideon has "sent a boy to do a man's job." Their previous positive attitude toward Gideon is crucial here, since any person - however bold - about to be executed, probably with a bronze weapon, would doubtless

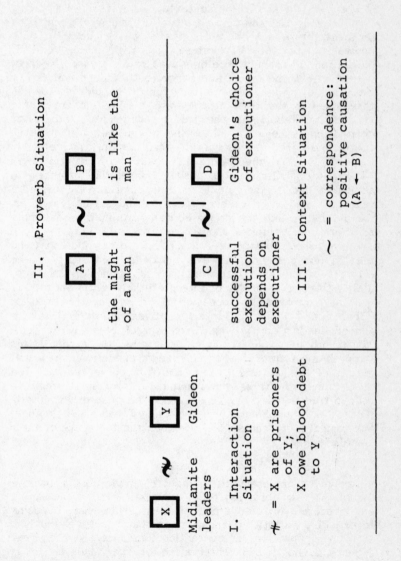

FIGURE 9: Proverb Performance in Judges 8:18-21

prefer to be dispatched by a mighty proven warrior than by an inexperienced, presumably weaker, youth.[71]

However, the key to the contextual referents of the saying must be sought in the context situation as a whole, since the prospect of a dishonorable death was doubtless more unpleasant to the Midianites than the simple fear of mutilation. The saying here employed refers to the choice of executioner to be made, and hence, both Gideon and Jether are implied, as they are the only logical candidates for the task given in the text, as they are the nearest kin of the victims on Tabor. As the saying applies to Jether, its correlation is negative, since the boy is not a man but a youth, and hence has less might than a man, and certainly less status than the valorous Gideon. With reference to Gideon, the saying is more positive, since the prisoners, in comparing him to their noble victims, have already formed a favorable evaluation of his capacities and status. However, the possibility that the saying contains an implicit challenge, as Hermisson thinks, should not be ruled out.[72] Such overtones should not be used as criteria to conclude that the text is not a saying, however, since a great part of the efficacy of use of a traditional saying resides in this very ability to yield a variety of interpretations. From our model, we may paraphrase the occasion of proverb performance as: Zebah and Zalmunna ("kings," captives, murderers) say to Gideon (leader, captor, legal executor of blood vengeance), "as the whole nature of a man determines the extent of his strength and prowess, so the choice of executioner now will determine the successful execution of blood vengeance." The conclusion of the verse shows that the prisoners' "strategy" in using a traditional saying to influence their captor was finally successful: "and Gideon arose and killed Zebah and Zalmunna, and took the crescents which were on the the necks of their camels."[73]

Comments

A number of observations might be made concerning the use of the traditional saying in our text. We find the saying employed, as we would expect, in a situation where opposing forces, of a variety of kinds, are in sharp conflict. Further, we find support for our contention that a saying in context appears as no neutral observation of fact, but rather is employed with specific motives in a purposeful - and here successful - way.

A very interesting feature emerges from our analysis of

the context of use. The text portrays the proverb performance as taking place _between_ two different population groups, the settled clan of Abiezer and the Midianite camel nomads.[74] The implications of this fact - that the narrator is able to envision an interchange between two conflicting groups who both understand and respond to the validity of "traditional lore" - will come as no surprise to the student of wisdom literature, with its strong international character and background. Such considerations might also be used to reflect, however, on the basis for guidance in everyday conduct among various tribal units in early Israel. If sayings, whatever their origin, could be conceived of as operating between groups, it is also likely that they were functional _within_ groups as part of the fabric which held society together and provided the raw material from which goals for social order were formed. One might question, too, whether or not the "diplomatic" use of wisdom could not also have begun at the tribal level, as illustrated in Jg. 8:2, 21, where the use of traditional sayings might have functioned with a rudimentary regulatory power even among hostile groups.

PROVERB PERFORMANCE IN 1 SAM. 16:7

Introduction

The problems involved in using the historical-critical method to investigate the materials in 1-2 Samuel are well known.[75] These difficulties stem in part from the efforts to evolve theories acceptable to the modern critical investigator which successfully account for the widely divergent accounts of the rise of the monarchy given in the books of Samuel, and the sad state of the text due to poor transmission places an added burden on interpreters.[76] While it is not the place here to discuss the various theories about the sources of 1-2 Samuel or the processes of complication which resulted in the final form of the text, a few words should be said about the time period and the events which form the context for the pericope in 1 Sam. 16:1-13.

The events covered in the Books of Samuel range from the birth of Samuel, the kingship of Saul (ca. 1020 B.C.E.) and David, to the struggle over David's successor, which concludes in 1 Kings 1-2, with Solomon as the victor (ca. 961). The "historicity" of the events narrated in Samuel varies greatly with the complex under consideration, but Hertzberg still feels it possible to affirm that "the Books of Samuel provide a mass of excellent material to illustrate the historical situation of about 1000 B.C."[77] The historical "context" for the activities related in the Books of Samuel is akin to that obtaining at the end of the Book of Judges: the tribes of "Israel" are still engaged in a struggle to the death to expand their holdings in Palestine, against the major threat of the Philistines. The Battle of Aphek near the end of the eleventh century left Israel in a drastically weakened position, and the Philistines in virtual control of the land.[78] It is against this backdrop that Saul, a Benjaminite, arises as a deliverer, much in the manner of the "saviors" in the Book of Judges who were called up by Yahweh to deal with a specific crisis or military threat.[79] Saul, however, is a "judge" with a difference - he is acclaimed king.[80]

Saul's kingship is a brief and tragic one: almost immediately after his election, he unwittingly (1 Sam. 14:24ff.) - or, with full knowledge, in a later tradition (1 Sam. 13:8ff.; 15:9) - transgresses.[81] His kingdom is quite literally torn from him (1 Sam. 15:27).[82] It is clear that the various traditions, regardless of their attitude toward the institution of the monarchy, realize that Saul, although the Lord's anointed, is not a "man after his (Yahweh's) own heart" (1 Sam. 13:14).[83]

The Pericope: 1 Sam. 16:1-13

1 Samuel 16: 1-13 effects the transition from the "Samuel and Saul" complex of narratives to those concerning "Saul and David," and, because it forms the bridge between the anointed who has been rejected and the anointed who has been chosen, it stands as an extremely significant introduction for the understanding of the overall attitude toward David. Although it is probably the latest and least "historically accurate" of the traditions which deal with David's rise to prominence and introduction into Saul's court (1 Sam. 16:14-23; 1 Sam. 17:1-18:5),[84] theologically, it is probably the most important.[85]

The passage, for all its lateness and introductory status, exhibits a close connection with the preceding chapter (the Gilgal tradition of Saul's anointing and rejection),[86] and its similarities in function and motif to the ingenuous tale of Saul's search for the lost she-asses (1 Sam. 9:1-10:16) bear the marks of fine literary craftsmanship, in both its composition and placement.[87] Although the secret choice and anointing of David in his early adolescence is not referred to by the other traditions concerning his rise to power (1 Sam. 16:14ff.; 17:1ff.; 2 Sam. 2:4; 5:3), the action portrayed here reflects elements which become standard in the traditional picture of David.[88]

Ashley Rose has seen in this pericope an affinity with the function of the "torah"-unit, and finds a pattern based upon a series of divine address-human response interactions which lead inexorably to final resolution in v. 13.[89] Perhaps most importantly for our discussion, Rose points out that the criteria by which selection is made as well as the literary methods, motifs, and vocabulary used to express those criteria, seem to be drawn from didactic "wisdom" concerns.[90] With this in mind, we will turn to an analysis of proverb performance in the narrative itself, where the saying "Man looks on the outward appearance, but the Lord looks on the Heart" is transmitted.

Only one alteration needs to be made in the text of the pericope: in verse 7, the second "kî" clause which precedes our saying in the MT reads "kî lōʲ ʲašer yirʲeh hāʲādām," which is clearly in error. Reading with the Septuagint and 4 Q Samb, we have restored the reading "kî lōʲ kaʲašer yirʲeh hāʲādām yirʲeh hāʲelōhîm," "for God does not see as man sees."[91] This restores the sense of the text.

(1) The Lord said to Samuel, "How long will you grieve over Saul, seeing I have rejected him from being king over Israel? Fill your horn with oil, and go; I will send you to Jesse the Bethlehemite, for I have provided for myself a king among his sons." (2) And Samuel said, "How can I go? If Saul hears it, he will kill me." And the Lord said, "Take a heifer with you, and say, 'I have come to sacrifice to the Lord.' (3) And invite Jesse to the sacrifice, and I will show you what you shall do; and you shall anoint for me him whom I name to you." (4) Samuel did what the Lord commanded, and came to Bethlehem. The elders of the city came to meet him trembling, and said, "Do you come peaceably?" (5) And he said, "Peaceably; I have come to sacrifice to the Lord; consecrate yourselves, and come with me to the sacrifice." And he consecrated Jesse and his sons, and invited them to the sacrifice. (6) When they came, he looked on Eliab and thought, "Surely the Lord's anointed is before him." (7) But the Lord said to Samuel, "Do not look on his appearance or on the height of his stature,

because I have rejected him; [for the God sees not as man sees]; man looks on the outward appearance, but the Lord looks on the heart." (8)Then Jesse called Abinadab, and made him pass before Samuel. And he said, "Neither has the Lord chosen this one." (9) Then Jesse made Shammah pass by. And he said, "Neither has the Lord chosen this one." (10) And Jesse made seven of his sons pass before Samuel. And Samuel said to Jesse, "Are all your sons here?" And he said, "There remains yet the youngest, but behold, he is keeping the sheep." And Samuel said to Jesse, "Send and fetch him; for we will not sit down till he comes here." (12) And he sent, and brought him in. Now he was ruddy, and had beautiful eyes, and was handsome. And the Lord said, "Arise, anoint him; for this is he." (13) Then Samuel took the horn of oil, and anointed him in the midst of his brothers; and the Spirit of the Lord came mightily upon David from that day forward. And Samuel rose up, and went to Ramah. (RSV)

I. The Interaction Situation.

In our passage, the ostensible Source (X) or user of the saying is Yahweh;[92] the Receiver (Y) or hearer of the saying is Samuel, his prophet, and it is the prophet's behavior, in his positive evaluation of Eliab, which has elicited the use of the saying. The relationship between them ($\mathcal{H}$) is one of great inequality, as the saying itself makes clear. Samuel, despite the awe which he is able to inspire in those around him (vv. 4-5), is the servant of the one god, whose qualities are so different from those of humans that the two may hardly be compared. Whenever any comparison is made - as is done in our pericope - it becomes clear that humans, in their abilities, evaluations, and actions, are grossly inferior by nature.[93] Samuel, although he is the prophet of God, and hence, has access to supra-normal guidance which might function to mitigate the usual state of human blindness, appears here to have gained little advantage from his special status. "Kingmaker" he may well be in the other traditions in the Book of Samuel, but in this passage, it is Yahweh, not Samuel, who chooses, decides and acts, and he must continually reprimand his truculent servant for his ineptitude in carrying through the divine purpose.[94]

II. The Proverb Situation.

The saying in verse 7, "Man looks on the outward appearance, but the Lord looks on the heart" (hā'ādām yir'eh la^cênayim waYHWH yir'eh lallēbāb) is one of the passages which Eissfeldt lists which "sounds like a proverb," and the saying is accepted as such by Fohrer.[95] Weiser cites this saying as an example of early "parallelismus membrorum" in the popular form and comments that "the prophets often made use of the popular proverb in their preaching and so, as all life became permeated with faith in Yahweh, it acquired a stronger religious colouring and served rather to throw light on spiritual and religious associations in life ...."[96] Hermisson, although he ad mits that the saying has the form of a proverb, denies that it might be of popular origin, since it appears in a passage likely to have been contaminated by wisdom influence from the Jerusalem court.[97]

The saying meets our own formal criteria in that we see complete syntax (with the more normal word order reversed by placing the subjects in "casus pendens") and two complete topic-comment units (topics: man, Yahweh; comments: sees outward form and inward form, respectively), which make it a multi-descriptive saying of the contrastive type (A ≠ B). The saying further shows a fine example of "elevated style" not only in its cadence, assonance and consonance, but also in the fact that its internal synonomous parallelism between lines produces external antithetic parallelism in thought (i.e., the structural form of the saying highlights the contrast in thought). Because of this deft literary craftsmanship, as well as the subtle way in which the verb "r'h," which supplies the verbal action for both topic-comment units, is used to provide a theme for the pericope, it is easy to see why some have excluded this saying from consideration as a folk proverb.[98] However, its occurrence here still has the marks of an "out-of-context" statement, and it is certainly susceptible to a number of applications other than the one found in our pericope.

The architectural formula along which the saying has been framed is one which uses identical syntax and contrasting word pairs (hā'ādām / YHWH; ^cênayim / lēbāb) to produce a contrastive saying. Structurally, the saying may be further broken down as follows:[99]

$$A \quad \neq \quad B$$
$$\text{Noun A - Verb - Object} \neq \text{Noun B - Verb - Object}$$
$$\text{waw-}$$
$$\text{disjunctive}$$

A multi-descriptive contrastive saying constructed along the same formula (A [N - V - O] = B [N - V -O]) may be found

99

in Pr. 16:9, "A man's mind plans his way, but the Lord directs his steps," which presents a similar evaluation of the contrast between human and divine conditions.[100]

The image used in the saying is one which makes use of human perceptual faculties to stress the great discrepancy between human and divine capacities, and hence, evaluations. It is not surprising to the reader of the Old Testament to find such physically based activities as "sight," "smell," or even "whistling" attributed to the Holy One - in fact, the tradition quite regularly ascribes such activities to its god.[101] However, there is also an exceedingly strong current which reflects the knowledge that such conceptualizations are just that - conceptualizations. The Old Testament "theologians" knew quite well that Yahweh and his creatures were very, very different.[102]

It is interesting, too, that the saying has formulated its observations in characteristically impersonal terms. The use of "hāʲādām" here is generic, rather than specific[103] (although its context of use gives it a very specific referent - Samuel). The theological statement in the saying contrasts creature with Creator in a general way; the context gives an example of how one is to modify his or her actions once the theological statement has been evaluated and affirmed.

The message of the saying, conveyed through the image of sight and the physical objects seen, has already been touched upon: humans, by nature, see only external features; Yahweh, by nature, sees the true essence of all things, no matter how deeply it may be hidden. While visible signs may often seem to be a fairly reliable source of information about those aspects of a thing which are invisible - especially, it seems in the wisdom literature - ultimately, anyone reflecting upon the matter must accept the limitations of human knowledge, especially when it stands over against divine knowledge.[104]

The "folk ideas" which underlie this saying in its basic form (as opposed to the folk ideas which underlie its application in context, which will be discussed below) center not only around a specific theological statement about Yahweh's perceptions as compared to those of humans, but are also closely tied to the ancient conception of the "heart."[105] In general usage, to speak of the heart of a thing is to refer to that which is "inaccessibly unexplorable ... anything that is quite simply impenetrably hidden."[106] In this respect, reference to "the heart of the sea," as in Pr. 23:34; 30:19; Ezek. 27:4, 25-27; 28:2, Ex. 15:8, etc., is an allusion to the unknowable, unfathomable depths. Similarly, the "heart of

100

the oak" (2 Sam. 18:14) and the "heart of heaven" (Dt. 4:11) refer to the inner, hidden part which is inaccessible by usual means. In the same way, reference to the human heart retains this nuance of that which is concealed from human sight and knowledge.[107]

However, the importance of the reference to the heart in our text is not confined to this hidden aspect. The heart "designates the whole essence and the character."[108] In many respects, the Old Testament conception of the heart is similar to the modern concept of the "mind": the heart is the seat of the emotions (Pr. 14:30; 23:17; Ps. 25:17; 1 Sam. 1:8; etc.); desires (Pr. 6:25; 13:12; Ps. 21:2); intellectual faculties such as "understanding" (Pr. 15:14; 16:23; Ps. 90:12, etc.), memory (Ps. 27:8; Dan. 7:28; etc.), and decision (Pr. 6:18; 16:9; Gen. 6:5; 2 Sam. 7:27).[109] From these broad range of meanings, it becomes clear that in a fundamental way, the heart may be taken as the measure of the person as a whole. In our saying, the heart certainly refers to those features of the personality which are hidden, since it stands in contrast to $c^\hat{e}$nayim, that which is visible and readily apparent (as is the earth's surface in Ex. 10:5, 15). But the statement means as well that God sees those hidden dimensions, plans and feelings. It is with this second, broader understanding of the use of "heart" in the saying, that we come to those criteria which doubtless cause one man to be rejected and another to be a man after Yahweh's own heart.[110]

The other major "folk idea" which surfaces in our saying concerns the theological affirmation "God looks on the heart." There is a strong recognition in the Old Testament that God's "sight" differs markedly from that of other creatures:

> The Lord looks down from heaven,
>> he sees all the sons of men;
> from where he sits enthroned he looks forth
>> on all the inhabitants of the earth,
> he who fashions the hearts of them all,
>> and observes all their deeds.
>
> Ps. 33:13-15[111]

Futhermore, this divine surveillance is continuous (although at times God may seem to have turned away his eyes): the "šōmēr-yiśrā'ēl" is always on duty, and "will neither slumber nor sleep" (Ps. 121:4). The prophets, knowing this, are openly derisive of those who say, "My way is hid" (Is. 40:27; cf. Jer. 16:17; Ezek. 9:9b, etc.). The "eye" of the Lord is on those who follow him to deliver them (Ps. 33:18-19), and he sees the day coming when the wicked will be requited (Ps. 37:13). When Job voices his plaintive cry, "Hast thou eyes of flesh? Dost thou see as man sees?" (Job 10:4), he is giving expression to the same folk idea which is found in the saying in 1 Samuel 16.[112]

Finally, we find that this awesome vision is turned upon the most intimate and constituent element of the human being - the heart. Yahweh "knows the secrets of the heart" (Ps. 44:21b); he searches the mind and tries the heart (Jer. 17:10; cf. Ps. 139:23; etc.). The wisdom tradition affirms this as well: "Sheol and Abaddon lie open before the Lord; how much more the hearts of men!" (Pr. 15:11); "Every way of a man is right in his own eyes, but the Lord weighs the heart." (Pr. 21:2).[113]

Parallels to the message of 1 Sam. 16:7 - that human "sight" is limited, especially in comparison to divine capacities - and the general reflections on the dichotomy between creator and creature which underlie the message are evident in the wisdom literature of Mesopotamia and Egypt. In the "Words of Ahiqar" we find similarities to our saying both in the images used and thought expressed:

> If God's eyes are on men, a man may chop wood in the dark without seeing, like a thief who demolishes a house.

> A man [knows not] what is in his fellow's heart. So when a good man [se]es a wi[cked] man [let him beware of him]. Let him [not] join with him on a journey or be a neighbor to him - a good man [wi]th a bad man.[114]

Similarly, the sufferer in the Babylonian "Ludlul bēl nēmeqi" reflects on the inability of human sight to see what a god sees, and understand divine purpose, which is so often hidden:

> Oh that I only knew that these things
>   are well pleasing to a god!
> What is good in one's sight is evil for a god.
> What is bad in one's own mind is good for his god.
> Who can understand the counsel of the gods
>   in the midst of heaven?
> The plan of a god is deep waters;
>   who can comprehend it?
> Where has befuddled mankind ever learned
>   what a god's conduct is?
> He who was living yesterday has died today:
> Instantly he is made gloomy,
>   suddenly is he crushed.

One moment he sings a happy song,
And in an instant he will moan like a mourner.[115]

The same thoughts are echoed in the Egyptian "Instruction for King Merikare" and the more "theological" Instruction of Amenemope:

Generation passes generation among men, and the god, who knows [men's] characters, has hidden himself.
Instruction for King Merikare

God is [always] in his success,
Whereas man is in his failure;
One thing are the words which men say,
Another is that which the god does.
Instruction of Amenemope[116]

The folk ideas which we find surfacing in these ancient works speak of human limitation and ignorance, when compared to the divine, and it is out of insights such as these that a saying like the one in 1 Sam. 16:7 is crafted.

We might summarize our analysis of the saying in 1 Sam. 16 as follows:

1 Sam. 16:7:   "Man looks on the outward appearance, but the Lord looks on the heart."
Type: Multidescriptive contrastive saying (A ≠ B)
Topics: A, man; B, YHWH
Comments: A, sees externals; B, sees internals
Architectural Formula: A (N - V - O) ≠ B (N - V - O)
Image: human physical capacities (sight)
Message: the essential nature of human and divine capacities (affects subsequent evaluations)
Parallels: formula - Pr. 16:9; 12:23; 13:6; 15:14, 18, 28
            image - Ps. 33; Job 10:4, etc., ancient Near East parallels
            message - Pr. 15:11; 21:2, etc.; ancient Near East parallels

III. The Context Situation.

As we have just seen, the contrast between human and divine vision described in the Proverb Situation is one which draws upon folk ideas common not only to the wisdom tradition, but to Israel's hymnic and prophetic traditions as well. Further, these ideas are ones which may be found in the literature of Israel's neighbors, as a survey of only the wisdom collections of Egypt and Mesopotamia shows. We must now turn to the context in which the saying is used, to see exactly "how" one might apply the theological statements of the saying to a specific situation.

The general background for the action related in this passage has to do with the rejection of Saul as a leader and the necessity of finding a proper replacement.[117] With the dismal failure of Saul, it has become obvious that the previous criteria for the selection of the anointed are clearly inadequate. Although the sources vary concerning the manner in which Saul was chosen as king, there are strong similarities to the fashion in which "saviors" arose in the Book of Judges as charismatic leaders, endowed with the necessary physical attributes for effective leadership. Not one, but twice, mention is made of Saul's outstanding physical qualifications: "There was not a man among the people of Israel more handsome than he; from his shoulders upward he was taller than any of the people" (1 Sam. 9:2; cf. 1 Sam. 11:23b).[118] In a world view, where "The soul is more than the body, but the body is a perfectly valid manifestation of the soul,"[119] greatness of stature might well be considered a reliable indication of greatness of "heart," as we understand it in its broadest sense. Yet with Saul, this was not the case, and "the Lord repented that he had made Saul king over Israel" (1 Sam. 15:35). It is the disheartening failure of this first attempt to establish permanent leadership for Israel which forms the canvas against which the success story of the Davidic election is painted.

We are told that Samuel, for all his brusqueness of manner, "grieved" over Saul (1 Sam. 15:35; 16:1), so much so, in fact, that it hindered him in inaugurating the search for Saul's replacement.[120] Yet, when God directs Samuel to visit Jesse and his sons to anoint the new king which the Lord has provided (rā'îtî (!), v. 1) for himself, Samuel is on the verge of repeating the errors of his past selection: "When they [Jesse's sons] came, he looked on Eliab and thought, 'Surely the Lord's anointed is before him'"(v.6). Only a divine rebuke, couched in the vetitive,[121] supplied with three motivations introduced by "kî," of which our saying is the last and perhaps the most important, averts the disaster of another unfortunate choice:[122]

Admonition: But the Lord said to Samuel,
Vetitive "Do not look ('al-tabbēṭ) on his appearance or on the height of his stature

104

Motivation

1.   because (kî) I have rejected him

2.   because (kî) the God does not see (yir'eh)
              as man sees[123]

3.   because (kî)
              man looks (yir'eh) on the outward appearance,
              but the Lord looks (yir'eh) on the heart.

1 Sam. 16:7

Our contextual referents, then are clearly defined: Samuel, in his previous choice of Saul and present evaluation of Eliab, is the man who does not see as God sees - he is guilty of "judging a book by its cover," by using external appearances as his guide for evaluation. For the Lord, who knows well enough that "serpent heart" may be "hid with a flow'ring face,"[124] there is only one true choice, based on the internal criteria to which only he has access: David, the shepherd after his his own heart. We might diagram the relationships in this interaction as in Figure 10.

The use of the traditional saying in this context in a literal way is an interesting one, because of the fact that the saying is a multi-descriptive one, and thus has more than one topic-comment unit, and this means that it yields an intricately crafted complex of contextual relationships. In this passage, both topic A (man) and topic B (Yahweh) are correlated with the participants in the interaction: Samuel (Y = A, C) is negatively correlated with the referents in II. and III. Further, both comments (A, sees externals; B, sees internals) are similarly correlated in negative and positive ways with Saul/Eliab and David, repectively.[125] Finally, the use of the saying as the final motivation given after the vetitive points clearly to its function: while the saying is evaluative with respect to Saul as the referent of Comment A (past time), even though he is not mentioned explicitly, the transmission of the saying is _affective_ as it applies to the immediate context when Samuel is evaluationg Eliab's claim (present time reference).[126]

It is interesting, too, to note how the saying functions to mediate between conflicting folk ideas which underlie the Proverb Situation and the Context Situation. In the first instance, the presupposition is that outstanding physical characteristics are both a measure of the inner person and a prerequisite for leadership. This evaluation represents the fruits of rational, human "wisdom," if you will; but this stands over against and ultimately falls before "divine wisdom,"

105

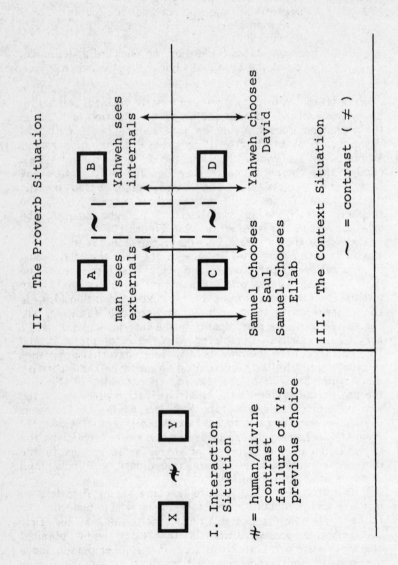

FIGURE 10: Proverb Performance in 1 Samuel 16:7

which is based on a knowledge infinitely superior to that of humans. In our context of use, all the traditional repositories of wisdom in human society - the "seer" Samuel, the elders (v. 4)[127], and the father - have not sufficient knowledge to make the proper choice. The "late" author of this masterly introduction to the shepherd of God's kingdom knew well enough who had chosen David, and might have given hearty assent to the wisdom affirmation, "No wisdom, no understanding, no counsel, can avail against the Lord!" (Pr. 21:30).

It is a subtle touch in our passage that when David is finally introduced, we do not find him lacking in the outward, physical signs of inward greatness (v. 12). His appearance is no less impressive than that of Saul or Eliab, although he is presumably smaller since he is the youngest son (cf. 1 Sam. 17:39). The author takes great pains to point out that "he was ruddy, and had beautiful eyes and was handsome" (v. 12).[128] The thrust of the use of the saying in our context is obviously not to gloss over some imagined defect in David's appearance, since his looks are specifically mentioned in a favorable way; rather, the saying points to the fact that those who judge David's election solely in the light of appearances are mistaken. This is made especially clear in the subsequent narrative in chapter 17 when David goes out as Israel's unlikely champion against Goliath. Although Goliath sees that David is handsome, he notes only his youth and size,[129] but does not see his greatness of heart: "When the Philistine looked, and saw David, he disdained him; for he was but a youth, ruddy and comely in appearance. And the Philistine said to David, 'Am I a dog, that you come to me with sticks?'" (1 Sam. 17:42-43). The giant champion discovers to his dismay that the outward trappings of power and impressive weaponry mean little to the Anointed who comes "in the name of the Lord of hosts," as David himself affirms in a response which sounds much like the teaching of the sages: "This day the Lord will deliver you into my hand...that all this assembly may know that the Lord saves not with sword and spear; for the battle is the Lord's and he will give you into our hand" (1 Sam. 17:46a, 47).[130] Even as human wisdom fails before divine choice, so does human might fall before divine purpose, manifested in one with whom the Lord is (1 Sam. 16:18b).

Comments

We have seen that in a period of general conflict and

uncertainty (the Philistine threat to Israel, the change from a tribal system to monarchy), the traditional saying appears in a context where it mediates between opposing folk ideas (external prerequisites for leadership vs. divine choice) to suggest that there is more to David's election than meets the human eye. The strategy of the use of the saying in its literary context is immediately successful: Samuel accepts the guidance of God in the choice rather than pursuing his own hasty evaluations.

The "indirection" afforded to the user of a saying surfaces in this pericope in an interesting way. Obviously, God as the Source of the saying has no need to mince words with his prophet, and does not do so (see v. 1, with its rather irascible challenge to Samuel's continued indulgence in sorrow over Saul). However, the author's intent in using the traditional saying shows a full awareness of the cloak which traditional language may afford its user. The passage, dealing as it does, with the first introduction of David in the Book of Samuel and his anointing as the true king, is especially important for the understanding of both subsequent events in the Book of Samuel, and Davidic covenant theology. The author, as is evident in the dramatic way in which the hearer/reader is kept ignorant of the anointed's identity until verse 12, wants to give his full attention to Yahweh's choice of David and the reasons for that choice. Yet, some comparison to the tragic figure of Saul, the rejected king, is inevitable, and even desirable. The author has been at great pains to establish subtle connections between this passage and what has gone before,[131] but the real contrast between Saul and David is to be found in the traditional saying as it is used in context. The author has rendered a favorable judgment on David and a negative one on Saul without having to share the stage with the rejected leader. It is through the use of the saying, with its internal ambiguity which nonetheless becomes explicit through the correlation with contextual referents, that this goal is achieved. The immediate referent may be Eliab, but he is a mere cipher for the figure whose downfall paves the way for David's success. Saul is evaluated and dismissed in favor of David, without the embarrassing necessity of explicit references, and the legitimacy of David is affirmed - a shrewd use of a traditional saying to further literary, political and theological ends.

PROVERB PERFORMANCE IN 1 SAM. 24:14 [13]

Introduction

The exchange of words between David and Saul outside a cave at En-gedi on the first occasion of David's "generosity" to the disturbed king provides an excellent example of the "strategic" use of the traditional saying in social interactions. Despite some small problems with the order of verses 5-8 [Hebrew; English, 4-7][132] and the close similarity which the pericope bears to Chapter 26, the second instance when David spares Saul, the vividness of the narrative, along with its "folksy" overtones[133] and the fortuitous designation of the saying in verse 14 as a "'māshāl' of the ancients," make it especially apt for the study of use of the saying in context.

Both chapter 24 and 26, generally acknowledged to be doublets, are set against the background of Saul's not wholly unfounded animosity toward young David, whom "all Israel and Judah loved" (1 Sam. 18:16a). Whether prompted by "an evil spirit from God" (1 Sam. 18:10) or by the growing conviction that David's popularity constituted a very real political threat (1 Sam. 18:8), Saul's earlier patronage to the comely hero is replaced by bitter enmity, and on a number of occasions (reflecting the usual tangle of sources generally found in the Book of Samuel), he attempts to get rid of his young rival by fair means (1 Sam. 18:20-28) or foul (1 Sam. 19:8-17, etc.). As usual, the sources disagree on the exact place to which David escapes in fear of his life,[134] but the picture is consistent in presenting David in mortal danger from Saul. Further, as is so often the case with outcast, handsome young heroes, "every one who was in distress, and everyone who was in debt, and everyone who was discontented, gathered to him, and he became captain over them" (1 Sam. 22:2). It is within this context of continued pursuit and flight, that Saul is seemingly "delivered" into David's eager hands in a cave in En-gedi.

The Pericope

We need not be unduly concerned with the relationship between chapters 24 and 26, since our major interest is with the interaction portrayed between David and Saul.[135] Neither need we take up the question of the relative "historicity" of the two accounts, since it is clear that whatever the nucleus of historical truth which may lie behind the events narrated, it has been overlaid in a programmatic way to stress certain theological perspectives on David's rise to kingship, and this is especially so of chapter 24, which shows more signs of reworking than does chapter 26.[136]

The picture described in the first narrative of David's generosity in sparing Saul is one which reflects the conflict of the times. Not only does the responsibility of dealing with the Philistine threat still lie heavily upon Saul (1 Sam. 24:2), but his desire to rid himself of David and his followers leads him on numerous fruitless chases (1 Sam. 19:22; 23:8, 14, 25). After dealing with a Philistine raid, Saul returns with a large force (3,000 men, in v. 3 [2] compared to David's following of 400 men in 1 Sam. 22:2b or 600 in 1 Sam. 23:13) to hunt the small band in the rough terrain surrounding En-gedi. A moment of perhaps unintentional comic relief occurs when Saul chooses to answer a call of nature in the outer portion of the very cave in which David and his men have sought shelter.[137] It is here that the immediate conflict begins.

David's men are, quite naturally, delighted with the situation, and choose to interpret Saul's proximity as an expression of divine favor toward David: "And the men of David said to him, 'Here is the day of which the Lord said to you, "Behold, I will give your enemy into your hand, and you shall do to him as it shall seem good to you'" " (v. 5). Certainly, on the basis of past performance, both David and his men are justified in believing that, were the situations reversed, Saul would not hesitate to turn his advantage to good account (cf. 1 Sam. 18:10-11, 17b; 19:9-11; 23:9; etc.). However, it is at this point that David's understanding of what it means to be "Yahweh's Anointed" intervenes to stop the execution of his men's precipitate justice. Still, he does cut off the hem of Saul's robe, an act for which his heart later "smites" him.

David's action should be seen in the light of Samuel's similar act in 1 Sam. 15:27:[138] in our present context. David, too, performs an act which symbolizes the Lord's rejection of Saul; and, like a blessing or curse in the ancient world, such an act was charged with power to effect the thing which it symbolized.[139] In this fashion, through the performance of the symbolic act, David has actually followed "... Samuel in rejecting Saul as Yahweh's anointed, and is accepting the theological justification for the attack on Saul's person which has been formulated by his men. But he immediately repents of this step; Saul is still Yahweh's anointed after all, and David is no longer convinced that either Samuel's act or his own can deprive him of his sacral status and open up the way for an attack on his person."140

(2) When Saul returned from following the Philistines, he was told, "Behold, David is in the wilderness of En-gedi." (3) Then Saul took three thousand chosen men out of all Israel, and went to seek David and his men in from of the Wildgoat's Rocks. (4) And he came to the sheepfolds by the way, where there was a cave; and Saul went in to relieve himself. Now David and his men were sitting in the innermost parts of the cave. (5a) And the men of David said to him, "Here is the day of which the Lord said to you, 'Behold, I will give your enemy into your hand, and you shall do to him as it shall seem good to you.'" (7) He said to his men, "The Lord forbid that I should do this thing to my lord, the Lord's anointed, to put forth my hand against him, seeing he is the Lord's anointed." (8a) So David persuaded his men with these words, and did not permit them to attack Saul. (5b) Then David arose and stealthily cut off the skirt of Saul's robe. (6) And afterward, David's heart smote him, because he had cut off Saul's skirt. (8b) And Saul rose up, and left the cave, and went on his way. (9) Afterward David also arose, and went out of the cave and called after Saul, "My lord the king!" And when Saul looked behind him, David bowed with his face to the earth, and did obeisance. (10) And David said to Saul, "Why do you listen to the words of men who say, 'Behold, David seeks your hurt'? (11) Lo, this day your eyes have seen how the Lord gave you today into my hand in the cave; and some bade me kill you, but I spared you. I said, 'I will not put forth my hand against my lord; for he is the Lord's anointed.' (12) See, my father, see the skirt of your robe in my hand; for by the fact that I cut off the skirt of your robe, and did not kill you, you may know and see that there is no wrong or treason in my hands. I have not sinned against you, though you hunt my life to take it. (13) May the Lord judge between me and you, may the Lord avenge me upon you; but my hand shall not be against you. (14) As the proverb of the ancients says, "Out of the wicked comes forth wickedness" ! but my hand shall not be against you. (15) After whom has the king of Israel come out? After whom do you pursue? After a dead dog! After a flea! (16) May the Lord therefore be judge and give sentence between me and you, and see to it, and plead my cause, and deliver me from your hand."

I. The Interaction Situation.

The Source of the traditional saying in this pericope is David (X); the Receiver (Y) is Saul, and it is David's behavior in verse 5b which elicits the use of the saying directed at Saul. The relationship between them ($\nmid\!\!\!\!/$) is one of polar extremes in almost every respect. David is the young hero, Yahweh's preferred anointed, upon whom "the Spirit of the Lord came mightily" (1 Sam. 16:13), and the leader of a small band of men who, for all their lack of numbers, are nonetheless quite efficient in dealing with the Philistines (1 Sam. 23:1-5, etc.). Saul, on the other hand, is the anointed who has been rejected, a man "of volatile temperament who was liable to be morose, suspicious and violently vindictive,"[141] and one who is "tormented" by an "evil spirit" from the Lord (1 Sam. 16:14). In his encounters with David, he has suffered the symbolic loss of his kingdom (1 Sam. 16:1, etc.), his prestige (1 Sam. 18:7-9), and has even been forced to witness the defection of his children (1 Sam. 18:20ff.; 19:1-6, 11-17; 20:30-34). Further, on a number of occasions, Saul has made attempts on David's life, and so, would have reason to expect violence at David's hands when the situation is suddenly reversed.

II. The Proverb Situation.

The traditional saying "Out of the wicked comes forth wickedness" (mēr^{e}šā^{c}îm yēṣē^j rešā^c) in verse 14a [13a] is one of the four sayings in the Old Testament outside of the wisdom literature which are explicitly designated as "māshāl."[142] Eissfeldt, for this reason, accepts it as a bona fide folk proverb (Volkssprichwort) as do others.[143] Hermisson, although correctly disagreeing with the position of earlier commentators who viewed verse 14 as a gloss to 13b [12b],[144] does not consider the passage to be a true saying, but sees it more properly as an example of a type of legal declaration.[145]

By our criteria, we find that 14a meets the minimum structural requirements for designation as a saying. Syntax is complete and typically brief, and the statement consists of one complete descriptive unit (topic: the wicked [A] ; comment: produces wickedness [B]). The saying exhibits both assonance and consonance achieved through the repetition of the root concept "r^s^{c}" and a balanced cadence (4/4 beat for topic and comment), which provides a reasonable example of the "elevated style" so familiar in sayings, whether popular or learned in origin. Furthermore, the saying is capable of numerous applications because of the generality of its image and message, and certainly appears here as an "out-of-context" statement.[146] Finally, the saying here is specifically identified as such by the introduction "as the 'mashal' of the ancients says ..."[147] While such an introductory formula does not necessarily mean that what follows is undoubtedly a saying, the use of a formula along with fulfilment of the other requirements posed makes the assumption that we are dealing here with a traditional saying, a fairly safe one.

The architectural formula used to construct the saying is one of identification with an aspect of causality (A → B), indicated in the relationship between the topic and comment. The grammatical structure may be further analyzed as "min" ("from") + N V N, and the placement of mērešācîm before the copula emphasizes the "wicked ones" as the true focus or topic of the saying. This is accomplished through the operation of the transformation rule (T-rule) permuta- tion, which, in this instance, shifts the grammatical agent (the wicked ones) or source into the position of logical subject. If the second half of the verse is included in consideration of the saying in 14a, we find roughly synonomous syntax used to build an external antithesis between the concepts of the saying and David's appraisal of that content with respect to his own actions:

| min | N | V | N |
| waw | N | V | PP (Prepositional Phrase) |

Parallels to this formula may be found in Pr. 12:14a, "From the fruit of the mouth of a man he is satisfied with good" (mippᵉrî pî ʾîš yiśbaᶜ-ṭôb), and Pr. 13:2a, "From the fruit of the mouth of a man he eats (what is) good" (mippᵉrî pî-ʾîš yōʾkal ṭôb).[148]

The image of the saying is one which is a special favorite in wisdom literature: the nature, activities, and ends of the wicked. The image of the wicked producing wickedness is in full harmony with wisdom's reflections on the subject, as the following representative statements from Israel and her neighbors show.

It is like sport to a fool to do wrong,
  but wise conduct is pleasure to a man of understanding.
                        Pr. 10:23

The thoughts of the righteous are just,
  the counsels of the wicked are treacherous.
                        Pr. 12:5

Deceit is in the heart of those who devise evil,
    but those who plan good have joy.
                    Pr. 12:20

A righteous man hates falsehood,
    but a wicked man acts shamefully and disgracefully.
                    Pr. 13:5

The mind of the righteous ponders how to answer,
    but the mouth of the wicked pours out evil things.
                    Pr. 15:28

The way of the guilty is crooked,
    but the conduct of the pure is right.
                    Pr. 21:8

The soul of the wicked desires evil;
    his neighbor finds no mercy in his eyes.
                    Pr. 21:10

When the wicked are in authority, transgression increases.
                    Pr. 29:16a

You are placed into a river
    and your water becomes at once stinking;
you are placed in an orchard
    and your date-fruit becomes bitter.
If the shoot is not right
    it will not produce the stalk, nor create seed.
                  Akkadian Proverb
                  K 4347, #53-55

As for the fool who will not hear, there is no one who
can do anything for him. He regards knowledge as
ignorance and what is beneficial as something harmful;
he does everything hateful, so that men are angry with
him every day. He lives on that whereby men die, and to
distort speech is his food. His character in this respect is
in the knowledge of the magistrates, dying alive every
day; men pass over his deeds because of the multitude of
troubles on him every day.
                  Maxims of Ptahhotep,
                  17, 5-9[49]

It should be noted, too, that in Biblical Hebrew the ancient
notion of "wickedness" carries the implication of violence and
illegitimate activities against the "proper" or right (civil)
authority (Pr. 4:17; 10:2; Ps. 141:4, etc.). Similarly, a "wicked
one" is someone who is judged to be guilty of such crimes

against proper authority (Ex. 2:13; Dt. 25:2; Pr. 17:23; 18:5; 19:28; 20:26; 29:12; Job 9:22,24; Jer. 5:26, etc.). Wickedness, then, does not refer simply to some theoretical or abstract evil, but to the kinds of activities which tear apart the very fabric of human society. Those who commit "wicked" deeds are condemned not so much because they are dedicated to some goal of evil, but because their actions (which, of course, stem from their character) disrupt society as a whole. Thus, leaders, who are especially responsible for ensuring the internal cohesion of society, must not only be on guard against those who challenge their own authority (i.e., "the wicked ones"), but must also be careful not to indulge in disruptive activities themselves. This is brought out in many of the "royal" wisdom sayings: "It is an abomination to kings to do wrong ($ca\check{s}\hat{o}t$ $re\check{s}a^c$) for the throne is established by righteousness" (Pr. 16:12); and "A wise king winnows the wicked, and drives the wheel over them" (Pr. 20:26).

The message of the saying operates on two levels, giving both a specific statement about the wicked as well as an insight into the ancient understanding of the relationship between inner essence and its tangible effect in outward actions (or, one might say, the relationship between actor and act). McKane has paraphrased this relationship as "there is a harmony between character and action," and goes on to comment: "It is more than a statement that an evil deed condemns its doer as evil, for it embraces the converse, that a good man will never perform an evil act. Hence it may be used to indict an evil man or dissociate a man of settled virtue from an evil act of which he is accused."[150] These observations are certainly true of wisdom's understanding of wickedness - that is, that the wicked person invariably produces wicked deeds.[151] One might also point out that these insights are often taken a step further: the very wickedness produced by the wicked person generally proves to be his or her downfall, as any act sets into motion a chain of reactions or consequences (see Pr. 10:24a; 11:3b, 5b, 6, 23b, 27b; 14:14, 32; 21:7; 22:8; etc.).

The implications of the message underlying the saying in verse 14a go beyond the culture's characterization of evildoers, however. The folk idea which finds expression in the relationship between the wicked person and the wicked act is beautifully stated in Pr. 20:11, "Even a child makes himself known by his acts, whether what he does is pure and right."[152] The impression here of the natural and human world is in keeping with other folk ideas embodied in sayings which we have already discussed. The picture is that of a simpler world, where outward appearance and performed actions offered a fairly reliable guide to knowledge of the inner nature, and vice versa. In this world, there was no need to discuss abstractions of evil and good, or the relation between actor and act - simple observation and experience of the world, along with a seemingly naïve trust in such endeavors, could provide all the information needed to make sense of persons and events.[153] Still, it would not do to censure the sages as shallow reductionists bent on finding harmony where none actually existed. The truly wise have always been aware that general "rules" may sometimes end in paradox,[154] that appearances may be deceptive and that glitter is not an invariable indication of gold - these insights also found expression in the "mešālim" of the wise.[155] To summarize, then, the conceptualization of the relationships which form the "kernel" of the saying in 14a and many similar wisdom sayings are significant not only because of their statements on the concrete images used in each individual saying (e.g., the ways of the wicked), but also because they provide an insight into the broader understanding of reality of those who coined and used them.

1 Sam. 24:14:
"Out of the wicked comes forth wickedness"

Type:	Identificational, positive causation (A→B)
Topic:	the wicked (A)
Comment:	produce wickedness (→B)
Architectural formula: min + A V B	
Image:	the wicked; human character
Message:	harmony between character and action
Parallels:	formula - Pr. 12:14a
	image - Pr. 13:5b; 15:28b; etc.
	message - Pr. 20:11; 25:23; etc.

III. The Context Situation.

Once more, we find the use of a traditional saying occurring in a situation which bristles with hostility and potential violence (see I. Interaction Situation), and one where appeals to "traditional wisdom" and common world view might well be employed efficaciously to mediate the various conflicts. The specific context of use is the interchange between David and Saul which takes place when Saul leaves the cave at En-gedi, only to be confronted by David and the realization of this narrow escape. David, here, disarms Saul, both with his extremely respectful actions, and by his arguments that he means Saul no harm. These are bolstered both by his disclosure of the hem which he cut from Saul's robe as evidence, and the traditional saying which he uses to lend credence to his favorable interpretration of the act. The contextual referents which are correlated with the topic (A, the wicked) and comment (B, produced wickedness) are the binary opposition between David's presumed nature (C) and his actual deeds (D). We may illustrate the situation as in Figure 11.

A general paraphrase of this interaction and use in context is "David, (X, the preferred anointed in an inferior position) says to Saul (the rejected anointed in a superior position), '"a wicked nature (A) produces wicked acts (B),' so if I were indeed wicked (C) as you believe (v. 10), I would have acted ($\sim$) wickedly toward you and killed you when I had the opportunity (D); since I did not commit this wicked deed, I must not be of a wicked nature." The time reference is to past events (David's actions inside the cave); the reference is clearly evaluative. The intent in David's direction of the saying at Saul is evident from the context (vv. 11-13): David purposefully introduces a loaded statement which carries the authority of traditional wisdom ("As the māshāl of the ancients says ...");[156] if Saul assents to the validity of the saying (which he does, because he shares the world view which underlies it), then he must carry this reasoning through to its logical conclusion, even though it may produce an affirmation which he would not normally care to champion (e.g., that David is not, in fact, wicked). David's strategy is quite successful, as is confirmed by Saul's response: "You are more righteous than I; for you have repaid me good, whereas I have repaid you evil. And you have declared this day how you have dealt well with me, in that you did not kill me when the Lord put me into your hands. For if a man finds his enemy, will he let him go away safe?" (vv. 18-20a [17-19a]). The scene ends with Saul's rather pathetic statement that he knows David will be his successor,[157] and a plea that David spare Saul's family. Once again, Saul has come away the loser in his encounters with David.

It should be noted that this interpretation of the use of the saying is in no way inconsistent with our earlier understanding of David's act of cutting Saul's robe as a symbolic action which figuratively "clips Saul's wings."[158] Even though this action is a grave one, about which David is subsequently regretful, the recognition of the true nature of the deed does not preclude David (and/or a later redactor)

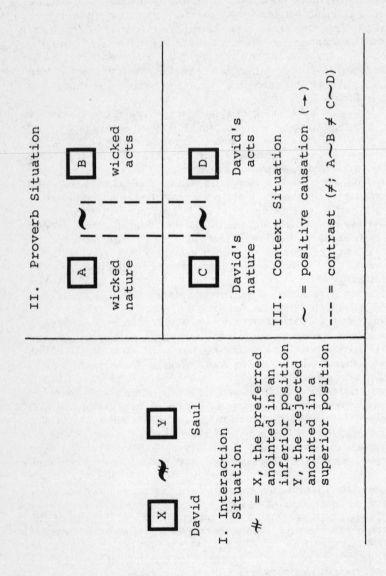

FIGURE 11: Proverb Performance in 1 Samuel 24:14 [13]

from placing the most favorable construction possible on the act, in order to minimize David's very real rebellion against Saul as the legitimate civil authority. Indeed, from what we know of David's personality, this is precisely what we would expect him to do.[159] David, the consummate opportunist, has a knack for turning his questionable actions into advantageous propaganda, so that we find even his murders can be tidily concealed beneath the pious cloak of retribution for blood guilt.[160]

Comments

As has been noted above, earlier commentators considered the use of the traditional saying in this context to be a later addition to the text, since "the introduction of such a proverb as we here find is particularly infelicitous, for it intimates that the wickedness of Saul would be his destruction. There is good ground therefore for suspecting the verse to be an interpolation."[161] Some recent commentators tend to take Saul as the contextual referent of the saying, and hence, share the evaluation that the use of a saying in this way to point up Saul's wickedness, is tactless enough to warrant the conclusion that David would not have used the saying.[162] Our understanding of the dynamics of proverb performance, however, provides a reasonable model by which the use of the saying may be properly understood. First, it must be realized that the very generality of a saying is one of the qualities which make its use in difficult situations so likely. It is quite possible that David may be using the saying to apply to both Saul (a negative correspondence, $Y \neq C$) and himself (a positive correspondence, $X = C$), but the "indirection" in the metaphorical use of a saying applied to the specific context[163] shields him against renewed hostility on the part of Saul. That is, David may be making a negative evaluation of Saul (i.e., "even though your acts have shown you to be wicked, I will not seek revenge"), but Saul, because of the generality of the saying, is not obligated to interpret its use in this way. The text seems to suggest that Saul, although he grants that David is the more righteous in their mutual dealings, does not see himself as overtly wicked; rather, he takes the saying as applying to David, and assents to its logic. We need not consider the saying a gloss simply because analysis of its use may yield a variety of interpretations. Rather, it should be recognized that this is precisely the reason why it is used.

Secondly, an investigation into the strategy of proverb use

contributes to our assumption of the integrity of the text in two ways. David's <u>intent</u> in using the saying is to force Saul to assent to a position which he must certainly find distasteful, and which, in other circumstances, he might even have refused to entertain (cf. 1 Sam. 20: 30-34). Saul is out-maneuvered by David's manipulation of traditional wisdom for his ends. His innermost feelings - his distrust of David - must be reassessed when confronted with the authority of the saying's logic. David, technically in the inferior position, uses indirection to force his superior to subscribe to his own (David's) interpretation of the situation. This is exactly the same strategy used by Nathan in 2 Sam. 12 when he forces David, now king, to acknowledge and judge his actions towards Bathsheba and Uriah the Hittite. Nathan cannot confront his king directly and hope for fair results; rather, he seeks the indirection of a parable to obtain a full hearing. The prophet's strategy is double-edged: he not only protects himself from David's anger,[164] but ensures that the king view the events objectively - a feat which could hardly have been accomplished if he had opened with a direct personal attack. The fact that the parable used by Nathan does not quite "fit" the context situation (David and Bathsheba) is clearly secondary to the benefits it provides as traditional language which is pointed yet indirect, and suited to the strategic needs of the context and intent of its user. Similar "strategy" is employed in 2 Sam. 14 by the "wise woman" of Tekoa to obtain David's reconciliation with Absalom.

Another way in which the strategy of proverb use operates in our text is in the specific technique which David uses to achieve his aims. David sets up a proposition ("there is a harmony between character and action") to which Saul tacitly agrees. This established, David proceeds to his second proposition which points out the contradictions between the view or folk idea expressed in the saying and its logical application to the contextual situation. Saul, having accepted the "truth" of the first proposition, is thus committed to the second - i.e., David must not be wicked after all, and Saul's wickedness is implicitly recognized.[165]

This "method" of proverb performance strategy - the introduction of a "fact" or premise which is then qualified, or perhaps contradicted - has been found by folklorist Peter Seitel in his studies of East Nigerian society to be one of the primary ways in which proverbs are "manipulated" in so- cial contexts to achieve personal ends.[166] His further suggestion that such strategy may hold true cross-culturally for proverb use in general, seems to be well taken, as the illustrations below demonstrate. However, a further refinement of this observation should be made: the qualification of the first proposition may occur either <u>within</u> the traditional saying itself (usually making it a contrastive or paradoxical saying); or it may occur <u>outside</u> of the saying proper, either by (a) the introduction of a second saying to provide the contrast or qualification or by (b) an appraisal made by the proverb user or hearer, usually drawn from the context situation, which need not take the form of a saying. Examples of sayings which show self-contained qualifications to "traditional" views may be observed in a variety of cultures:

Good speech is more hidden than malachite,
yet it is found in the possession of women slaves at the millstones.
Maxims of Ptahhotep

By nature, men are nearly alike;
by practice, they get to be wide apart.
Confucius

Do not praise a man for his good looks,
    nor loathe a man because of his appearance.
The bee is small among flying creatures
    but her product is the best of sweet things.
Ben Sira 11:2-3

A toad does not run in the daytime -
    unless something is after its life.
Ibo saying from East Nigeria

Time is a merciless enemy,
    as it is also a merciless friend and healer.
Gandhi

Gold goes in any gate - except Heaven's.
English saying

All men must die, but death can vary in its significance. The ancient Chinese writer Szuma Chien said, "Though death befalls all men alike, it may be heavier than Mount Tai or lighter than a feather." To die for the people is heavier than Mount Tai, but to work for the fascists and die for the exploiters and oppressors is lighter than a feather.
Mao Tse-Tung[167]

In each of the sayings given, the strategy for using traditional wisdom to challenge the hearer is the same. One quite naturally assents to the observations that polished rhetoric is a difficult art, that there is a certain natural equality among persons, that the bee is tiny and the toad not given to sunbathing and strenuous activity during the day, that time is a relentless force, money a universal key to opening doors, and that all must die. The qualifications that follow - that there are "good" and "bad" deaths, that time, the enemy, is also time, the friend, and so on - are all the more striking because of the hearer's tacit response to the initial statement. The paradoxes often revealed in traditional genres wield the power to confront the hearer with seeming contradictions and by doing so, encourage reflection, evaluation, and an attitude of openness toward the world of events.

One may also point to numerous cross-cultural examples, where a saying is qualified through juxtaposition of a contrasting saying or an appraisal rising out of a given context. This strategy, too, highlights perceived contradictions, and in general, the second element in the contrast is the one favored by the proverb user, or at least felt to represent the actual (contextual) situation.

A. Juxtaposed Sayings

I thought "wisdom is better than prowess,"
    but "the wisdom of the poor man is despised and his
    words are not heard."
                          Ec. 9:16

"Wisdom is better than weapons of war"
    but "one fool destroys much good."
                          Ec. 9:18

(You say) "With aged men is wisdom,
    and length of days is understanding;"
(I say) "With Him is wisdom and might;
    He hath counsel and understanding."
                          Job 12:12-13

Something happened to the smoke which caused it to
    enter the bush and become mist.

A leopard conceals his spots.
                          Anang judicial proverbs[168]

Chapter III : Proverb Performance

B. Saying-Appraisal

It is the eater who tastes, and he who is questioned answers; it is the sleeper who sees the dream - As for the judge who ought to be punished, he is a pattern for the wrongdoer.

Tale of the Eloquent Peasant

A brick may move from beneath its companions, but I will not move from beneath the two feet of the king, my lord.

Amarna letter EA, #292,
lines 14-15

I thought, "Days should speak, and many years teach wisdom;" but it is the spirit in man and the breath of the Almighty, that brings insight.

Job 32:7-8

As people say: "Man is the shadow of a god, and a slave is the shadow of a man;" but the king is the mirror of a god.

Akkadian letter to Esar-haddon (?)
ABL, No. 652, lines 10-13

You have heard that it was said, 'An eye for an eye and a tooth for a tooth.' But I say to you, Do not resist one who is evil. But if anyone strikes you on the right cheek, turn to him the other also.

Mt. 5:38-39

Wei Cheng of the Tang Dynasty also understood the error of onesideness when he said, "Listen to both sides and you will be enlightened; heed only one side and you will be benighted." But our comrades often look at problems one-sidedly, and so they often run into snags .... For all objective things are actually interconnected and are governed by inner laws, but, instead of undertaking the task of reflecting things as they really are, some people look at things one-sidedly or superficially and know neither their interconnections nor their inner laws, and so their method is subjectivist.

Mao Tse-Tung

"Short cuts make long delays," argued Pippin .... "That settles it! " said Frodo. " 'Short cuts may make delays,' but inns make longer ones ...."

Hobbit "proverb performance"
The Lord of the Rings[169]

The "context" of the Egyptian peasant's appraisal of the saying (whose message is that those engaged in certain endeavors perform activities appropriate to those endeavors) is his contention that the magistrate from whom he had sought redress for a crime refuses to render a fair judgement, the activity appropriate to the one who occupies the position of judge. The context of the Amarna letter quoted is that Ba^{c}lu-shipti, the Canaanite governor of Gezer, will continue to try to hold the Egyptian territories of Pharaoh Akhenaton in Canaan, despite the growing difficulties of that task. In fine proverbial language, Ba^{c}lu-shipti states that even if it is a time in which a brick might be displaced from beneath the structure which it upholds (an extremely unlikely occurrence!), his own steadfastness will not alter, even in perilous times. The writer of the Adakkian letter to (probably) Esarhaddon states a common "folk idea" about the human condition of limitation, with an added flattering appraisal that such limitations do not apply to the king. Similarly, Elihu appraises the folk idea that the greatest wisdom is possessed by the aged, in light of his own intent within the context of wishing to join the discussion between Job and his friends. It might be argued that the statements in Matthew 5 should be understood more properly as legal statements rather than as traditional sayings. However, our definition of a traditional saying does not preclude a legal statement from functioning as a saying in a given context, and the use of the statement made in Matthew provides a good example of this traditional method of arguing (see also Lk. 4:23-24). The "midrash" of Chairman Mao on an extant Chinese saying to dramatize organizational problems needs little comment, nor does the incidence of the "saying-appraisal" method of proverb performance among hobbits to settle the problems of decision making.[170]

Thus, we have seen from a variety of contexts, that proverb users may use a strategy of "supposition-qualification" to achieve their ends. This may be achieved by a selection of an apt saying which contains a paradox, juxtaposition of contrasting sayings, or saying-appraisal which draws attention to the contextual correlation. This latter form of the strategy - the saying-appraisal - is the type of argument David advances toward Saul in our passage. The text is correct as it stands.

Several other "folk ideas" undergird the use of the traditional saying in its present context. The first we might mention, the Hebrew understanding of "yăd," hand, is in keeping with our earlier remarks concerning the ancient conception of the body, where individual parts (limbs, organs, stature, etc.) may represent the person or certain aspects of the person as a whole.[171] The "hand" is used in this respect, and is the part of the body most often mentioned in the Old Testament.[172] The "hand," quite reasonably in view of its dexterity and importance in all forms of physical action, comes to represent the strength or power of the whole person (Jos. 8:20; Jg. 7:2; Job 2:6; Is. 1:12; etc.). Wolff comments, "... in the case of 'yād,' the notion of a bodily limb recedes entirely into the background, generally speaking, giving way to the meaning "strength," which belongs to the hand as the primary means of power ...."[173] David's statement in his appraisal of the saying in 14a, that his hand will not be against Saul, is thus not simply a statement that, even if given the opportunity, he will not raise his hand in violence against Saul. On a broader level, David asserts that he will not use his considerable powers (as the recipient of God's blessing and spirit) against Saul.

Two important theological presuppositions provide the motivations for the action related in the context situation: the concept of the sacral king ("Yahweh's Anointed"), and the popular belief in Yahweh as judge. In Israel, we find some distinctive elements in the understanding of the sacrality of the king, a basic folk idea which she shared with her neighbors. However, where the inviolability of the king in the ancient Near East usually stemmed from the belief that he was a descendant from the god(s), and hence was himself divine,[174] in Israel, the sacrality of the king could not be understood in this way. Yahweh was the only true god, and although the king might be understood to have been "adopted" by god (Pss. 2:7; 110; etc.), he was never conceived of as personally divine. "His divinity depends on the equipment he has received by his election and anointment and on the force flowing to him through the holy rites of the cult, according to Yahweh's free will and depending on the king's loyalty and obedience towards Yahweh's commandments."[175] It was the cultic act of anointment, charged with power to transmit the Sacred, which made the person of the king sacrosanct, and "as a result, he was now thought to be a channel for the operation of the divine 'Spirit' ..."[176] David, himself the Anointed of Yahweh, respects the power communicated in that rite even if he may not respect its recipient. Careful to avoid entanglements whenever possible, David is even more desirous of avoiding any guilt which might be attached to anyone unwise enough to do violence to Yahweh's Anointed.[177] Even when faced with the necessity of doing away with possible rivals from Saul's family, David is careful to arrange that his machinations incur no technical guilt (2 Sam. 21), and used "the very sacredness of the royal family to get rid of its members."[178] Whether this idea of the inviolability of the sacral king and his family was indeed in evidence at the time of Saul and David, or is a later interpolation by the tradition to push the doctrine of the sacrality of the Davidic king back into the period of the inception of the monarchy,[179] this perception of Yahweh's Anointed constitutes one of the primary motivations for the events presented in the text.

Closely tied to the idea of the sacrality of the king, the second theological "folk idea" which forms the background for our context is the belief in Yahweh as the judge of an individual's actions. Given this view, David must be content to call upon God to judge between himself and Saul and execute whatever vengeance may be necessary (vv. 13, 16, 20), since he can do nothing against the sacral king. This affirmation that God will judge, holds firm even in cases where human observation might conclude otherwise, as Eichrodt comments:

> It is recognized that the murderer is cursed of God, even though no man's hand may be raised against him (Gen. 4:11f.). It is possible to say of an act of violence, for which no expiation has been made, that "Yahweh will punish it" (2 Sam. 3:39). Indeed, because it is known that Yahweh judges those offences with which no human judge is concerned, his wrath is feared even before his punishment is made manifest (1 Sam. 24:6; 2 Sam. 12:13; 24:10).[180]

In 1 Sam. 24, we once again find a traditional saying surfacing in exactly the type of situation we might expect: the conflicts between David and Saul are temporarily resolved, due in great part to David's masterful use of the saying with an appended appraisal relating it to the context. Indirection, ambiguity, and the appeal to a common understanding of reality aid David's interpretation of events, and Saul is, for the moment, convinced. Perhaps most interesting for our investigation, we see here a "folk idea" believed to be characteristic of "wisdom thought"[181] nestling comfortably between the theological affirmations of the sacral king and Yahweh as. judge. Wisdom (whether popular or courtly in <u>origin</u>) seems to be perfectly well at home in a variety of places, once one begins to investigate its <u>application</u> in specific contexts.

PROVERB PERFORMANCE IN 1 KINGS 20:11

Introduction

The Hebrew Book of Kings presents the scholar with a fine example of the manipulation of historiographic sources to further other ends than that of "history" writing. Covering the history of the kingdoms of Judah and Israel up to the fall of the southern kingdoms in the sixth century B.C.E., the work is an obvious amalgam of sources. These sources have been welded together and placed within a framework whose specific attitudes and evaluations towards the events recounted are frankly judgmental and fall far outside the realm of objective reportage. For this reason and others, the "historicity" of the events narrated is often called into question, and in certain cases, the theological "program" of the editor(s) has caused a distortion of the various reigns under discussion.[182] The events related in the book give ample indication of the continual upheavals and pressures which beset the political and religious history of the two kingdoms. It is from one such period in the history of Israel that our pericope in 1 Kg. 20:1-21, comes and thus we should not be surprised if "traditional wisdom", encapsulated in the saying genre, did not play some part in the understanding and management of events.

The Pericope

Nestled within the Elijah cycle (1 Kg. 17-19; 21; 2 Kg. 1) which tells the story of that exceedingly zealous Yahwist's conflict with the non-exclusivist forces in Israel, we find two accounts of (supposedly) Ahab's wars with Aram-Damascus under the leadership of the king "Ben-hadad" in chapters 20 and 22. A number of striking features are immediately apparent when these two complexes are read together: the source which relates Ahab's conflict with Ben-hadad is very positive indeed in its evaluation of Ahab, as compared to the more typical judgments made in chapters 17-19; 21; 2 Kg. 1; there is no mention made at all in 20 and 22 of Elijah, but rather reference is made to an anonymous prophet in chapters 20 and 22, even though Elijah suddenly reappears in

2 Kg. 1; and there is a discrepancy concerning the nature of Ahab's death (cf. 1 Kg. 21:29 and 1 Kg. 22:34, 37-40). These differences, along with the difficulty in constructing a coherent sequence of the events of the Syrian wars given our information from extra-biblical sources, have led biblical scholars to a variety of conclusions.[183] The most "conservative" position adopted simply rearranges the order of the chapters to place Chapter 20 and 22, the war accounts, after the story of Naboth's vineyard in chapter 21, but retains the association of the wars with Ahab.[184] Even though we must regard the identification of Ahab as the "king of Israel" involved in the battles as suspect, the pericopes in 1 Kg. 20 no doubt go back to a period of time not far removed from the period when the actual events took place, and probably give a fairly accurate representation of the interchanges which took place between the besieged king of Israel, entrenched in Samaria, and the arrogant king of Aram-Damascus.[185]

Ben-hadad the king of Syria gathered all his army together; thirty-two kings were with him, and horses and chariots; and he went up and besieged Samaria, and fought against it. (2) And he sent messengers into the city to Ahab king of Israel, and said to him "Thus says Ben-hadad: (3) 'Your silver and your gold are mine; your fairest wives and children also are mine.' " (4) And the king of Israel answered, "As you say, my lord, O king, I am yours, and all that I have." (5) The messengers came again, and said, "Thus says Ben-hadad: 'I sent to you, saying, "Deliver to me your silver and your gold, your wives and your children"; (6) nevertheless I will send my servants to you tomorrow about this time, and they shall search your house and the houses of your servants, and lay hands on whatever pleases them, and take it away.' " (7) Then the king of Israel called all the elders of the land, and said, "Mark, now, and see how this man is seeking trouble; for he sent to me for my wives and my children, and for my silver and my gold, and I did not refuse him." (8) And all the elders and all the people said to him, " Do not heed or consent." (9) So he said to the messengers of Ben-hadad, "Tell my lord the king, 'All that you first demanded of your servant I will do; but this thing I cannot do.' " And the messengers departed and brought him word again. (10) Ben-hadad sent to him and said, "The gods do so to me and more also, if the dust of

Samaria shall suffice for handfuls for all the people who follow me." (11) And the king of Israel answered, "Tell him, 'Let not him that girds on his armor boast himself as he that puts it off.' " (12) When Ben-hadad heard this message as he was drinking with the kings in the booths, he said to his men, "Take your positions." And they took their positions against the city. (13) And behold, a prophet came near to Ahab king of Israel and said, "Thus says the Lord, Have you seen all this great multitude? Behold, I will give it into your hand this day; and you shall know that I am the Lord." (14) And Ahab said, "By whom?" He said, "Thus says the Lord, By the servants of the governors of the districts." Then he said, "Who shall begin the battle?" He answered, "You." (15) Then he mustered the servants of the governors of the districts, and they were two hundred and thirty-two; and after them he mustered all the people of Israel, seven thousand. (16) And they went out at noon, while Ben-hadad was drinking himself drunk in the booths, he and the thirty-two kings who helped him. (17) The servants of the governors of the districts went out first. And Ben-hadad sent out scouts, and they reported to him "Men are coming out from Samaria." (18) He said, "If they have come out for peace, take them alive; or if they have come out for war, them alive." (19) So these went out of the city, the servants of the governors of the districts, and the army which followed them. (20) And each killed his man; the Syrians fled and Israel pursued them, but Ben-hadad king of Syria escaped on a horse with horsemen. (21) And the king of Israel went out, and captured the horses and chariots, and killed the Syrians with a great slaughter.

I. The Interaction Situation.

In our text, the Source (X) of the use of the traditional saying is the "king of Israel" whom we find identified as Ahab in v. 2, although historical-critical analysis tends to support an identification with Jehoahaz or Joash of Israel. The Receiver (Y) of the saying is Ben-hadad, king of Aram, and it is his challenge to the Israelite king which has prompted the use of the traditional saying in v. 11. We may further identify Ben-hadad as either Hadadezer (Ben-hadad II), Ahab's contemporary, or as Ben-hadad III, the son of the usurper Hazael, who probably succeeded his father towards the end of Jehoahaz's reign.[186] The relationship between the two kings ($\cancel{H}$) is one of considerable inequality, as portrayed in the pericope, since the Syrian king has successfully forced the king of Israel and his followers to take refuge inside the city of Samaria. Although the two kings are technically equal in status, the history of the conflicts between Aram and Israel gives the Syrian the advantage in the present situation, since the constant oppression of Israel by Aram-Damascus usually ended with Aram in the more powerful position (v. 34), whether one sets this during Ahab's reign or the time of Jehoahaz/Joash. If one places this pericope during Ahab's time, whether at the beginning or end of his reign, then one should assess the "status" of Israel's leader as generally less weak with respect to the Aramean contingent than if one places the pericope within the context of the end of Jehoahaz's reign or at the beginning of Joash's.[187] It should be added as well that the interchange between the two rulers in vv. 2-4 is tantamount to an admission of vassal status on the part of the Israelite king,[188] which obviously gives Ben-hadad the greater status. However, from the biblical perspective, we must acknowledge the king of Israel's superior position (even in the Deuteronomist's view!) as the leader of the people of Yahweh. This is apparent from the subtle way in which the interaction itself is presented: we find the king of Israel soberly taking counsel with "all the elders and all the people" (v. 8) and later being aided by a prophet; the braggart Ben-hadad, on the other hand, is outside the city indulging in a bit of pre-victory revelry with his cohorts - no doubt one of the reasons why his forces make such a poor showing in the following battle (vv. 12, 16-21).

Another factor should be taken into account in our understanding of the Interaction Situation: the growing might of the Assyrian military machine which cast its shadow across the political and economic history of the ninth century. Whether we set this interaction within the context of the reigns of Ahab or Jehoahaz/Joash, Assyria "was now in a state of military ascendancy when pillage practically replaced the regular trade exchange."[189] It is this common, greater threat which dictates the manner in which the kings of Israel and Aram attempt to settle their differences, as we shall see below in the Context Situation.

II. The Proverb Situation.

The traditional saying in verse 11, "Let not one who girds on (his armor) boast himself as one who takes (it) off" ('al-yithallēl ḥōgēr kimpattēaḥ) is one of the passages which Eissfeldt cites as "sounding like a proverb," and most wisdom scholars and commentators concur.[190] The saying meets our criteria for designation as a traditional saying, since it shows complete syntax and topic-comment unit (topic: one girding on; comment: should not boast like one ungirding), a logical relationship between its terms, and may lay some claim to "elevated style" in its cadence, use of comparison and vivid images to build a corresponding image or form (Gestalt) for the Receiver.[191] The occurrence of the saying in the interchange between the two leaders concerning the terms of the surrender of Samaria causes it to appear as an impersonal "out-of-context" statement, although the image and message of the saying fit the context admirably.

The saying, couched in the vetitive form (which provides an indication of the Source's evaluation of the relationship between the topic and comment) is of the multi-descriptive contrastive type (A ≠ B) The basic recognition between the topic and its comment (i.e., the core or kernel) - that boasting before completion of a task is not equivalent to boasting after the completion of a task - is positively evaluated by the proverb user, and this positive evaluation of the message is expressed by the adjunction of the vetitive to the phrase-structure of the topic-comment unit. This addition, which expresses the modality of "obligation" or "necessity" derived from the favorable evaluation of the message,[192] "transforms" the basic contrastive message into the form of a "negative causational" or "causal oppositional" saying (i.e., A ↛ B: A should not/does not B). The elementary transformation of the contrastive kernel (A does not equal B, A ≠ B) into a negative causational form (A should not/does not B; A ↛ B) is possible only because the Source has tacitly agreed with the proposition "A does not equal B."[193] The proposition "A ≠ B" expressed in the example here comes from the tension of "chronological displacement" - in this case, the tension between the contrasting concepts "before" (completion of a task) and "after."[194]

The architectural formula upon which the saying has been framed, VET + A + k^e B, is a complex one from the standpoint of derivation, due to the implicit problems which one must face when dealing with imperatives, especially those which embody a negation of the command or wish.[195] The simplest form of the negative admonition consists of the vetitive alone ($^{\prime}$al + jussive). This basic formula may be expanded by the addition of a motivation for the vetitive nucleus, thus altering the structure of the simple form. The appended motivation "transforms" the basic structure and may be actualized in one of two ways.[196] The motivation may be implicit; that is, derived solely from the content of the kernel (Baukern) (A∼B) and the speaker's evaluation of it, as in our example here:

Kernel (A ≠ B) + evaluation ⟹ ("rewritten as," "yields")

Derived S (A↛B)

The second type of expansion of the admonition is that which is formed by the adjunction of an explicit motivation, in Biblical Hebrew usually introduced by a causal "kî" clause, etc., which explicates the relationship of the kernel in a specific way.[197]

The image of the traditional saying in 1 Kg. 20:11 is drawn from the military world, as well as from an astute evaluation of human conduct in such circumstances. The terms "ḥāgar" and "pātaḥ" are used elsewhere in the Old Testament as specific, technical terms for arming and disarming.[198] The nuances to be found in these terms also incorporate the idea of "getting ready to do X" which is so common to the idiom "to gird up one's loins" (2 Kg. 4:29; 9:1; cf. Job 38:3; 40:7 where " ʾzr" is used rather than "ḥgr"). The grammatical forms which constitute the referents of the image contribute nicely to its force: the use of participles conveys the impression of ongoing, habitual, and hence, unfinished action, the use of which enhances the ideas embodied in the saying. Similarly, the use of the Hithpaᶜel here, with its reflexive, intensive overtones of actions performed "with regard to or for oneself, in one's own special interest"[199] is especially appropriate of boasting about oneself - particularly when the self-aggrandizement takes place before one has performed any action about which one might legitimately boast.

The message of the saying, which is conveyed through the use of military images and heightened by the use of apt grammatical forms, is one that is immediately familiar to paroemiologists, and might be paraphrased as "planning does not equal doing" (A ≠ B). The contrastive relationship between planning and doing is achieved through the use of the antithetical word pair "ḥgr"/"pth," girding on and ungirding, which are roughly equivalent to the "before"/"after" opposition. The well-attested ambiguity of life with all its random occurrences which forms the kernel (Baukern) of this traditional saying, has found its way into the world's proverbial lore. Parallels to this nuclear kernel may be seen in "Don't count your chickens before they hatch," "There's many a slip twixt cup and lip," "Ne triumphum canas ante victoriam," the Sumerian saying "He did not (yet) catch the fox, (but) he is making a neck stock for it," and so on.[200] The transformation of this basic relationship between planning and doing into a recommendation for action (i.e., one who is planning should not boast as if he or she had already completed what was planned) expands on a major theme in ancient wisdom literature - the imprudent nature of boastfulness.

Parallels to the message and image may be found in Pr. 27:1, "Do not boast about tomorrow, for you do not know what a day may bring forth." We read similarly in the Instruction of Kagemni:

Let your name go forth
While your mouth is silent.
When you are summoned, don't boast of strength
Among those your age, lest you be opposed.
One knows not what may happen,
What god does when he punishes.[201]

The Instruction of Amenemope from the New Kingdom contains similar recommendations:

Do not say: "Today is like tomorrow,"
How will this end?
Comes tomorrow, today has vanished,
The deep has become the water's edge.[202]

The "folk ideas" which find expression in the traditional saying in 1 Kg. 20:11 and its ancient parallels - that life is uncertain with respect to human plans and their ultimate achievement, and that this perception should modify one's behavior accordingly - are quite interesting in view of the concept of a regular "world order" which is so often posited as the world view which underlies Ancient Near Eastern wisdom literature. Once again, we find that careful analysis of the text and appropriate parallels reveals considerably more flexibility in viewing the events of life than scholars have previously recognized. This perception of life's vagaries was apparently felt with such great force that purposeful admonitions were formulated to point out the most appropriate and sensible responses to this aspect of the human condition.

1 Kg. 20:11:   Let not one who girds on (his armor) boast
himself as one who takes (it) off.

Type: Multidescriptive contrastive (negative causation;
              $A \neq B \Rightarrow A \nrightarrow B$)
Topic: One girding on (his armor)
Comment: Should not boast as one ungirding
Architectural Formula: VET + A k^e B
Image: Military; chronological discontinuity
Message: Planning is not the same as doing; therefore one
              who plans should not boast until completion
Parallels: Image - Pr. 27:1
              Message - Pr. 27:1; ancient Near East parallels

III. The Context Situation.

As we have come to expect, the Context Situation for the traditional saying in 1 Kg. 20:11 is one filled with conflict. Ben-hadad, the powerful king of Aram, has already gained the upper hand in the present military engagement, forcing Ahab to retreat within the safety of Samaria.[203] Indeed, Ben-hadad is so contemptuous of his antagonist that he shows his lack of concern over the outcome of the siege by celebrating the upcoming victory without even bothering to achieve it (vv. 12, 16). He first sends messengers to Ahab to receive the Israelite king's affirmation of his status as Ben-hadad's vassal (v. 3), to which Ahab accedes willingly enough (v. 4). Apparently, the mere assertion of Israel's vassalage is insufficient tribute to Ben-hadad's ego: he sends to Ahab a second time, demanding the surrender of his (Ahab's) personal wealth, the members of his family for hostages, and the right to loot Samaria.[204] At this point, the king of Israel, after consulting with the "elders of the land," sends a negative answer to Ben-hadad. Ben-hadad's response is predictable: in colorful language, he threatens to destroy Samaria so thoroughly that there will be insufficient dust for his numerous followers to carry away by handfuls.[205] To this, Ahab responds with the use of the traditional saying, whose contextual correlation is immediately evident to Ben-hadad. We might fill in our model of proverb performance as in Figure 12.

Paraphrasing our model, we obtain "Ahab (X, vassal in inferior military position) says to Ben-hadad (Y, suzerain with current military advantage), 'Even as one girding on armor (A) should not boast ($\nrightarrow$) as one ungirding (B), so should you not boast as present (C, $\nrightarrow$) until you have attained victory (D).' As one might expect, Ben-hadad has no difficulty in breaking the proverbial "code" of the traditional saying, and he responds to the challenge implicit in Ahab's contextual use

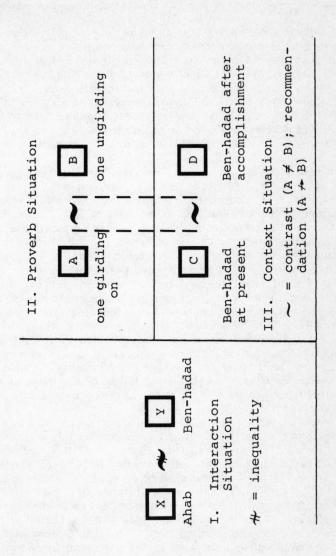

FIGURE 12: Proverb Performance in 1 Kings 20:11

135

of the saying: "When Ben-hadad heard this message as he was drinking in the booths, he said to his men, 'Take your positions.' And they took their positions against the city" (v. 12).

Ahab's use of the traditional saying is <u>evaluative</u> with reference to Ben-hadad's past demands and threats. We note also that the correspondence between the Receiver (Y) and the Context referent (C) is a negative one (i.e., Y = A,C; Ben-hadad is correlated both with the proverb referent A and the Receiver Y of the saying). However, it is also true that the outcome of the incident of proverb performance in the text is <u>affective</u>; Ben-hadad takes up the challenge to "put his money where his mouth is" due to Ahab's purposeful use of the saying.

A few words should be said about the "strategy" of proverb use in our pericope. One naturally wonders why a vassal, presently in an extremely precarious position, would send a message to his overlord which contains so overt an insult. Although the traditional saying makes typical use of "indirection" through its employment or the third person singular jussive rather than the more common second person singular, and the use of nominalized participles as the major referents of the image, its message in context (that Ben-hadad should "put up or shut up") is quite unmistakable and the Source probably had little fear that it would be misunderstood. The application to the Context Situation is literal - the referents of the Proverb Situation (A,B) and Context Situation (C,D) are identical in terms of image (preparing for battle) and message (inadvisability of boasting before accomplishment), so the possibility of distortion of the "proverb performance meaning" is reduced even further in our context of use.

There are at least two ways to understand the strategy of proverb use in our pericope, and these are roughly equivalent to the affective and evaluative functions of the contextual use of sayings. In the first interpretation (affective), the king of Israel may well be trying to bring matters to a head and force Ben-hadad into taking some action. Given that Samaria is besieged by a force which far outnumbers its defenders (vv. 1, 13) and that the king and elders have decided that Ben-hadad's demands should not be met (v. 8), prolongation of a siege would ultimately work to the detriment of Samaria's defenders, since the resulting shortages of food and material caused by a drawn-out siege would weaken the position of those inside the city.[206] Also, the use of a saying to insult

Ben-hadad might favor Israel in another way, by making the Aramean king angry enough to impair his judgement and cause him to make mistakes which he would not normally make if he were to remain "cool-headed."

If one stresses the evaluative function, the traditional saying operates to express the king of Israel's reading of the context situation - that Ben-hadad has yet to make good his boasts. Closely connected with this, it is possible to understand the use of the traditional saying as an example of the stubborn defiance often exhibited by those who are ensnared by a greater force demanding ignominious surrender.[207] If this is indeed the case in our pericope, then the use of the traditional saying is similarly apt, since, in the event of defeat, one might later claim to have made a general observation which was misinterpreted by the Receiver.[208] However, since the contextual referents are so obvious in this interaction, indirection plays a less important role here than it usually does in performance strategy. It is also possible to view the use of the saying as a way of mitigating the insult which Ahab received from Ben-hadad's high-handed demands. As Eissfeldt has pointed out, the ironic or satiric use of a saying is closely related to the "taunt," one of the later meanings of "māshāl."[209] However one chooses to interpret the strategy underlying the use of the saying here, the purposeful manipulation of traditional wisdom in context is exactly what one would expect from a deft, cosmopolitan king.

The folk ideas which underlie the use of the saying in context consist of an amplification of the proverb message. While it is true that Israel's rout of the arrogant Syrian forces may be attributed to shrewd tactics in the placement of Israel's smaller forces,[210] it is clear that our pericope attributes the victory to another cause: "And behold, a prophet came near to Ahab king of Israel and said, 'Thus says the Lord, have you seen all this great multitude? Behold, I will give it into your hand this day, and you shall know that I am the Lord.' " (v. 13). It is Yahweh, through the word of this prophet, who determines the outcome of the battle, and the defeated Arameans evidently thought so too (v. 23). The plans of humans may never be realized, and therefore one should not boast prematurely, but in our context, this folk idea is subordinated to Israel's conception of God and God's plans. For Israel, victory comes from Yahweh, who needs no great multitudes to win battles. This is the true reason why Ben-hadad should refrain from boasting - the outcome of all human activities lies in the hands of God.[211] Once more we find the folk idea of the traditional saying used in close connection with the theological "folk idea" which provides the interpretive key for the pericope.

Comments

In the context for the event of proverb performance in 1 Kg. 20, we find a situation analogous to that in Jg. 8:21, where we saw "traditional wisdom" operating between different population groups, at the tribal level. In 1 Kg. 20, the traditional saying is once more directed between groups, but this time, during the monarchic period, the saying is transmitted and received by kings instead of tribal leaders.[212] We suggested above[213] that such use of wisdom between tribal groups might be the precursor of the "diplomatic" use of wisdom in court settings. In the present context, we find such traditional wisdom, now at "court," but operating in the same purposeful way as it did in the tribal setting.

Another feature emerges from our contextual study of the use of 1 Kg. 20:11, which connects it with the development and use of Old Testament wisdom traditions. It is indeed noteworthy that Ahab transmits the saying to Ben-hadad after he has conferred with the elders. Despite the fact that this seems a bit out of character from the usual autocratic picture given of Ahab, it points to the continuing role of the elders as repositories and mediators of the traditional wisdom which helped form the fabric of daily life.[214] Our context also stresses the importance of the role of "counsel" in decision making,[215] and provides a graphic illustration of the saying in Pr. 15:22: "Without counsel, plans go wrong, but with many advisors they succeed."

Chapter IV

WISDOM AT WORK:
TOWARDS AN UNDERSTANDING OF
THE CONTEXTUAL USE OF THE TRADITIONAL SAYING
IN THE OLD TESTAMENT

METHODOLOGICAL CONSIDERATIONS

We have seen from our textual studies that the traditional saying is used in context in a purposeful way to further the strategic interactional aims of its user.[1] While it is true that our analyses revealed many of the features of proverb performance which we had been led to expect from our survey of anthropological and folklore studies, it is only proper to consider now whether or not our emphasis on contextual use is an appropriate focus for our inquiries of the text. A major shift in recent folklore studies emphasizes the desirability of "fitting" the methodology to the text studied. Modern folklorists are no longer willing to violate the objects of their investigations by ruthlessly forcing a text into alien (Western) analytic categories which have no inherent relation to the item studied.[2] Biblical scholars using inter-disciplinary approaches have also responded to the obligation to respect the internal integrity of the materials with which they deal.[3] Thus, it is fitting to raise the question of the ancient understanding of the use and function of the traditional saying.

Ancient Perspectives on "Proverb Performance"

It was suggested above that folkloric genres may be a powerful societal force for a variety of reasons. Specifically, it was pointed out by William Bascom that certain folklore genres, especially those like the traditional saying which are often used in educational settings, are valued and used not only because of the "controlling" power which they exercise to uphold the norms, institutions, rituals, and beliefs of a given society, but also because of their actual informational content.[4] To put this observation another way, the message of a specific item of folklore may be as important to a culture as is any given application or strategic use to which that item may be put.

We may observe this same important interaction between content (message) and context (use) in the wisdom literature of the ancient Near East. This is especially true in those places where "wisdom" reflects upon itself. In the "Epilogue" of the Instruction of Ptahhotep, we read the following justification for the making of the instruction:

> If you listen to my sayings,
> All your affairs will go forward;
> In their truth resides their value,
> Their memory goes on in the speech of men,
> Because of the worth of their precepts;
> If every word is carried on,
> They will not perish in this land.[5]

The instruction for King Merikare, which comes from the difficult period of the transition from the Old to the Middle Kingdom, expresses similar respect for the messages encapsulated in the culture's traditional sayings and those with the wit to make use of them.

> Be a craftsman in speech, (so that) thou mayest be strong, (for) the tongue is a sword to [a man] and speech is more valorous than any fighting. No one can circumvent the skillful heart .... They who know his wisdom do not attack him, and no [misfortune] occurs where he is. Truth comes to him (fully) brewed, in accordance with the sayings of the ancestors. Copy thy fathers and thy ancestors .... Behold, their words remain in writing. Open, that thou mayest read and copy their wisdom. (Thus) the skilled man becomes learned.[6]

The well-known wisdom composition from the New Kingdom, the Instruction of Amenemope, continues these thoughts concerning the value of the content of traditional sayings, as we see in the following excerpts from the "Prologue" and first chapter.

> Prologue
>
> Beginning of the teaching for life,
> The instructions for well-being,
> Every rule for relations with elders,
> For conduct toward magistrates;

Chapter IV : Wisdom at Work - Contextual Use

Knowing how to answer one who speaks,
To reply to one who sends a message.

He says: Chapter 1
Give your ears, hear the sayings,
Give your heart to understand them;
It profits to put them in your heart,
Woe to him who neglects them!
Let them rest in the casket of your belly,
May they be bolted in your heart;
When there rises a whirlwind of words,
They'll be a mooring post for your tongue,
If you make your life with these in your heart,
You will find it a success;
You will find my words a storehouse for life,
Your being will prosper upon earth.[7]

Here we see the high value which ancient sages placed upon their work, and upon the most fundamental representative of that work, the saying. The "truth" in a traditional saying is valued for a variety of reasons in these texts. First, the saying represents the wisdom of the "ancestors," and part of its authority derives from this relationship to those admired forerunners who have communicated their knowledge and experience to the ones who come after. Second, "In their truth resides their value" - that is, the actual message of a saying is of great importance, since it adds to the information of the hearer or user. Thus, the saying is remembered and preserved not only out of deference to the "ancestor" who supposedly coined it, but also because of its content.[8] Finally, the sages held a very high opinion of the <u>function</u> of the traditional saying: its truth might come to the hearer/user "fully brewed" and distilled from the experience of tradition, but the claims made concerning function of that truth are the most striking in their scope. Those who "hear" the message of the saying find that their activities are more apt to be successful; the "craftsman in speech" discovers that such wisdom found encapsulated and ready for use in the saying offers its hearers and users immunity from the little misfortunes and aggravations of life. In a "whirlwind of words," the traditional saying provides a reliable and traditionally sanctioned chart for navigation through the murky waters of human interactions. The ancient scribe knew his subject well when he described sayings as a "storehouse for life."

It might be pointed out that one might naturally expect a person to praise his or her own profession,[9] but that this does not necessarily reflect a "popular" evaluation of "good speech" or the usefulness of the traditional saying. However, the surviving materials from the ancient Near East do give some indication that the positive value attached to the skilled speaker, the user of sayings, may not have been confined solely to a professional scribal class. Certainly, the court circles recognized the worth of the "craftsman in speech" as would naturally be expected. The famed "good counsel" of the "wise scribe" Ahiqar was popularly held to have earned him a death sentence,[10] and we read in the Old Testament of the sage Ahithophel whose counsel was "as if one consulted the oracle of God" (2 Sam. 16:23). The astute user of language and traditional argument was appreciated, though, wherever he or she might be found - however far away from the court. The plot of the Egyptian "Tale of the Eloquent Peasant" is specifically contrived to display the "beautiful speech" of that loquacious representative of the "folk,"[11] and we must assume that the local "wise women" of 2 Samuel 14 and 20 were esteemed and considered "wise" for their adroitness in the use of traditional language to deal with conflict-ridden situations. Perhaps the most complete statement of how greatly the art of "good speech" was valued - and the practical uses to which such an art was put - comes from the Middle Kingdom Stele of the Chamberlain Intef, son of Sent. While Intef obviously speaks of success which was achieved in court circles, the virtues of which he boasts are ones which must have been positively regarded at all levels of society.

> I am cool, free of haste,
> Knowing the outcome, expecting what comes.
> I am a speaker in situations of strife,
> One who knows which phrase causes anger....
> I am a straight one in his lord's house,
> Who knows flattery when it is spoken....
>
> I am knowing to him who lacks knowledge,
> One who teaches a man what is useful to him.
> I am a straight one in the king's house,
> Who knows what to say in every office.
> I am a listener who listens to the truth,
> Who ponders it in the heart....

I am kindly in the offices,
One who is calm and does not [roar].
I am kindly, not short-tempered,
One who does not attack a man for a remark.

I am a knower who taught himself knowledge,
An advisor whose advice is sought.
I am a speaker in the hall of justice,
Skilled in speech in anxious situations.[12]

While it is true that Intef does not mention the use of sayings specifically, it is hard to imagine that one acknowledged to be "skilled in speech in anxious situations" would not have followed the recommendations of the sages and made use of the traditional saying in difficult contexts. Intef's catalogue of virtues recalls strongly the teachings of the wise men of the ancient Near East; he "knows" what phrase causes anger and what soothes, and he makes shrewd use of this knowledge in his activities at court. We cannot doubt that the skillful use in context of the traditional wisdom of one's culture was a recognized and valued ability.

Turning to the wisdom literature of ancient Israel, we find a very similar picture. In the "introduction" to the Book of Proverbs (Prov 1:2-6), we find the goals of wisdom instruction openly stated:

That men may know wisdom and instruction,
    understand words of insight,
receive instruction in wise dealing,
    righteousness, justice, and equity;
that prudence may be given to the simple,
    knowledge and discretion to the youth -
the wise man also may hear and increase in learning.
    and the man of understanding acquire skill,
to understand a proverb and a figure,
    the words of the wise and their riddles.[13]

The objectives of wisdom, then, are explicit: through education a person is trained to nurture and uphold those qualities, such as righteousness and justice, of which the society approves. But exactly how does one train another to carry through these goals in daily life? We would suggest that this is accomplished in a two-fold way: through understanding (and hence, internalization) of the content (message) of the teachings of the wise, and through the subsequent application of that content in daily contexts of use.[14] That this is the way wisdom "worked" in everyday life may be seen in the attitude of the wisdom teachers toward the one on whom instruction is wasted - the fool.

We know that the sages' opinion of the "fool" was not too high: "It is like sport to a fool to do wrong" (Pr. 10:23a); the fool is one who "despises his father's instruction" (Pr. 15:5a) and thinks his "way" right (Pr. 12:15). Indeed, the sages suggest that an encounter with a she-bear robbed of her cubs is better than coming upon a "fool in his folly" (Pr. 17:12). Interestingly enough, a good number of the observations of the wise have to do with the "verbal" activities of the fool:

> Wise men lay up knowledge,
> but the babbling of a fool brings ruin near.
> > Pr. 10:14

> The talk of a fool is a rod for his back,
> but the lips of the wise will preserve them.
> > Pr. 14:3

> Leave the presence of a fool,
> for there you do not meet words of knowledge.
> > Pr. 14:7

> The tongue of the wise dispenses knowledge,
> but the mouths of fools pour out folly.
> > Pr. 15:2

> The mind of him who has understanding seeks
> > knowledge,
> but the mouths of fools feed on folly.
> > Pr. 15:14

> Fine speech is not becoming to a fool;
> still less false speech to a prince.
> > Pr. 17:7

> Even a fool who keeps silent is considered wise;
> when he closes his lips, he is deemed intelligent.
> > Pr. 17:28[15]

The fool's use of language, then, is imprecise and perverse. Where the speech of a wise man reveals his wisdom (Sir. 4:24), the speech of a fool is apt to bring only punishment or disdain - indeed, the fool is better off keeping quiet, for then he or she might be mistaken for a sensible person! To the discerning observer, it is apparent from the words and actions of a fool that the fool does not understand the content of instruction: "The mind of a fool is like a broken jar; it will hold no knowledge" (Sir. 21:14). It is not only in the realm of the understanding and internalization of the messages of the saying or instruction that the fool is deficient, however. The fool is also unable to apply the content of wisdom teachings, as we see from the following sayings.[16]

> Like a lame man's legs, which hang useless,
>> is a proverb (māshāl) in the mouth of fools.
>>> Pr. 26:7

> Like a thorn that goes up into the hand of a drunkard,
>> is a proverb (māshāl) in the mouth of fools.
>>> Pr. 26:9

> A proverb from a fool's lips will be rejected,
>> for he does not tell it at its proper time.
>>> Sir. 20:20

The images used by these wisdom sayings to convey their messages are delightfully apt, both in their portrayal of the fool's ineptitude in the realm of performance and also in the nuances of the purposefulness of the saying genre which they bring out. The dangling, useless legs of the lame evoke a picture of functional units which cannot fulfill their natural purpose - the physical movement of their possessor from point "A" to point "B." The comparison of the disfunctional vehicles of human locomotion to the māshāl as used by the fool could not convey more clearly the purposeful nature of the saying. The saying, whether popular or literary, is a form which is designed for use; a form which, when employed properly (i.e., in an appropriate context), moves its user from point "A" to point "B" in daily interactions. The fool cannot make effective use of the saying form, whether from an improper understanding of its message, or the inability to apply it to a proper context at the right time. Thus, it becomes dangerous to its would-be user. This explains the fool's predilection for aggressive behavior (see Pr. 14:17; 18:6; 19:23; 26:6; 27:3; 29:9, 11). Fools resort to violence to handle conflict because they know no other way. The fool's orientation toward the world precludes true competence and hence, successful performance is impossible.

While we have discussed ancient wisdom's reflections on the fool's inability to make proper use of a saying, our real purpose has been to focus on the understanding of the use and function of the saying genre. It seems reasonable to assume that if the sages took the time to discuss what we might label "improper proverb performance," that there must have been some corresponding notion of "proper" proverb performance as well. Although this positive understanding of the way to use a traditional saying is less explicit in ancient wisdom literature than its negative counterpart (misuse of a saying), it may well be that it is just such a notion as "appropriate" use which underlies wisdom's preoccupation with discerning "the right time." The key to effective "proverb performance," as we have seen from our contextual studies, lies in the understanding of the message of a traditional saying and discerning the proper time and way in which to apply it to a given context. Both of these considerations are to be found in the writings of the ancient sages, and we may assume that even if they might not have been impressed by a grandiose analytical category of interactions such as "proverb performance," the features and functions of that type of interaction were well known to them. Ben Sira sums up these reflections:

> Do not slight the discourse of the sages,
>   but busy yourself with their maxims;
> because from them you will gain instruction
>   and learn how to serve great men.
> Do not disregard the discourse of the aged
>   for they themselves learned from their fathers;
> because from them you will gain understanding
>   and learn how to give an answer in time of need.
>   Sir. 8:8-9

Proverb Performance in the Ancient Near East

One of our fundamental methodological presuppositions in applying a model of proverb performance to ancient texts was that even where the texts containing interactions using traditional sayings might be judged to bear little relation to actual historical events (as in 1 Sam. 16), the use of the traditional saying in such a text must roughly approximate the way sayings were actually used in "real life" or else their occurrence in a text would be unintelligible to their first audiences.[17] It is fitting here to point out that support for this presuppostion may be found by surveying some of the "correspondence" which survives from the world of the ancient Near East. As we would expect, the traditional saying makes its appearance in these examples of folk speech (i.e., the actual discourse of native speakers) to further the strategic aims of its writers,[18] as the letters of Egypt and Mesopotamia amply demonstrate.

The Mari letters from the period covering the late 19th to

mid-18th century B.C.E. contain a number of interesting examples of "proverb performance."[19] Indeed, two of the traditional sayings used are specifically cited by their Sources as "proverbs" (teltum).[20] The traditional sayings which are transmitted in context[21] all occur as complete statements which seem to be "out-of-context." A number of features which we associate with proverb performance are discernible: the use of the saying is elicited by a conflict situation (many of them having to do with military strategems); indirection is used to protect the participants in the interaction (although this feature does not seem to be as important in the Mari letters as it is in the Old Testament); and most importantly, the use of the traditional saying in context is purposeful, operating in both evaluative and affective ways. A single example should be sufficient to illustrate. King Šamši-Adad I writes the following to his son Yasmaḫ-Adad, his appointed ruler of Mari:

> You are thinking up strategems to beat the enemy and maneuvering for position against him and the enemy is likewise thinking up strategems and maneuvering for position against you, just as wrestlers are constantly seeking for tricks against each other. I hope you will not do now as the old proverb says: "The bitch in her passing back and forth (?) gave birth to lame (?) puppies." I hope that the enemy will not maneuver for position against you ... [broken text for 3 1/2 lines] Do not be in continual distress about approaches to my city. Don't keep going to and fro so much. The time for the expedition is near; until I go on it, take care of the supervision of the troops.
>
> ARM, 5:10-13 lines 4-23[22]

While there are some difficulties in translation, the purposeful nature of the proverb performance is clear, just as it is in the other instances in the Mari letters and our Old Testament examples.[23]

The Amarna letters, which date to the last years of the reign of Amenophis III through the reign of Amenophis IV (Akhenaton), offer not only dramatic insights into the troubled states of Egypt and Syro-Palestine in the mid-fourteenth century B.C.E., but also two interesting examples of proverb performance, elicited by conflict situations. The Source in letter EA, No. 252, is the scoundrel Labʲayu, the ruler of Shechem, who appears to have been universally disliked by his peers, and who is frequently accused of treason by the other correspondents in

Traditional Sayings in the Old Testament

Palestine.[24] In EA, No. 292, Ba^clu-shipti, prince of Gezer, is the Source. In both cases, the Sources have been accused of disloyalty and treason to the Egyptian king; both make use of a traditional saying to proclaim their innocence or strengthen their justification of questionable acts.[25]

The proverb performance which occurs in Lab'ayu's letter is of special interest. Not only is the letter written in a cuneiform which bears a closer relationship to Canaanite than it does to Akkadian, but there is also mention in the other Amarna correspondence that Lab'ayu was associated in some way with the enigmatic ^cApiru,[26] who were so troublesome to the Egyptian authorities in Palestine. Lab'ayu protests in his letter to the Egyptian ruler that his military actions were all taken in self defence:

> Further, when (even) ants are smitten, they do not accept it (passively), but they bite the hand of the man who smites them. How could I hesitate this day when two of my towns are taken?

> Further, even if thou shouldst say: "Fall beneath them, and let them smite thee," I should still repel my foes, the men who seized the town, and my god, the despoilers of my father, (yea) I would repel them.
>
> EA, No. 252 lines 16-30[27]

Lab'ayu makes use of a traditional saying whose image is drawn from observation of the natural world in order to justify his aggressive actions. While we may have good cause to doubt that Lab'ayu's actions and motives were quite so unimpeachable as he would have his detractors believe,[28] the message which he transmits to the powers that be is one of great significance, coming as it does from a period of social unrest. We might paraphrase the message as "even the smallest of creatures will defend themselves"; the contextual correlation is clear as well - humans, too, regardless of their status, have the same urge to defend themselves from attack, and will defend themselves when attacked. It is intriguing to find traditional "wisdom" of this sort employed as a legitimation for the struggle against oppressive authority, and circulating in "pre-Conquest" Palestine. It is interesting to speculate that wisdom, too, may have made a contribution to the social and theological legitimations for the overthrow of traditional but repressive structures of society.[29]

We have seen, then, that sources for both the concept of "proverb performance" (the apt and purposeful transmission

148

of a traditional saying in a social interaction) and the strategic types of proverb performance actually found in the Old Testament may be seen as well in some of the extant materials from the neighboring societies of the ancient Near East. The cross-cultural validation of this particular perspective on the use of traditional wisdom is gratifying, but hardly surprising: wisdom, after all, has always been recognized as an international phenomenon, and we would expect to find it used in context in similar ways in neighboring societies. We would contend, as well, that traditional wisdom cannot be viewed as the sole possession of the "elite" - even female slaves may possess the ideal of "good speech."[30]

The Use of Structural Analysis

The question might be raised concerning the desirability or necessity of incorporating an interdisciplinary approach into the analysis of the traditional saying as it occurs in the Old Testament. Indeed, at first glance, it might seem that the use of structural analysis leads to even more fragmentation of the text than do the classic techniques of (biblical) literary and historical criticism. However, a number of advantages of the use of this method (as we have adapted and supplemented it from folklore stories) for the study of the saying genre might be pointed out.

First, by "waiving" the question of origin and authorship, we have been free to concentrate on the specific items of the genre which occur in the Old Testament without falling into the trap of asking unanswerable questions concerning the "intent" and identity of the original author of the saying, and then postulating "appropriate" content suited to that intent and identity. Through our examination of the interaction between code (form), message (content), and use (context) in the traditional saying, we have been able to ask not only the question of "what does it mean?" but also the questions of "how does it mean?" and "why does it mean?" These interactions are crucial elements in the sensitive analysis of any genre, but they are especially important to the discussion of the saying form, since the genre is a "compressed" one, which, when considered apart from a context of use, may be opaque to the modern investigator.

Paul Ricoeur has discussed the saying genre as a subspecies of metaphorical or poetic language which "does not say literally what things are, but what they are like"; for him, the "ordinary function" of the proverb and saying is that of "originating life."[31] The <u>function</u> of a genre is a critical factor in understanding its form, and one must seek to grasp both aspects together to truly comprehend the processes at work in the formation and use of a given genre. We might describe the traditional saying as the "working class" of metaphorical language: its function is to orient its Source/Receiver towards the experiences of life, and it achieves this by making explicit in its form the web of relationships encountered in daily life. Structural analysis, by allowing one to distinguish between messages, and the vehicles which convey those messages (architectural formulae and images), provides a way to look at the "how" and "why" of the genre, promotes discussion of the true content as opposed to its expressive, stylistic vehicles, and facilitates cross-cultural and cross-generic comparisons. Finally, the insistence of structural analysis on the importance of the interconnections between features of the surface structure and deep structure of an item is of extreme interest to the student of the saying, where destruction of the vehicle of a message destroys the form as a whole and renders the message ineffectual.[32] The recognition of this interdependence of surface features and the message they express validates the observation of Old Testament scholars that <u>style</u> is a constituent rather than ornamental feature of the genre, and forces the responsible investigator to deal with the form as an organic whole. For this reason, the method of analysis we have adopted promotes a cohesive rather than an atomistic approach to the text.

RESULTS OF THE CONTEXTUAL STUDY OF THE TRADITIONAL SAYING IN THE OLD TESTAMENT

Nature and Form of the Traditional Saying

Our contextual investigation has supported both Old Testament and folkloric perspectives on the traditional saying. The logical relationships between the terms of the traditional saying constitute the content of the form, and allow it to function in a paradigmatic way, as the proverb users and receivers correlate these terms with contextual referents. These logical relationships do not consist simply of a hodge-podge of juxtapositions, however, but incorporate notions of cause and effect, paradox and ambiguity, positive and negative correspondences. The traditional saying gives linguistic expression to the operational categories of a culture; their function is not so much to discover some pre-existent "world order" as it is to <u>create</u> and consolidate (cultural) order. Discussions of the "observational" nature of the traditional saying should be qualified somewhat, according to our understanding of the function of the genre. The creative act of explicating the relational aspects between the proverb terms is itself not merely an observation, but reflects an orientation towards the propositional content (the "Baukern" or kernel, A ~ B) as well.33 The alleged "observational" nature of the traditional saying is compromised even more seriously when use in context is considered. As we have shown, use in a social context is <u>always</u> purposeful, and use may condition the meaning of the message, as specific intent of proverb performance varies from context to context.

From the perspective of function, our genre designation of "traditional saying" to cover a wide variety of forms seems a valid one. Whether cast as an interrogative, imperative, or simple indicative statement, items tend to be manipulated in context in the same way, to further the same types of interactional ends. Hermisson's exclusion of all but the simple "Aussage" from consideration as a folk proverb is derived from presuppositions about the nature of the folk proverb which, by and large, find little support in paroemiology, folklore studies, or the ancient understanding of what may count as a "māshāl." The problems encountered by Hermisson in his survey underscore the difficulty of pinpointing a life setting for the origin of a saying and serve as an example of the ethnocentricity which has hindered research on folk genres in the past.

The Style of the Traditional Saying

Our investigations into the style of the traditional saying have essentially confirmed previous research on this "homely" genre. The traditional saying may be as brief as only two or three words, but these generally display some type of "elevated style," achieved through the use of a variety of poetic devices (alliteration, rhyme, cadence, ellipsis, etc.). The "working class" metaphors found in the traditional saying may not be as well developed from a literary perspective as the images found in the wisdom saying, but they may be just as vivid and forceful.

The style of the traditional saying is an extremely important element of the form. Usually, the stylistic features of a saying provide the first indication that one is, indeed, dealing with a traditional saying. Style aids identification of the genre, and acts to facilitate appropriation, memorization and subsequent recall, thus ensuring that the traditional saying will be readily available for use in future contexts. Another important way in which the style of the traditional saying operates is found in its ability to create a thoughtful attitude of inquiry and expectation in its receivers.[34] Because the style often violates regular syntatic patterns - deleting some normal features, juxtaposing and rearranging others, etc. - the hearer is struck by the unusual sound patterns, and forced to "process" what has been heard and supply the missing elements to obtain an intelligible grasp of the content which is being conveyed. Once the receivers of a saying have processed the item which has been transmitted, supplying the necessary features which have been omitted or transformed in some way, and providing the cultural framework against which the saying must be understood, it is quite natural to move a step further in this "instant" cognitive analysis and supply the "hidden" referents to which the saying used in context is applied. The use of a saying challenges the receiver to break the cultural and linguistic code of the form, release its semantic content, and supply its immediate contextual referents. Hence, aside from its mnemonic uses in aiding identification and recall, the style of the traditional saying also enhances the function of the genre by encouraging reflection on the message conveyed by its image, and its probable correlations. In a similar way, style plays a part in the strategic use of the saying, since the "indirection" afforded by the use of a saying is derived in part from the ambiguity of its style, as well as from the saying's status as "traditional" wisdom (which protects the Source from the burden of defending its content as if it were one's own creation). The ambiguity to which the style of the traditional saying contributes may be an active deterrent to the paroemiologist's discovery of "the" ultimate meaning of the saying, but it is one of those features of the traditional saying which suits it so well to its task.

The Content of the Traditional Saying

Image

The images used in the traditional saying are those which are familiar to the culture (or subculture) in which the saying circulates. In our contextual studies, we saw the use of agricultural (Jg. 8:2), military (1 Kg. 20:11), and human images and relationships used as vehicles for messages. It should also be noted that the realm of divine-human interactions is not excluded from encapsulation in the images and messages of the traditional saying. This is true not only of the proverbial stock of Israel and her neighbors, but of other cultures as well.[35] The experience of the Holy, the paradoxical and often frightening ambiguity of events, are all part of daily life, and as such, are just as much "proper" content for the traditional saying as agricultural or mundane observations.

At times it is tempting to try to fix a specific life setting for the origin of a given saying on the basis of its image. Thus, one might conclude that the saying in 1 Kg. 20:11 ("Let not him who girds on [his armor] boast himself as him who ungirds") was originated in military (court) circles, and so on. While such observations might very well be true, they are doomed to remain inferential since there is very little possibility of proving them. Aside from this difficulty, there is an even stronger consideration which must militate against the attribution of a saying to a given life setting strictly on the basis of its image: the image is not the message itself; rather it is the carrier or vehicle of the message. The saying in 1 Kg. 20:11 may make use of military terms, but its message is not confined to this sphere alone. In general, one must exercise extreme caution in assigning life-setting for the origin of a traditional saying solely on the basis of images used.

Message

The messages encapsulated in the traditional saying which were examined in context all tended to revolve around basic identifications and contrasts, and their respective causational variations. The semantic types ($A = B$, $A \rightarrow B$; $A \neq B$, $A \nrightarrow B$) may be realized by a variety of syntactical frameworks ($k^e + B = A$; ṭôb A min B; etc.), but the messages always consist of the relationship between the proverb terms. Such relationships make explicit logical connections which might be inferred and validated from observations.[36] They are not neutral observations, but insights which have been filtered through and conditioned by the world-view of the culture in which the traditional saying originates and achieves currency.[37] Thus, examination of the message of a traditional saying, because it witnesses to the folk ideas of a society, provides insight not only into the content of the saying, but into the world-view of those who made use of it as well.

Function and Use in Context
of the Old Testament Traditional Saying

Several patterns emerge when we look at the uses of the traditional saying in context as a group. In terms of <u>literary function</u>, each incident of proverb performance in the texts which we examined served to bring about the final denouement of the action in the pericope. In Judges 8, Gideon's use of a saying appeases the Ephraimites, resolves the conflict, and paves the way for the narrative which tells of his pursuit of the Midianite chiefs. Similarly, the Midianites' transmission of a saying precipitates their execution by Gideon, a worthy executioner of heroic stature, and provides a link with the next literary unit where Gideon uses the spoil from the Midianite engagement to make an ephod (Jg. 8:26). In 1 Samuel 24, David's strategic use of a traditional saying brings about a momentarily peaceful resolution of the specific conflict with Saul at En-gedi, and also prompts Saul's recognition of David as his rightful successor (1 Sam. 24:21 [20]). The king of Israel's use of a saying in the negotiations in 1 Kings 20 acts in a similar way to bring matters to a head, and thus introduces the "real" point of that narrative - Yahweh's gift of victory through the medium of his prophet. In 1 Samuel 16, the saying occupies a more central position in the pericope, linking the anointment of the king which God has chosen for himself to the past failure with Saul, and the future success with David. Even though we might suspect that the saying in 1 Sam. 16:7 appears strategically as pro-Davidic propaganda rather than as an "actual" example of proverb performance, it is crucial to the development of the unit and serves as the introduction and legitimation of David, thus bringing about the denouement of his anointment. We may conclude, then, that the use of the traditional saying in the texts mentioned is a purposeful one on a narrative level, since it acts as a literary device to bring about the final conclusion and "set up" the introduction of the action which follows.

At the level of personal interactions between the actors involved in the events of proverb performance, patterns of use may also be observed. In each case, the stimulus which elicits proverb performance is a situation in which conflict is felt on the part of the Source between the "true" state of affairs (as the Source understands the context) and the "perceived" state of affairs (as seen from the perspective of the Receiver).[38] In other words, where the Source and

Receiver disagree over the proper interpretation of the Context Situation, the Source initiates proverb performance to hightlight those differences in perspective and make a traditionally sanctioned case for his own side (see Table 2). Also, in each case, with the exception of 1 Sam. 24:14,[39] the "Object" of the proverb performance - that is, the person whose behavior has prompted the use of the saying - is always the Receiver, the one at whom the saying is directed in the Interaction Situation (O = Y). Once again, this confirms the purposeful nature of the transmission of the saying.

Several other interesting features of the Source's role in Old Testament proverb performance might be pointed out. First, the Source(s) are, in every case, those whom we might naturally expect to have some acquaintance with and mastery of the proverbial stock of their cultures.[40] All are seasoned leaders of various types, used to settling disputes and rendering judgments on a wide range of topics. Thus, we find that those making use of the traditional sayings in context are exactly the ones whom we would anticipate to show a flair for persuasive, traditional argument. Since "source-reliability" and credibility is an important factor in the Receiver's acceptance of a message,[41] the Source's familiarity with and appropriate use of a stock of sayings is by no means an inconsequential consideration in proverb performance.

Secondly, in each case of proverb performance, the conflict found in the Interaction and Context Situations is concrete as well as abstract. All of our examples of proverb performance are not only set against a broad background of cultural conflict and instability ("tribal" repulsion of nomadic raiders; intratribal conflicts; the transition from charismatic to monarchic, hereditary leadership; war between bordering states), but in each, aspects of these general abstract conflicts surface in concrete, specific ways.[42] Each event which we discussed presented an example of a way in which the use of a traditional saying might diffuse the aggressive potential of the context situations. It should be noted that the resolution provided through proverb performance does not necessarily include a total elimination of violence; rather, the transmission of the traditional saying works to set the aggressive or improper intentions of the Receivers in their proper perspective (e.g., animosity between bordering clans is felt to be undesirable; the Midianites present their feelings that they deserve a fitting executioner; Samuel's fears (and perhaps the discontent of pro-Saul factions) must be

TEXT	SOURCE	CONTEXT SITUATION			RECEIVER
	X	Source's Evaluation	≠	Receiver's Evaluation	Y
Jg. 8:2	Gideon	Ephraimites achieved superior victory	≠	Ephraimites feel slighted	Ephraim-ites
Jg. 8:21	Midian-ite chiefs	Midianite chiefs deserve death commensurate with status	≠	Gideon delegates execution to youth (low status)	Gideon
1 Sam. 16:7	God/pro-Davidic author	choice of anointed by internal (divine) criteria	≠	choice of anointed by external (human) criteria	Samuel/traditions concerning David-Saul conflict over succession
1 Sam. 24:14	David	David's dealings with Saul are not wicked	≠	David's dealings with Saul are wicked	Saul
1 Kg. 20:11	king of Israel	Battle not yet fought	≠	Ben-hadad boasts as if battle had already been won	Ben-hadad

TABLE 2: Conflicting Interpretations of the Context Situation as the Stimulus for Proverb Performance

subordinated to Yahweh's choice; etc.). This, in turn, allows the participants in the Interaction Situations to formulate and enact a more appropriate course of action.

In the Interaction Situations in Judges, 1 Samuel 24, and 1 Kings, we find that although the Sources are roughly equivalent in status to their Receivers from an overall perspective (e.g., Jg. 8:2, tribal leader to rival tribe; Jg. 8:21, nomadic leaders to tribal leaders; 1 Sam. 24, anointed to anointed; 1 Kg. 20:11, king to king), within the given context, the Sources all occupy the inferior position or are in some way disadvantaged in the present situation (i.e., $X \leq Y$).[43] This subordinate status makes the Source vulnerable, and thus provides an insight into the <u>motivation</u> for the employment of a traditional saying. The "indirection" inherent in the saying protects its user, and lessens the risk of worsening matters for the Source whose situation is already rather precarious. Traditional wisdom can provide a valuable weapon for the "underdog" who knows how to make proper use of a traditional saying in context. Here, proverb performance serves an egalitarian function, if you will, by providing the weak with a relatively "safe" way to confront the strong.[44]

Another factor might be mentioned which contributes to the motivation to make use of traditional sayings in conflict situations. Psychological studies on the motivation for certain types of problem-solving and interactional behaviors have paid special attention to human responses to ambiguous context (i.e., contexts where two or more alternate strategies or interpretations may be proposed as appropriate). In general, it has been shown that "...the greater the ambiguity or lack of structure or clarity of the object, place, or <u>event</u> (stress mine) to be observed, the greater the influence of inner or behavioral determinants on the percepts that emerge."[45] This is one of the basic theoretical propositions which has led folklorist Roger Abrahams to conclude that incidences of proverb performance offer a guide to the "trouble spots" in a society.[46] When faced with an ambiguous, conflict situation, one is generally apt to "fall back on" the rules and recommendations encapsulated within the traditional saying or other familiar genres to deal with the situation. In traditional societies with a vigorous proverbial stock, the proverb and saying play a primary role in the education of children, and continue to exercise a good deal of influence throughout the adult life. When proverb performance occurs, it is purposeful, and its stimulus may generally be inferred to be situations which are ambiguous and filled with dissension. Traditional genres, because of their familiarity from youth and their stamp of authority, are thus employed to categorize the new situation in a culturally approved way. Where a saying occurs in context, we are justified in expecting to discover that a stressful situation is the stimulus of proverb performance.

One final point should be made about the Sources in our texts: in every case, the Sources are successful in achieving their goals within the context. A number of factors no doubt contribute to this success on the part of the proverb users. As we pointed out above, each Source is one for whom we may posit familiarity with and understanding of traditional sayings (competence), and the pericopes provide ample witness to their abilities to make appropriate use of the sayings (performance). Because the Sources make use of traditional arguments which appeal to the generally acknowledged authority of tradition, provide indirection and the possibility of multiple meanings, and encourage the Receiver to reevaluate the Context Situation, they attain their specific ends and achieve success. Recent studies in psycholinguistics have investigated the effect of linguistic style of persuasion on the Receiver, and have concluded that, in general, stylistic devices (such as the use of metaphor, analogy, proverb, etc.) do have an effect on the Receiver's response to the message sent by the Source.[47] In particular, Receivers are most apt to respond positively to a message when they perceive, via the use of style, a similarity between themselves and the Source.[48] To put this another way, Sources are most successful in achieving their ends when their style is felt to be similar to that of the Receivers (i.e., when Source and Receiver have access to and make use of the same "code"). As we have seen, this is precisely the way that traditional saying operates in context: it presents a message "coded" in traditional (and hence, "authoritative") language. The Receiver responds because of the familiarity with the culture's proverbial stock (the code) and acceptance of the folk ideas which it embodies (the message). The aspect of code commonality between Source and Receiver is crucial if communication, much less persuasion, is to take place.[49] The traditional saying, because of its broad currency and aura of authority, finds a natural place in the "koine" of daily human interactions.

Other Features of Proverb Performance
in the Old Testament

Table 3, "Features of Proverb Performance in the Old Testament," summarizes the results of our contextual investigations. Both identificational and contrastive sayings seem equally likely to be used in proverb performance, and, as we suggested in Chapter II, the identificational sayings may be minimal (one topic-comment unit) or multi-descriptive (two or more topic-comment units), but contrastive sayings must be multi-descriptive in order to create their oppositions. As we pointed out, the four semantic types $(A = B, A \neq B, A \rightarrow B, A \nrightarrow B)$ may be realized syntactically by any number of architectural formulae, and even our necessarily limited sample displays a good deal of diversity in this respect. Our interpretations of the messages transmitted in context have not even begun to exhaust all of the potential contextual applications to which each saying might be put; we would not even suggest that we have offered the "only" possible interpretation of the proverb performance meanings for the contexts which were investigated. This is not necessarily due to the failure of our method, but rather to the nature of the form upon which the method was employed. Paroemiological and folklore studies clearly show that one of the essential and enduring features of the saying genre is its ability to act as the vehicle for many messages. No one paraphrase can really do justice to the wide range of meanings inherent in the kernel (Baukern) of a saying,[50] and contextually specified meanings may be just as diverse. Regardless of this built-in difficulty in pinpointing one overarching message for a given traditional saying, our investigations have demonstrated that transmission of a saying in social interactions is purposeful and serves the general function of orienting the participants toward the events of the Context Situation and resolving conflict. The following features may be observed in our sample of Old Testament Proverb performance.

The Interaction Situation

We have alluded above to the interesting occurrence of proverb performance taking place between different population groups, during both the settlement and monarchic periods. In the same way, the interactions between Saul and David, and Yahweh/later author and Samuel reflect the transmission of a saying between a Source and Receiver of different backgrounds. The fact that each interaction takes

Text	Semantic Type	Descriptive Units	Architectural Formula	Image Referents	Message
Judges 8:2	Contrastive (>)	multi-descriptive	Q ṭob A min B	agriculture/specific	effort of strong > effort of weak
Judges 8:21	Identification-al (→)	minimum	$k^e + B = A$	human capacities/general	parts commensurate with whole
1 Sam. 16:7	Contrastive	multi-descriptive	A (N V O) ≠ B (N V O)	human-divine dichotomy/general	human-divine dichotomy affects judgments
1 Sam. 24:14	Identification-al[1] (→)	minimum[2]	min A Vcop B	human nature/general	correspondence between act and actor
1 Kg. 20:11	Contrastive (-→)	multi-descriptive	VET + A k^e B	military/general	planning is not equivalent to achievement

Text	Status (X to Y)	Application to context	Referent Relationships	Strategy-Intent	Object-Receiver Correlation
Judges 8:2	X ≤ Y	identificational	X=B,D; negative Y=A,C;positive	resolution through paradox; evaluative/affective	0=Y
Judges 8:21	X ≤ Y	identificational	Multiple[4]	evaluative/affective	0=Y
1 Sam. 16:7	X > Y	identificational	X=B,D;positive Y=A,C;negative	evaluative/affective	0=Y
1 Sam.24:14	X ≤ Y	contrastive[5]	X≠A,C;positive	evaluative/affective	0=X
1 Kings 20:11	X ≤ Y	identificational	Y=A,B,C,D; negative	evaluative	0=Y

[1] Appraisal transforms the type to Contrastive   [2] Appraisal transforms the saying to multi-descriptive
[3] Appraisal transforms the image from general to general/specific
[4] Y=B,D; negative; or Y=B,D; positive; Z(third person)=A,C or B,D, negative; X=A,C; positive
[5] Appraisal transforms application from contrastive to identificational

TABLE 3: Features of Proverb Performance in the Old Testament

place between members of different groups but for whom a commonality of proverbial stock between groups must be assumed in order to have any basis for the intelligibility of the interchange is striking, to say the least. We have already suggested that courtly, "political" wisdom may have had its beginnings in Israel in the tribal period, long before the monarchy appeared. We might also suggest that it is extremely significant that throughout a good portion of her history Israel's traditions present her using traditional wisdom presented in traditional sayings to deal with both internal and external conflicts. Whether the disputes take place between Israelites of different backgrounds or Israelite and non-Israelite groups, wisdom seems equally at home and equally as necessary to regulate the events of daily life. Whether the events of proverb performance which we have discussed actually took place becomes a secondary consideration beside the obvious fact that the ancient authors seemed to view such "between-group" exchanges of traditional wisdom as commonplace. While we may hesitate to argue for the historicity of any given incidence of proverb performance, the inference that similar types of proverb performance probably <u>did</u> take place on a fairly frequent basis seems well founded. We have not attempted the impossible task of pinpointing a life setting (Sitz im Leben) for the origin of the traditional sayings found in the Old Testament, but have been able to suggest an outline of the life setting of the <u>use</u> of the traditional saying. The elitist courts and schools - the ancient ivory towers - cannot claim wisdom as their exclusive possession, in terms of use. There may be more truth than poetic license in the "theological" introduction to the Book of Proverbs in Chapters 1-9 which tells us that Wisdom's voice may be heard in the street or the marketplace, on the walltops and at the city gates. On the basis of our contextual studies, we are inclined to agree.

Image Referents in the Proverb Situation

The terms of the Proverb Situation (A,B) are primarily general ones, dealing with familiar features of everyday life, which might be applied in a variety of ways. The two exceptions occur in Jg. 8:2, where Gideon's reference to Ephraim/Abiezer and gleaning/vintage have much more specific content and apply to the given context of use exactly; and in 1 Sam. 24:14, if one appends David's appraisal ("but my hand shall not be against you") to the nuclear saying, "out of the wicked comes forth wickedness."[51]

Although the referents of the Proverb Situations are fairly

general and capable of multiple applications, they tend to be applied in a rather simple-minded fashion. That is, the proverb referents and their contextual referents (C,D) are correlated in a literal way: military images are used in a military setting; strength and a man's military prowess are correlated with a situation where there is a dispute over the most fitting execution for a military leader, and so on. The major exception in this pattern of use occurs in Jg. 8:2, where the proverb referents are applied metaphorically to the contextual referents. If the more common "method" of proverb performance in ancient Israel was to select a traditional saying for use whose contextual referents could be related to the proverb reference in a fairly literal way, perhaps this may be one of the reasons why Gideon felt the obligation to provide an immediate "exegesis" of the traditional saying which he employed.

Correlations between Proverb Situation and Context Situation

In the models of proverb performance which we investigated, the Source generally tended to make fairly literal correlations (symbolized by - - - in our model) between the Proverb Situation as a whole $(A \sim B)$ and the Context Situation $(C \sim D)$. In Jg. 8:2, 21; 1 Sam. 16:7, and 1 Kg. 20:11, the Source identified the state of affairs obtaining in the Proverb Situation as corresponding exactly to the state of affairs found in the Context Situation. We might summarize this by saying that the Source contends that $A \sim B = C \sim D$. For example, in 1 Kg. 20:11, the Source, the king of Israel, contends that the message of the Proverb Situation (that one should not boast prior to accomplishment) reflects the true state of affairs in the Context Situation (i.e., that Ben-hadad should not boast until he has won his battle). In the four examples mentioned above, then the Source uses the Proverb Situation as a traditionally-phrased statement of his reading of the Context Situation, and makes an identification between the two. In 1 Sam. 24:14, the pattern changes: here the Source claims that the Proverb Situation (which reflects the Receiver's attitude towards the Source's actions) does not accurately reflect the Context Situation (i.e., $A \sim B \neq C \sim D$). Here David uses the message of the Proverb Situation (that wicked persons produce wicked acts) to disassociate himself from the wickedness imputed to him in the context. However, by appending David's appraisal to the nuclear saying, we find the same identificational relationship between the Proverb Situation and the Context Situation which we find in our other examples.[52]

The typical correspondences between correlations of the participants in the Interaction Situation and the referents of the saying and context which Peter Seitel observed in East Nigerian proverb performance (positive correspondence when X = A,C; negative correspondence when Y = A,C) do not appear to hold true for all of our examples in the Old Testament. The major factors which seem to determine whether or not the participants in the interaction are positively or negatively correlated with the proverb and contextual referents is the intent and strategy of the Source. Thus, when Gideon wishes to flatter his receivers, he slights himself and his achievements by a negative correlation with the less valued terms of the proverb and context situations. (B, vintage of Abiezer, and D, rout of the Midianite forces). We might summarize here by stating that the Source generally transmits a saying to further some end of his own, but that specific correlations, positive or negative, between the actors in the Interaction Situation and the referents of the Proverb and Context Situations are flexible and determined more by the requirements of the context and the strategy of the Source than by any fixed "law" of correlations between Source, Receiver, and referents. Often, too, multiple correlations are possible for a given context, so circumspection and attention to the broader cultural context are required in assigning possible correspondence.

Strategy and Intent

By strategy in proverb performance, we are referring to the method by which the source attempts to use a saying to resolve conflict; by intent, we mean the purpose for which the saying is strategically transmitted. The two favorite strategies for proverb performance are (1) highlighting the similarities between the Proverb Situation and Context Situation (Jg. 8:2, 21; 1 Sam. 16:7; 1 Kg. 20:11); and (2) pointing out the contrast between the Proverb Situation and Context Situation in order to redirect the attitudes of the Receiver (1 Sam. 24:14; see also Appendix C). The stable element in these strategies consists of the Source's statement of either identification or contrast between the kernel ($\sim$) exhibited in the Proverb Situation and the relationships between the "hidden" contextual referents, as perceived by the Source.

Folklorists studying proverb performance in African societies posited two types of intent which might be present in these types of interactions: the desire to render an evaluation of the context, or the intent to affect behavior.[53] Our contextual studies in the Old Testament point to a closer connection between the two types of intent than is perhaps the case in African contexts. The evaluative intent is closely related to affective proverb performance, since the evaluation rendered presumably becomes part of the Source/Receiver's body of knowledge and experience, and thus has (or should have) an influence on subsequent behavior. In the same way, affective proverb performance displays an interdependence with the evaluative function, since one generally makes the decision to try to affect a course of action or chain of events on the basis of some previous evaluation. The time reference of the events or actions which are evaluated or affected is of some importance here, since one is seldom able to affect the course of events which have already transpired. Still, any evaluation of past events contains an implicit, affective orientation toward analogous happenings in the present and future. We would prefer to adopt the term "orientation" to describe the purpose of proverb performance in the Old Testament, since this may encompass features of both evaluative and affective intent without creating artificial distinctions.

Conclusions:
The Structure of Old Testament Proverb Performance

We have commented at length on those aspects of proverb performance in the Old Testament which confirmed or contradicted our expectations, based on paroemiological and folklore studies. At this point, it is appropriate to make a few final remarks about the interactions in the Old Testament which we have designated as "proverb performance."

It was suggested by folklorist Alan Dundes that any approach to the cross-cultural study of the saying genre must begin by proposing an adequate, yet flexible definition for the form. Dundes attempted to do this by breaking the genre down into its component elements: the vehicles which convey the content (architectural formula and image) and the actual semantic content itself (message and corresponding "type" classification). In general, his system is successful in that it provides a fairly convenient means for distinguishing and communicating exactly what features of a given item are under discussion. In particular, his definition of the genre as a form which, in its minimum requirements, consists of a complete "descriptive unit" of one topic (A) and one comment ($\sim$B),[54] is quite helpful as a basic criterion for identification of sayings (as opposed to proverbial comparisons, phrases, or riddles).

Once the topic-comment unit has been accepted as the basic structural model of the genre, then it becomes possible to explain the development of more complex forms - the multi-descriptive sayings of the various types are all built up from basic elements inherent in the simple topic-comment unit, realized through a great diversity of syntactical concatenations. So, too, is proverb performance composed of an interconnected series of topic-comment units, which Sources everywhere manipulate in a variety of ways to serve countless purposes. The structure of <u>proverb</u> <u>performance</u> simply reflects a more complex version of the structure of the saying form itself.

The saying which exists in a collection or by itself without a context of use has a discrete nucleus located in its topic and comment. This is the context-free kernel (Baukern), and the ultimate source for all subsequent applications, since this core is the carrier of the message, however mundane or profound. The casual reader of collected sayings, however, is usually inundated by the countless topics rapidly passing by, and rarely perceives the ingenious way in which a traditional saying may replicate its simple structure when it is set free from the prison of paroemiological lore, and given life in contextual use.

Proverb performance, we have said, is purposeful. Its purpose is to orient the Source/Receiver toward the elements of the Context Situation in such a way as to achieve a resolution of the conflict (perceived in the context by the Source) which acted as the primary stimulus for the transmission of the saying. It achieves this purpose by making a seemingly apt comment on the events of the context. The Context Situation, then, with all its conflicts and ambiguity, is the "Topic" of proverb performance. The "Comment" in an event of proverb performance is the traditional saying itself, which the Source relates in some cohesive way to the "Topic"-context. In general, the more complex the "Comment"-saying (i.e., the greater its number of complete descriptive units), the more intricate its contextual correlations (its comments on the "topic"-context) will be. Let us illustrate the way proverb performance replicates the structure of the saying, using contextual examples of a "minimum" traditional saying drawn from the Old Testament. First, the structure of the minimal saying in 1 Sam. 24:14 should be outlined.

Traditional Sayings in the Old Testament

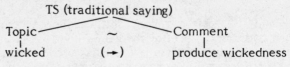

~ = →, positive causation

Figure 13: Topic-Comment Structure of 1 Sam. 24:14

Using our stuctural model of proverb performance, we obtain the diagram in Figure 14. The correspondences become more complex with the addition of more topic-comment units to the minimum saying, but the structural pattern remains the same.[55] The structure of proverb performance then, at least as it is found in the Old Testament, is simply an extension of the structural components of the traditional saying as the "comments" on a context situation (the "topic" of a proverb performance).

PERSPECTIVES ON TOPICS IN OLD TESTAMENT WISDOM

The Origins of Wisdom

Older discussions concerning the origins of wisdom in Israel made heavy use of the "international" character of wisdom and wisdom's close association with the court in the areas of the education of officials, and political, diplomatic counseling. Although some indigenous wisdom traditions among the "folk" were conceded, it was generally assumed that wisdom first succeeded in establishing itself in a truly significant way during the reign of Solomon, whose court bureaucracy was modelled after Egyptian institutions. In this view, (necessarily simplified here) wisdom was seen as something of a "foreign import" which was in many ways thought to be inimical to "genuine" Yahwism. Court and temple schools in Israel were postulated on analogies (albeit faulty ones) with the cultures of Egypt and Mesopotamia, and the elite court, with its rivalries, bureaucratic needs and diplomatic intrigue, was seen the primary life setting for Israel's wisdom.[56]

More recent works on the origins of Israel's wisdom have begun to stress other sources than that of the court at Jerusalem as possible life settings for wisdom. In particular, the work of Erhard Gerstenberger has made an extremely provocative case for the origin of certain wisdom forms (the prohibitive) in tribal society, where such forms were used to enforce and preserve the communal life of the clan. Hence, the ethos of the tribe (Sippenethos) has been tentatively recognized as a contributing life-setting for the origins of

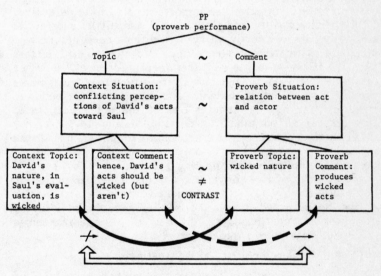

= Source's contrastive correlation between the Topic-context and
Comment-saying

FIGURE 14: Topic-Comment Structure of Proverb Performance in 1 Samuel 24:14

wisdom. The works of Jean-Paul Audet, Christa Bauer-Kayatz, and Claus Westermann have all dealt with the possibility, although from different perspectives, and the hypothesis of the tribal origin of some of Israel's wisdom traditions has gained a reasonable degree of acceptance in Old Testament wisdom studies.[57]

Our contextual studies offer a certain amount of support for the existence of some type of wisdom at this settlement stage of Israel's history. The instances of proverb performance in the Book of Judges, although perhaps not historically accurate or verifiable, do seem to point to the use of traditional wisdom during this stage of Israel's history as a means of settling both inter- and extra-tribal disputes. Similar- ly, our discussion of proverb performance in the Amarna letters suggests that the use of traditional sayings and the wisdom found in them was in evidence in the indigenous population groups of Palestine in the troubled "pre-Conquest" period. The inviting conclusion that traditional wisdom played an important part in the daily lives of a whole variety of groups who had little substantial contact with the courtly wisdom traditions need not depend on an identification of the "ᶜApiru" of the Amarna letters with the Hebrews of the Old Testament "Conquest." In times of cultural ambiguity and unrest, traditional societies make use of traditional argument, and the wisdom found in traditional sayings constitutes one of the chief weapons in this arsenal aimed at the reduction of anomie. It is not difficult to conjecture that traditional wisdom (via purposeful proverb performance) not only served the function of cementing the cultural solidarity of various groups (since it acted as an authority to which all might appeal in disputes), but may also have raised an eloquent voice in the articulation of the "social rage" engendered by the "governmental" abuse of power and continuous exploitation of the disenfranchised classes of Late Bronze Age society.[58]

Wisdom Influence on the Texts Investigated

The recent trend in biblical studies has been to find "wisdom influence" in a variety of canonical contexts from which wisdom had previously been excluded. The problem with such claims are many, as James Crenshaw pointed out some time ago. There is no real standardization in the meaning or use of the term "wisdom influence," nor is there much agreement on what criteria must be fulfilled before "wisdom influence" may be said to exist in a given text.

Deriving from and compounding these difficulties is the fact that no two scholars seem to make use of the same method to investigate a text for wisdom influence.[59] Since it is not possible to discuss the ramifications of these problems here, our comments will, of necessity, be brief.

If one takes "wisdom influence" to mean direct literary influence on a text by a representative of the "wisdom movement" (another problematic term!), whether as author, editor, or instructor of the author, then, with the possible exception of 1 Sam. 16, no such influence can be claimed for the pericopes which were investigated. If, on the other hand, one means by wisdom influence that a text shows affinities with the general values and goals of the sages - or, to use von Rad's terminology, if wisdom influence means that a text shares the same "understanding of reality" (Wirklichkeits-verständnis) as that held by the tradents of Israel's wisdom, then we might claim some degree of wisdom influence in our texts. The folk ideas which underlie the traditional sayings we have seen used in context also find expression in the Old Testament wisdom materials. "Wisdom thought," then, conceived of as a particular approach and response to reality, does find expression in these texts; direct literary influence by the wisdom movement does not.

The question might be raised as to whether or not the texts under consideration might be considered "example stories (Beispielerzählungen) written to illustrate the didactic goals and insights of the wisdom movement.[60] The discussion of each "Proverb Situation" for the texts studied mentioned parallels in the wisdom literature to the messages expressed in the traditional sayings transmitted in context, and one might easily cite other wisdom sayings whose message is illustrated in our texts. David's confrontation with Saul in 1 Sam. 24, for instance, puts one in mind of Pr. 20:22, "Do not say, 'I will repay evil'; wait for the Lord and he will help you" and Pr. 29:26, "Many seek the favor of a ruler, but from the Lord a man gets justice." Similarly, Pr. 20:18, "Plans are established by counsel; by wise guidance wage war," is nicely illustrated in 1 Kings 20, and so on. Each of the texts discussed do present a graphic representation of the message of the traditional sayings they contain: Gideon's military strength or prowess is commensurate with his person as the competent charismatic leader; Ben-hadad would have been better off had he spent his time planning strategies rather than boasting (and carousing); David does not kill his pathetic rival at En-gedi. Given Wisdom's rather high opinion of itself and the fact that each proverb user is ultimately successful in achieving his goals, may we then assume that these texts are "example stories" written for the express purpose of illustrating both wisdom themes and the efficacy of wisdom? Probably not; it seems far more likely that the similarities between wisdom concerns and the content and outcome of the various texts come from a shared worldview, as we suggested above, rather than from an overt intention to illustrate the teachings of the sages. That the Sources are generally successful in achieving their goals, and the importance of counsel and such attitudes as temperence and forbearance are so nicely demonstrated must be attributed to the fact that the ancient authors found the values hawked by the sages to be of true worth in the "real world," and naturally expected that those able to make wise use of a saying would be successful in their activities.

Wisdom at Work in Israel

We have seen that there are a marked number of similarities in content, structure, and function between the wisdom sayings cultivated by the sages and the traditional sayings found in use in narrative texts. The controlling power and authority of wisdom did not end outside the precincts of the court of Jerusalem; rather, traditional wisdom may be seen at work at various levels of society, resolving conflicts, orienting its users to respond to life's ambiguities and paradoxes in a wholesome, integrative way, so as to maximize the goal of "shālôm" in daily life. Such modest, daily wisdom needed no appeal to creation or special revelation to legitimate its existence: its authority derived from its recognized utility - a utility which had been validated through generations of use. "Proverb performance" is only one of the ways in which such traditional wisdom served society. Doubtless, wisdom made itself useful in other ways - in the education of children, as entertainment, etc. Traditional wisdom - the little insights drawn from shrewd observation and openness to experience - functioned as a vehicle for cultural solidarity, honing the inchoate presuppositions of the society into tools ready for "active duty" in the maintenance of culture. We may never construct a fully satisfactory picture of all of the life settings out of which Israel's wisdom grew; we can, however, point to a variety of life settings for the subsequent use of such wisdom. In a very real way, the "Sitz im Leben" of wisdom at work must be located in the familiar challenges of everyday life.

NOTES
APPENDIXES
BIBLIOGRAPHY
INDEXES

NOTES

NOTES TO CHAPTER I

A Survey of Scholarly Opinion on
Traditional Sayings in the Old Testament

1   The designation "traditional saying" will be used here in a neutral way. Chapter II will present a detailed discussion of the problems involved in defining the saying, and a specific definition of the traditional saying, encompassing Old Testament and folklore studies' perspectives, will be given there.

2   Otto Eissfeldt, Der Maschal im Alten Testament, BZAW 24 (Giessen: Alfred Töpelmann, 1913), p. 33.

3   Ibid., p. 6.

4   Ibid., pp. 12-13. A considerable amount of diversity exists in the terms used to designate the various types of wisdom and popular saying forms. For our purposes, we will adopt the following translations of the German terms:

Aussage, Ausspruch, Spruch - saying.
>These terms usually refer to sayings which are indicative in form, and may consist of either one or two lines.

Kunstsprichwort - artistic saying.
>This is usually used to refer to sayings of two lines which purportedly exhibit signs of literary polish, and parallelism.

Lehrgedicht - wisdom poem.

Mahnwort, Mahnrede, Mahnung - admonition.
>This may refer to both positive and negative forms.

Rede - speech.

Sprichwort - proverb.
>This form may be either one or two lines, and includes the idea of currency among a given group.

Spruchdichtung - epigrammatic poetry.

Volkssprichwort - folk proverb or saying.
>This presumes an origin, as well as currency, among the folk.

Weisheitsspruch - wisdom saying or aphorism.
>This refers to a two line saying exhibiting parallelism, and presumes an origin from wisdom circles.

5   Ibid., p. 12.   6   Ibid., p. 13.

7   Ibid., p. 7 passim.   8   Ibid., pp. 45-47.

9   See below, pp. 11, 16.

Notes to Chapter I

10   Eissfeldt, pp. 48-49. This observation is taken up by others who claim that parallelism per se did not develop from an early, popular epigrammatic or proverbial poetry (Spruchdichtung).

11   Ibid., pp. 48-49.   12   Ibid., p. 50.

13   Ibid., p. 51.

14   Aage Bentzen, Introduction to the Old Testament, 2 vols. (Copenhagen, 1957), 1:169; J. Schmidt, Studien zur Stilistik der alttestamentlichen Spruchliteratur, ATA 13/1 (Muenster: Verlag der Aschendorffschen Verlagsbuchhandlung, 1936), pp. 1-36; Ernst Sellin and Georg Fohrer, Introduction to the Old Testament, trans. David E. Green (Nashville: Abingdon Press, 1968), pp. 313-15.

15   As might be expected, Eissfeldt's treatment of the popular proverb in his later works draws heavily upon his earlier discussions as may be seen in his book, The Old Testament: An Introduction, trans. Peter Ackroyd (Oxford: Basil Blackwell, 1965; reprint ed., New York: Harper and Row, 1976), pp. 81-87. The folk proverb, which is, in his thinking, the forerunner of the artistic wisdom saying, "enjoyed very great popularity" in Israel in early times, and although it was later replaced in part by the wisdom saying, it did not totally cease to exist (p. 82). His remarks on the style of the popular proverb follow the lines of his earlier research, although he comments on the lack of parallelism and longer metrical constructions: "Thus the metrical form which properly belongs to the later artistic saying - normally, as we have seen, a double triplet - was not an absolute essential of the ancient proverb, though this does not of course exclude the possibility that the popular proverb also made use at an early date of that parallelismus membrorum which existed early in Israel's environment, and of the rhythmic structure which no doubt always existed with it" (p. 82). One need not look for specific, sociological settings in life for the "garden variety" saying, since "the whole of life is shot through with such sayings," but it is highly likely, in Eissfeldt's view, that Israel's popular sayings borrowed much from her environment, especially since the content of such sayings is "of general human interest" which renders them particularly open to crossing cultural boundary lines (p. 83).

16   Christa Bauer-Kayatz, Studien zu Proverbien 1-9, WMANT 22 (Neukirchen-Vluyn: Neukirchener Verlag, 1966); William McKane, Proverbs: A New Approach, Philadelphia: The Westminster Press, 1970), pp. 117-50; Hans-Jürgen Hermisson, Studien zur israelitischen Spruchweisheit,

173

WMANT 28 (Neukirchener Verlag, 1968), pp. 38-52.

17   Hermisson, pp. 27-36; and Paul Hernandi, Beyond Genre: New Directions in Literary Classification (Ithaca, N.Y.: Cornell University Press, 1972), pp. 83-85.

18   André Jolles, Einfache Formen, 3rd ed. (Tübingen: Max Niemeyer Verlag, 1965). The forms described are Legende, Sage, Mythe, Rätsel, Spruch, Kasus, Memorabile, Märchen, and Witz. These correspond to the basic types of folklore outlined by Alexander Krappe in: The Science of Folklore (London: Methuen Co., 1930). See Chapter II for Krappe's discussion of the saying which differs markedly on the evaluation of the importance of didacticism for the understanding of the form.

19   Jolles, pp. 1-22.   20   Ibid., pp. 16-20.
21   Ibid., p. 150.   22   Ibid., p. 153.
23   Ibid., pp. 150-55.   24   Ibid., p. 154.
25   Ibid., pp. 154-56, 167. Actualization of the saying as a proverb is not the only form of realization possible for the simple form of the saying. A "speech" (Rede) is produced if a different "verbal gesture" is made, for example. However, Jolles feels that the proverb is the realized simple form which best exhibits the essence of the saying. (Spruch).

26   Ibid., p. 158.
27   See Chapter II, "The Content of Proverbs and Traditional Sayings," p. 38.
28   Jolles, p. 164.   29   Ibid., p. 165.
30   Ibid., p. 167.   31   Hermisson, p. 36.
32   Ibid., p. 36.   33   Ibid., p. 36.
34   Ibid., p. 37.
35   Ibid., p. 40. See Chapter III for discussion of specific passages.
36   Hermisson, pp.43-44.   37   Ibid., p. 44.
38   Ibid., pp. 46-52.   39   Ibid., pp. 36, 113.
40   Ibid., pp. 113-36 passim.
41   See Pr. 25:23, 25:14, 27:17, 26:11, 26:20 and so on.
42   So with Roland E. Murphy, "Form Criticism and Wisdom Literature," CBQ 31 (1969): 482; or, to state this observation concerning the content "appropriate" to a given group in proverbial terms, "a cat may look at a king."
43   Erhard   Gerstenberger,   "Zur   alttestamentlichen Weisheit," Verkündigung und Forschung 14 (1969) : 41.
44   Hermisson, pp. 57, 66, 77.
45   Gerstenberger, p. 41.
46   See Chapter II, p. 38-41.
47   "We   are   not   able   to   proceed   from   a   positive

characterization of the folk proverb, but must ask much more: what is possible in a folk proverb, and what is not, and to define what is out of the presuppositions of the "wise," what lies outside their areas of interest." Hermisson, p. 51.

48   Erhard Gerstenberger, Wesen und Herkunft des sogenannten "apodiktischen Rechts" im Alten Testament, WMANT 20 (Neukirchen-Vluyn: Neukirchener Verlag, 1965). A similar position is advocated by Jean Paul Audet in: "Origines comparées de la double tradition de la loi et de la sagesse dans le Proché-Orient ancien," Acten Internationalen Orientalisten-kongresses (Moscow), no. 1 (1962), pp. 352-57.

49   R. N. Whybray, The Intellectual Tradition in the Old Testament, BZAW 135 (Berlin: Alfred Töpelmann, 1974), pp. 33-43.

50   James L. Crenshaw, "Prolegomenon" in: Studies in Ancient Israelite Wisdom, Selected with a Prolegomenon by James L. Crenshaw (New York: Ktav Publishing House, 1976), p. 14 (hereafter cited as SAIW).

51   Murphy, "Form Criticism," p. 483.

52   Sellin-Fohrer, p. 311.

53   Ibid., p. 311. 1 Sam. 24:14 (English, 24:13) is an example of a saying attached to a specific historical context.

54   "Problematic" because students of the proverb are as yet unable to reach consensus as to "why" and "how" one is usually able to identify a statement as a proverb or saying, although such identification does occur. See Chapter II, "Definition of the Proverb and Traditional Saying," pp. 32-34.

55   Sellin-Fohrer, p. 311.   56   Ibid., pp. 311-313.

57   Contrast 1 Sam. 16:7 and Pr. 10:5, 11 to Zeph. 1:12.

58   Sellin-Fohrer, p.311.   59   Ibid., p. 315.

60   Bentzen, I: 168.   61   Ibid., I: 168-69.

62   Ibid., I: 168-69, 175-76.

63   McKane, Proverbs, pp. 10-33.

64   Ibid., pp. 25-33.

65   See Chapter II, "The Function and Context of Proverbs and Traditional Sayings," p. 43.

66   McKane, p. 414.

67   Ibid., pp. 23, 414 passim.

68   Ibid., p. 11.

69   Gerhard von Rad, Wisdom in Israel, trans. James D. Martin (Nashville: Abingdon Press, 1974), p. 24.

70   Ibid., p. 26.   71   Ibid., p. 27.

72   Ibid., p. 31.   73   Ibid., p. 30.

74   Ibid., pp. 33-34.   75   Ibid., p. 30.

76   Ibid., p. 26.   77   Ibid., p. 26.

78   Roland E. Murphy, "The Interpretation of Old Testament Wisdom Literature," Interpr 23 (1969) : 289-301; "Wisdom Theses," in: Papin Festschrift: Wisdom and Knowledge, ed. J. Armenti, 2 vols. (Philadelphia: Villanova University, 1976), 2:187-200.
79   Murphy, "Form Criticism," p. 478, and "Theses," p. 194.
80   Murphy, "Interpretation," p. 301.
81   Murphy, Ibid., pp. 300-301, and "Theses," pp. 194-95.
82   Murphy, "Theses," p. 193.
83   Ibid., pp. 193-95.
84   Murphy, "Interpretation," pp. 295-96.
85   Claus Westermann, "Weisheit im Sprichwort," in: Schalom: Studien zu Glaube und Geschichte Israels, Festschrift Alfred Jepsen zum 70. Geburtstag, ed. Karl-Heinz Bernhardt (Stuttgart: Calwer Verlag, 1971), 73-85.
86   Ibid., pp. 80-81.   87   Ibid., pp. 74-75.
88   Ibid., pp. 74-75, 77, 84-85.
89   Ibid., pp. 80-81.   90   Ibid., 81-82.
91   Ibid., p. 81.   92   Ibid., p. 74.
93   Robert B. Y. Scott, "Folk Proverbs of the Ancient Near East," Transactions of the Royal Society of Canada 55 (1961) : 47-56, reprinted in: SAIW, pp. 417-26; The Way of Wisdom in the Old Testament (New York: Macmillan Publishing Co., 1971), pp. 12-18, 63-70; and "Wise and Foolish, Righteous and Wicked," VTS 23 (1972) : 146-65.
94   Scott, Way, pp. 12, 67; and "Wise," p. 155.
95   Scott, "Folk Proverbs," p. 418; and "Wise," pp. 155-56.
96   Scott, "Folk Proverbs," p. 418; Way, p. 63; "Wise," p. 155.
97   Scott, "Folk Proverbs," p. 418.
98   Scott, "Folk Proverbs," p. 418; Way, p. 63.
99   Scott, "Wise," p. 154.
100   Ibid., p. 156.   101   Ibid., pp. 156-57.
102   Scott, Way, p. 18.   103   Ibid., p. 12.
104   Ibid., pp. 12-18; "Folk Proverbs," p. 417.
105   Scott, "Folk Proverbs," p. 419.
106   Ibid., pp. 419-26.
107   James L. Crenshaw, "Wisdom," in: Old Testament Form Criticism, ed. John H. Hayes (San Antonio, Texas: Trinity University Press, 1974), pp. 226-64; and "Prolegomenon," pp. 1-60.
108   Crenshaw, "Prolegomenon," p. 13.
109   Crenshaw, "Wisdom," p. 231.
110   Ibid.   111   Whybray, pp. 33-43.
112   Crenshaw, "Prolegomenon," p. 16; "Wisdom," p. 233.

113   Crenshaw, "Wisdom," p. 236.

114   Ibid., p. 233.   115   Ibid., p. 231.

116   See Semeia 5 (1976) for a number of articles which attempt an interdisciplinary approach to biblical problems with oral literature. For an application of anthropological material to the problem of the function and formation of biblical genealogy, see Robert R. Wilson's study, Genealogy and History in the Biblical World, Yale Near Eastern Researches, no. 7 (New Haven: Yale University Press, 1977).

117   Angel Marzal, Gleanings from the Wisdom of Mari, Studia Pohl, no. 11 (Rome: Biblical Institute Press, 1976). For a discussion of George Milner's work, see below Chapter II, "Structural Studies of the Proverb and Traditional Saying."

118   Bendt Alster, The Instruction of Suruppak, Mesopotamia: Copenhagen Studies in Assyriology, no. 2 (Copenhagen: Akademisk Forlag, 1974); and Studies in Sumerian Proverbs, Mesopotamia: Copenhagen Studies in Assyriology, no. 3 (Copenhagen: Akademisk Forlag, 1975).

119   Alster, Studies, p. 37.   120   Ibid., p. 102.

121   Glendon E. Bryce, " 'Better'-Proverbs: An Historical and Structural Study," SBL Seminar Paper, 108, 2 (1972) : 350.

122   Robert Gordis, "Quotations in Biblical, Oriental, and Rabbinic Literature," HUCA 22 (1949) : 157-219, reprinted in: Robert Gordis, Poets, Prophets and Sages: Essays in Biblical Interpretation (Bloomington: Indiana University Press, 1971), pp. 104-59.

123   Ibid., p. 131.

NOTES TO CHAPTER II

Paroemiology and Folklore Studies
on the Proverb and Saying

1   Žbynek Žaba, Les Maximes de Ptahhotep (Prague: Editions de l'Academie Tchecoslovaque des Sciences, 1956), p. 45, line 368.

2   Aristotle, Rhetorica 2. 21. 11, quoted in: Bartlett Jere Whiting, "The Nature of the Proverb," Harvard University Studies and Notes in Philogy and Literature 14 (1932) : 277. This work presents an excellent survey of the history of proverb studies.

3   Archer Taylor, "The Study of Proverbs," Proverbium 1 (1965) : 3.

4   Henry Peacham, The Garden of Eloquence, A Facsimile Reproduction with an Introduction by William G. Crane (London, 1593; reprint ed., Gainesville, Fl. : Scholar's Facsimiles & Reprints, 1954), p. 30.
5   The works of Johann von Herder, for example, contain much that today would be considered "folklore studies."
6   Alan Dundes, "Who Are the Folk?", in: Frontiers of Folklore, ed. William R. Bascom, AAAS Selected Symposium, no. 5 (Boulder Co. : Westview Press, 1977), p. 18.
7   Dundes, "Folk," p.21.   8   Ibid., p.22.
9   Ibid., p. 23.   10   Ibid., p. 29.
11   For an excellent review of current trends in folklore studies, see Richard Dorson's "Introduction" in: Folklore and Folklife: an Introduction, ed. Richard Dorson (Chicago: University of Chicago Press, 1972), pp. 3-50.
12   Archer Taylor, "Problems in the Study of Proverbs," JAF 47 (1934) : 21.
13   Archer Taylor, The Proverb and an Index to the Proverb, 2nd ed. (Copenhagen and Hatboro, Pennsylvania : Rosenkilde & Baggers, 1962), p. 3.
14   Ibid., pp. 5, 10, 35 passim; Taylor, "Problems," p. 10.
15   Krappe, p. 143.
16   Ibid., pp. 143-48; Taylor, Proverb, p. 135.
17   Bengt Holbek, "Proverb Style," Proverbium 15 (1970) : 470.
18   Ibid.   19   Ibid.
20   Ibid., p. 471.   21   Ibid., p. 472.
22   Marjorie M. Kimmerle, "A Method of Collecting and Classifying Folk Sayings," WF 6 (1947) : 353.
23   Ibid., pp. 363-64.
24   For a complete discussion of proverb image, message, and framework, see Alan Dundes, "On the Structure of the Proverb," in: Analytic Essays in Folklore, ed. Alan Dundes, Studies in Folklore, no. 2 (The Hague: Mouton & Co., 1975), pp. 103-18, and discussion below on structural studies of the proverb, pp. 34-38.
25   Dundes, for example, finds such definitions of limited use, since "other genres of folklore may share the same function(s) of proverbs." Ibid., p. 104.
26   "Structural analysis," as it is used by folklorists, should be understood in the broad sense as a method which looks for "a combination and relation of formal elements which reveal their logical coherence within given objects of analysis." Jacques Ehrmann, "Introduction," in: Structuralism, edited with an Introduction by Jacques Ehrmann (Garden City, N.Y.:

Doubleday & Co., 1970; Anchor Books, 1970), p. ix.

27   Dundes, "Structure," pp. 104-6.

28   Ibid., p. 105. See also Matti Kuusi, "Ein Vorschlag für die Terminologie der parömiologischen Strukturanalyse," Proverbium 5 (1966) : 98.

29   Dundes, "Structure," p. 108.

30   Ibid.   31   Ibid.

32   Ibid., p. 109. For example, "Time flies" might be a saying, but "Time" could not.

33   Ibid., pp. 109-110.   34   Ibid., p. 110.

35   Ibid.

36   Ibid. The same observation is also true of sayings cast in interrogative form. E.g., "Is the Pope Catholic?" is a transformation of a simple equational saying, consisting of one topic (the Pope) and one comment (Catholic).

37   Ibid.   38   Ibid., p. 111.

39   Ibid., p. 112.   40   Ibid., pp. 112-15.

41   Ibid., p. 111.   42   Ibid., p. 115.

43   These genre distinctions reflect the terminology of Archer Taylor, The Proverb, p. 4. It should be noted that he, as well as Dundes, makes no distinction between the metaphorical and non-metaphorical, the folk and learned proverb for purposes of analysis, since the problems which occur in the study of all types of sayings are fundamentally the same, regardless of the origin of saying. See Dundes, "Structure," pp. 109-110.

44   Dundes, "Structure," p. 104.

45   Matti Kuusi, "Toward an International Type-System of Proverbs," Folklore Fellows Communications (Helsinki), no. 211 (1972), pp. 5-41.

46   Grigory Permyakov, Izbrannije poslovitsi i pogovorki narodov Vostoka [Selected proverbs and sayings of the people of the East] (Moskva, 1968).

47   Kuusi, "Type-System," pp. 16, 41.

48   Ibid., pp. 14-15.

49   George Milner, "Quadripartite Structures," Proverbium 14 (1969) : 379-83.

50   Ibid., pp. 379-80.

51   For a further discussion of the difficulties inherent within Milner's system of analysis, see Dundes, "Structure," pp. 106-8.

52   Nigel Barley, "A Structural Approach to the Proverb and the Maxim," Proverbium 20 (1972) : 739.

53   Ibid. It is for this reason that Barley feels that the

maxims of a foreign culture are essentially more intelligible to outsiders than are its proverbs.

54   Ibid., pp. 737-40. "The leopard cannot change his spots" may be used to refer to a broad range of situations, although its structural basis, "One-time membership in category A implies permanent possession of distinctive feature 'a' " is similar to the structural description of "once a thief, always a thief", as "One-time membership in category A implies permanent membership in category A."

55   Ibid., p. 739.   56   Ibid., p. 740.

57   Ibid., p. 739.

58   Ibid., p. 741. Notice, too, that Barley uses structural analysis of the proverb image to explicate the proverb message, but pays scant attention to the architectural formula (contra Dundes).

59   Ibid., p. 744; Dundes, "Structure," p. 115. See also the discussions of the work of Kimmerle and Milgren above, pp. 34, 37.

60   Bartlett Jere Whiting, "Proverbs and Proberbial Sayings: an Introduction" in: The Frank C. Brown Collection of North Carolina Folklore, gen. ed. Newman Ivey White, 7 vols. (Durham, N.C. : Duke University Press, 1957-64), I:343.

61   Taylor, Proverb, p. 12.

62   Roger Abrahams, "Such Matters as Every Man Should Know and Descant Upon," Prov 15 (1970) : 426; Anna B. Rooth, "Domestic Animals and Wild Animals as Symbols and Referents in Proverbs," Prov 11 (1968) : 286-88; Taylor, Proverb, pp. 13-15, 66-134. Examples of new sayings coined by a subgroup of a larger community may be found by examining the "street language" of the "counterculture" of the later 1960's, e.g., "Make love, not war."

63   Taylor, Proverb, p. 171.

64   Dundes, "Structure," p. 105. Compare, for example, the sayings "He who is bitten by a snake fears even a rope" (English) and "A scalded cat fears even cold water" (French), which have different images but the same message.

65   Nigel Barley, "The Proverb and Related Problems of Genre Definition," Prov 23 (1974) : 881.

66   Bartlett Jere Whiting, "The Origin of the Proverb," Harvard University Studies and Notes in Philology and Literature 13 (1931) : 80.

67   Roger Abrahams, "Introductory Remarks to a Rhetorical Theory of Folklore," JAF 81 (1968) : 151; Barley, "Approach," pp. 737-40; Dundes, "Structure," pp. 103-5; Heda Jason, "Proverbs in Society: The Problem of Meaning and

Function," Prov 17 (1971) : 617-23; Barbara Kirshenblatt-Gimblett, "Toward a Theory of Proverb Meaning," Prov 22 (1973) : 821-27.

68   Barley, "Approach," pp. 739-40. In The Proverb, Taylor concludes that "a sentence comes to mean far more than the sum of the words composing it. 'New brooms sweep clean' is a housewife's observation of fact, but as a proverb it may find use in any field" (p. 10).

69   Barley, "Approach," p. 739.

70   Jason, p. 621.

71   Abrahams, "Introductory Remarks," p. 740.

72   Taylor, Proverb, p. 10; Barley, "Approach," p. 740.

73   "Metaphorai ap'eidous ep'eidos," Aristotle Rhetorica 3.11.14, quoted in: Whiting, "Nature," p. 277. It is unfortunate that Aristotle did not discuss this at greater length, although it is clear from the context that he is addressing the <u>application</u> of a proverb which moves away from the specific image to differing context situations.

74   S. J. Sackett, "Poetry and Folklore: Some Points of Affinity," JAF 77 (1964) : 149; Barley, "Approach," p. 740.

75   Sackett, pp. 149-51.

76   Ibid., p. 150; Roger Abrahams, "A Rhetoric of Everyday Life: Traditional Conversation Genres," SFQ 32 (1968) : 48; Whiting, "Nature," p. 277.

77   Barley, "Approach," pp. 737-50; Carolyn Ann Parker, "Aspects of a Theory of Proverbs: Contexts and Messages in Swahili" (Ph.D. dissertation, University of Washington, 1973).

78   Jerome S. Bruner, Jacqueline J. Goodnow, and George A. Austin, "Categories and Cognition," in: Culture and Cognition: Rules, Maps, and Plans, ed. James P. Spradley (San Francisco: Chandler Publishing Co., 1972), p. 169.

79   Ibid., p. 178-79.   80   Pr. 12:15; 13:20; etc.

81   Jerome S. Bruner et al., p. 174.

82   Ibid., p. 177.

83   Alan Dundes, "Folk Ideas as Units of Worldview," JAF 84 (1971) : 95-96. Obviously, the discussion of the categorization at work in the formation and use of proverbs has important implications for Old Testament wisdom studies which often postulate "world order" as the underlying premise of wisdom literature.

84   Eastman, pp. 197-98.

85   A. I. Hollowell, "Myth, Culture, and Personality," AA 49 (1947) : 544-45; Bronislaw Malinowski, Myth in Primitive Society (London: Kegan Paul, Trench & Trubner, 1926).

86   Holbek, p. 470.   87   Malinowski, pp. 19, 29.

88   William R. Bascom, "Four Functions of Folklore," JAF 67 (1954) : 333-49, reprinted in: The Study of Folklore, ed. Alan Dundes (Englewood Cliffs, N.J.: Prentice Hall, 1965), pp. 279-98.

89   Ibid., p. 290.   90   Ibid., p. 293.

91   Ibid., p. 295.   92   Ibid., p. 293-94.

93   George Herzog, Jabo Proverbs from Liberia (London: Oxford University Press, 1936), p. 2.

94   Bascom, p. 295.   95   Krappe, pp. 143, 147-48.

96   Taylor, "Study," p. 7.

97   Herzog, p. 9. Although Herzog makes no specific reference to the role of proverbs in the education of children, it is apparent from the short explanation appended to each proverb text that such a function does indeed exist.

98   John C. Messenger, Jr., "The Role of Proverbs in a Nigerian Judicial System," SJA 15 (1959) : 64-73, reprinted in: Dundes, Study of Folklore, pp. 299-307; Raymond Firth, "Proverbs in Native Life with Special Reference to Those of the Maori," FL 37 (1926) : 134-53, 254-70.

99   Krappe, p. 151.

100   Alan Dundes and Ojo Arewa, "Proverbs and the Ethnography of Speaking Folklore," AA 66 (1964) : 70-85, reprinted in: Dundes, Analytic Essays, pp. 35-49.

101   Ibid., p. 36.

102   Ibid. See also Roger Abrahams, "Proverbs and Proverbial Expressions," in: Dorson, Folklore and Folklife, p. 119. For a statement of the "Contextualist" approach to folklore, which calls for a move from identification to interpretation, see Richard Bauman, "Settlement Patterns on the Frontiers of Folklore," in: Bascom, Frontiers, pp. 121-31. For studies which pay special attention to the use of proverbs in context, see Eleanor Forster, "The Proverb and the Superstition Defined," (Ph.D. dissertation, University of Pennsylvania, 1968); Peter Seitel, "Proverbs and the Structure of Metaphor Among the Haya of Tanzania," (Ph.D. dissertation, University of Pennsylvania, 1972); and the studies of Dundes and Arewa, Firth, Herzog, and Parker cited above.

103   Forster, pp. 15-18.

104   "Proverb performance" here refers to a situation in which a certain stimulus (usually human behavior, whether proposed or completed) has elicited the application of the proverb to the situation. Such an application is usually heard or read by an addressee, but it is possible to quote a proverb to oneself as well.

105 Forster, p. 16. The interplay between these three levels of context might be illustrated in an event of proverb performance in which a mother quotes "If you lie down with dogs, you get up with fleas" to a child concerning the child's choice of friends. Context A refers to the actual references of the proverb (dog, fleas) and its message (Activity A causes effect B; A → B). Context B, the micro-context, refers to the situation which elicits the proverb; in this case, the mother's disapproval of her offspring's choice of friends. Context C, the macro-context, represents the cultural milieu which underlies the event. In this example, we might point to the "folk ideas" that a person may be known by the company he or she keeps, and that bad companions may "contaminate" the innocent but unwary.

106 Abrahams, "Rhetoric," p. 45.

107 Jason, p. 620. 108 Ibid., p. 619.

109 Ibid., p. 617. 110 Ibid.

111 Kirshenblatt-Gimblett, p. 821.

112 Ibid., p. 822.

113 Ibid., p. 823. For a discussion of the "enactment theory" of folklore, see William R. Bascom, "Frontiers of Folklore: An Introduction," in: Bascom, Frontiers, pp. 1-16.

114 Parker, p. 80. 115 Ibid., pp. 79-82.

116 Ibid., p. 89. 117 Ibid., p. 84.

118 Ibid., p. 88. 119 Ibid., pp. 119-22.

120 Abrahams, "Introductory Remarks," p. 146.

121 Ibid., pp. 146, 148.

122 In recent writings, Abrahams has adopted the term "enactment" to replace "performance", since many of those things being discussed in performance terms were "stretching the idea of performance somewhat out of shape." Roger Abrahams, "Toward an Enactment Centered Theory of Folklore," in: Bascom, Frontiers, p. 80.

123 Roger Abrahams, "The Complex Relations of Simple Forms," Genre 2 (1969) : 114-16.

124 Abrahams, "Rhetoric," pp. 50-56.

125 Abrahams, "Proverbs," p. 121.

126 Abrahams, "Rhetoric," p. 48.

127 Ibid., pp. 47-48.

128 Abrahams, "Introductory Remarks," p. 151.

129 Alan Dundes, "The Study of Folklore in Literature and Culture: Identification and Interpretation," JAF 78 (1965) : 136-142; Daniel Hoffman, "Folklore in Literature: A Symposium," JAF 70 (1957) : 1-24; Wolfgang Mieder, "The Essence of Literary Proverb Study," Prov 23 (1974) : 888-94.

130 Mieder, p. 892.

131 Richard M. Dorson, "The Use of Printed Sources," in: Dorson, Folklore and Folklife, pp. 465-78.

132 Ibid., p. 465.   133 Ibid., pp. 473-77.

134 Ibid., p. 466.   135 Ibid., p. 41-77.

136 Taylor, "Problems," p.20.   137 Ibid.

138 Mieder, p. 888.   139 Ibid., p. 889.

140 Ibid., pp. 890-91.

141 Ibid., p. 891. For example, a study of the use of proverbs in the poetry of John Donne has identified 267 different proverbs used 352 times in a variety of ways: for allusion, amplification of imagery, and presentation of an argument from authority. Arthur W. Pitts, "John Donne's Use of Proverbs in His Poetry," (Ph.D. dissertation, Louisiana State University, 1966), pp. i-iii.

142 Mieder, p. 891.   143 Ibid., p. 892.

144 Whiting, "Origin," p. 50.

145 Bartlett Jere Whiting, Proverbs in the Earlier English Drama, Harvard Studies in Comparative Literature, no. 14 (Cambridge: Harvard University Press, 1938), p. 4.

146 Dorson, "Printed Sources," p. 472.

147 Chinua Achebe, Things Fall Apart (London: Heinemann, 1958); Suleiman Omar Said Baalawy, Hadithi za Bibi Maahira (Nairobi, Kenya: Evans Brothers, 1969); and Ebrahim N. Hussein, Kinjeketile (East Africa: Oxford University Press, 1971).

148 Parker, p. 22.

149 Carol Eastman, "The Proverbs in Modern Written Swahili Literature: an Aid to Proverb Elicitation," in: African Folklore, ed. Richard M. Dorson (Garden City, N.Y.: Doubleday Anchor, 1972), pp. 201-2.

150 Eastman, p. 207; Parker, p. 21; and Peter Seitel, "Proverbs: A Social Use of Metaphor," Genre 2 (1969) : 143-61, reprinted in: Folklore Genres, ed. Dan Ben-Amos (Austin: University of Texas Press, 1976), pp. 125-43.

151 Seitel, "Social Use," p. 127.

152 See above, pp. 46-47.

153 Seitel, "Social Use," pp. 126-27.

154 Ibid., p. 128.   155 Ibid.

156 In other terminology, the "proverb situation" would constitute Forster's "literal context," (see above, p. 47), or the proverb message conveyed by means of its image.

157 Seitel, "Social Use," p. 133.

158 Note that the saying here quotes Job 12:11, where we find the same image expressed as a didactic question ("Does

not the ear try words as the palate tastes food?"), and employed in the service of Job's sarcastic reply to the dogmatic assertions of his friends. Note also that the following verse, 12:12, ("Wisdom is with the aged, and understanding in length of days") is taken up by Elihu in 32:9 and refuted for the same strategic reasons that 12:11 is used in 34:3 (i.e., Elihu has a right to speak, regardless of age).

159   "Or because my argument is a later addition to the text (!)."

160   Job 32:2-3, 5ff.

161   Hans Walter Wolff, Anthropology of the Old Testament, trans. Margaret Kohl (Philadelphia: Fortress Press, 1974), pp. 123-27.

162   Norman K. Gottwald, The Tribes of Yahweh: A Sociology of the Religion of Liberated Israel 1250-1050 B.C.E., (Maryknoll, NY: Orbis, 1979).

163   Ibid., pp. 679-99.

164   Ibid., p. 698. Gottwald would argue that the later prophetic movements were born out of the struggle of early "monoYahwism," with all its distinctive social features, against the move toward a centralized, statist social order (the monarchy). Yahweh's touching statement to Samuel in 1 Sam. 8:7b ("For they have not rejected you, but rather me they have rejected from ruling over them") concerning the people's request for a king reflects this tension.

165 See Chapter I, above, pp. 23-24.

NOTES TO CHAPTER III

Proverb Performance in the Old Testament

1   See Chapter II, pp. 48-52, 57-63.

2   See above, pp. 54-58.

3   Thus, we have excluded from consideration here: Gen. 10:9, because it lacks complete syntax and contextual information; 1 Sam. 10:12 (1 Sam. 19:24) and 2 Sam. 5:8 because contextual data has clearly been subordinated to etiological interests; 2 Sam. 20:18 because of its occurrence in the literary composition of the Succession Narrative, which may make it more likely to have been presented in a way consistent with the author's intent; etc.

4   See above, pp. 57-60.

5   Robert G. Boling, Judges: Introduction, Translation and Commentary, AB (Garden City, N.Y.: Doubleday & Co., (1975), pp. 7-29; John L. McKenzie, The World of the Judges (Englewood Cliffs, N.J.: Prentice-Hall, 1966), p. 11.

6   Boling, pp. 11, 29, 36, 130; Eissfeldt, Introduction, pp. 257-67.

7   Boling, p. 5. This is certainly true, regardless of what model one uses to understand the "Conquest."

8   Charles Fox Burney, The Book of Judges with Introduction and Notes (London: Rivingtons, 1918), pp. 227-34; Eissfeldt, Introduction, p. 260; George Foot Moore, A Critical and Exegetical Commentary on Judges, ICC, vol. 7 (New York: Charles Scribner's Sons, 1895), p. xxi; Gerhard von Rad, "The Beginnings of Historical Writing in Ancient Israel," in: The Problem of the Hexateuch and Other Essays, trans. E. W. Trueman Dicken (New York: McGraw-Hill; Edinburgh and London: Oliver & Boyd, 1966), p. 172; Cuthbert A. Simpson, Composition of the Book of Judges (Oxford: Basil Blackwell, 1958), pp. 33-39; and C. F. Whitley, "The Sources of the Gideon Stories," VT 7 (1957) : 158. The sources may also represent a confusion of two separate figures, Gideon and Jerubbaal, as discussed by Herbert Haag, "Gideon-Jerubbaal-Abimelek," ZAW 79 (1967) : 305-14.

9   Boling, pp. 6-7, but see Jotham's statement about his father in Jg. 9:17.

10   A. D. H. Mayes, "The Period of the Judges and the Rise of the Monarchy," in: Israelite and Judaean History, ed. John H. Hayes and J. Maxwell Miller (Philadelphia: Westminster Press, 1977), p. 315; see also Boling, pp. 15, 126; and McKenzie, pp. 130-31.

11   Boling, p. 23, contra Mayes, p. 322.

12   Boling, p. 31; McKenzie, p. 11. Eissfeldt relates the old narratives more closely to the "saga" because of the tribal concerns and character evidenced in the stories (Introduction, pp. 264-65). von Rad, although noting that the Gideon hero-saga is a "conglomeration" of a variety of materials, still believes that "Neither their own historicity, nor the scene of their activities, nor the reality of the political conflicts in which they are involved can be impugned" ("Writing," p. 172).

13   Boling, p. 32; McKenzie, p. 133.

14   See Chapter II, pp. 52-53.

15   Those who feel the two narratives to be different accounts of the same raid are Burney, pp. 182-83; and H. W.

Hertzberg, Die Bücher Joshua, Richter, Ruth, ATD, Teilband 9 (Göttingen: Vandenhoeck & Ruprecht, 1953), p. 196. Those supporting the latter alternative, which is followed here, are Boling, pp. 148-58; John Gray, Joshua, Judges and Ruth, CB (London: Nelson, 1967), p. 226; Hugo Gressmann, Die Anfänge Israels (von 2. Mose bis Richter und Ruth), SAT I/2 (Göttingen: Vandenhoeck & Ruprecht, 1922), p. 208; McKenzie, pp. 130-34; Mayes, p. 315; Moore, p. 176; and von Rad, "Writing," p. 175.

16   Boling, p. 151; McKenzie, p. 149; and Moore, p. 216.

17   A good deal of recent discussion of the socio-political organization of early Israel casts serious doubts on Martin Noth's hypothesis of the existence of a tribal amphictyony in Israel. For a summary, see The Interpreter's Dictionary of the Bible, Supplementary Volume, s.v. "Amphictyony," by Michael C. Astour. Similarly, the term "tribe" (perhaps better understood as "clan" in the Hebrew Bible) may no longer be used solely as a designation of a nomadic or ethnic group, but must be interpreted more as a reference to a social organization which may have little to do with actual common ancestors or pastoral life-style. In our texts, it is clear that one of the underlying motivations for unified action on the part of the "tribes" is the pressing need to defend territory from outside incursions. So with George Mendenhall, in IDB/S, s.v. "Tribe." It may be best here to interpret the narrated action within the tradition where Gideon appears as a "local hero" leading primarily men from his own clan, rather than as a judge of "all Israel." So with Boling, pp. 138-51; Burney, p. 227; von Rad, p. 175; and Whitley, "Sources," p. 158.

18   The location of Beth-barah is unknown, but the factors necessary for the postulation of a logistically feasible site for the action has led some to suggest the Wadi Far^cah as a possible location. So Boling, p. 151; and Moore, p. 214.

19   von Rad, "Writing," p. 175. "Rock of Oreb" may reflect an error in the text, where "bswr" may have been confused with "bṣyr" (as in Zech. 11:2), which occurs later in 8:2. The text perhaps should read "the Gleaning of Oreb," which makes better sense in the context. So with Frank Zimmermann, "Reconstruction in Judges 7:25-8:25," JBL 71 (1952) : 111-12.

20   Gray, Judges, p. 226. Verses 23 and 25 may both be editorial additions which attempt to harmonize this action with what follows in 8:4-21. So with Boling, p. 151; Burney, Judges, p. 182; Moore, pp. 213-27; and C. A. Simpson, p. 33.

21   Jg. 7:23-8:3.

22   For a discussion of the roles inherent in proverb performance, see Chapter II above, pp. 50-52, 58-60.

23   The reasons for the importance of the clan of Ephraim are many: they seem to be part of the Yahwistic core of the Israelite "settlers"; their territorial holdings are among the most productive of all of the clans; they may have been guardians of a central shrine; and a number of important figures (Joshua, Samuel) in early Israel are associated with them. The picture of the Ephraimites as zealous in guarding their position and prerogatives is fairly consistent throughout the biblical narratives. So with Boling, p. 151; McKenzie, pp. 85-86; and Moore, p. 216.

24   The situation here is not simply one where the Ephraimites feel that they have been slighted and have suffered a diminution in "honor." Rather, their exclusion from the major portion of military action would also result in a loss of a share of the spoils. McKenzie offers the interesting suggestion that perhaps Ephraim, as the leading "tribe" in the "amphictyony," claimed special authority in instigating military action (p. 149). Whitley has suggested that the quarrel between Gideon and the Ephraimites should be interpreted as a response of the Ephraimites objecting to a local hero usurping their particular rights in instigating military action ("Sources," p. 158).

25   Moore suggests that Gideon must have been accompanied during the interaction by men of his own clan rather than the greater grouping of Manasseh, since it is likely that the Ephraimites would have been more temperate in their accusations if Gideon has sufficient troop strength to back him up (p. 213).

26   Eissfeldt, Maschal, pp. 46, 51.

27   Boling remarks that "he is either coining a proverb or adapting an old one, more likely the latter, in view of his early education at the cult place of 'Joash the Abiezerite' (6:11)" (p. 151). Gray and Moore both comment on the figurative aspects of the verse (Gray, Judges, p. 225-26; Moore, p. 216), while Gressmann refers to the saying as "a word spoken in jest" (Scherzwort) which undercuts the anger of the Ephraimites (p. 208).

28   Hermisson does deny that this passage is an authentic saying on the basis of its interrogative form. There are a number of considerations which should be raised with respect to Hermisson's conclusions (pp. 42-45). First of all, the interrogative form has always been particularly associated with wisdom forms - (a) because of its use in didactic

settings: Johannes Fichtner, "Isaiah Among the Wise," in: SAIW, pp. 429-38; Johannes Lindblom, "Wisdom in the Old Testament Prophets," VTS 3 (1960) : 201-2; Gerhard von Rad, "Job XXXVIII and Ancient Egyptian Wisdom," in: Problem of the Hexateuch, pp. 281-91 (reprinted in: SAIW, pp. 267-77); Hans Walter Wolff, Amos the Prophet: the Man and His Background, trans. Foster R. McCurley, with an Introduction by John Reumann (Philadelphia: Fortress Press, 1973), pp. 8-16; - or (b) because of its connection with the riddle: Johannes Hempel, Die althebräische Literatur und ihr Hellenistisch-Jüdisches Nachleben, Handbuch der Literaturwissenschaft (Wildpark-Potsdam: Akademische Verlagsgesellschaft Athenaion M.B.H., 1930), pp. 44-49. Secondly, it might be pointed out that the ancient Israelites themselves apparently felt that an interrogative form might operate as a saying, since "Is Saul among the prophets?" in 1 Sam. 10:12 (1 Sam. 19:24) is both clearly marked as a question and designated by the text as a "māshāl." Third, from a structural point of view, even though the features of Q (interrogative) originate at the level of the DS (deep structure), they do not alter the relationship expressed between the terms of the saying, but rather reflect the Source's orientation towards that expressed relationship (for further discussion see note 192 below). This is true whether one translates "hălōʼ " simply as "is not" or as "surely," both of which seem to expect an answer in the affirmative. For a discussion of this idiom, see Arthur E. Cowley, trans., E. Kautzsch, ed., Gesenius' Hebrew Grammar, 2nd English ed. (Oxford: Oxford University Press, 1910), §150e (hereafter cited as GKC). For a representation of the relation of Q to the DS of the propositional content of the nuclear S (sentence), see Appendix B, Fig. 9, "Syntactic Structure of Jg. 8:21." Many sayings often assume interrogative form without experiencing a loss of their "proverbial" status, even when they are regarded as "rhetorical questions." In our context, the use of a traditional saying marked as a Q, rather than a simple comparative statement, must be viewed as a functional strategy (see Context Situation, Section III) rather than a variation which affects the message of the saying. So with Eissfeldt, who states that a saying may be cast in interrogative form, for greater force (Maschal, p. 52). See also folklorist Alan Dundes' remarks on the structural similarities between literal and metaphorical sayings, which are applicable as well to interrogative sayings ("Structure," pp. 109-10).

29   For a discussion of the "Better-than" saying (tôb-Spruch) in Israel and Egypt, see Glendon Bryce's survey, cited above in Chapter I, p. 23.

30   One might, of course, conceive of this saying functioning in a general way to highlight Ephraim's view of its superiority over other clans, even though it refers to a specific historical situation out of which it probably arose. From modern times, an example of such a saying, coined by reference to a concrete event and later finding at least limited currency, may be found in the English saying, "The battle of Waterloo was won on the playing fields of Eton." Although this saying came out of a specific setting - the English system of education and the close interplay between the ideals of "good sportsmanship" and "teamwork," which worked to help win that particular battle. (A more cynical comment on Wellington's quip might be that by the time his "infamous army" fought the crucial battle in Belgium, they had already been seasoned by several years of fighting on the Iberian peninsula, and thus, the gentlemanly approach to war "games" instilled by the English public school system had very little to do with the victory.) Still, with respect to the saying in Jg. 8:2, one can hardly posit the same broad acceptance and use for this type of saying as one might postulate for a more general statement such as "like mother, like daughter."

31   Hermisson, p.58.

32   Similar forces seem to be in operation in the use of other genres in the Old Testament. See, for example, von Rad's discussion of the prophetic use of traditional forms to express new insights, in: Old Testament Theology, trans. D. M. G. Stalker, 2 vols. (New York: Harper & Row, 1965), 2:326 (hereafter cited as OTT).

33   The word used here for "gleaning" refers only to the gleaning of olives or grapes, rather than the gleaning of wheat (lqt). So with Burney, Judges, p. 227; and Moore, p. 217.

34   See above, note 18. Note also that the names Oreb and Zeeb, literally "raven" and "wolf" respectively, are particularly apt ones for the leaders of nomadic raiders who commonly preyed upon settled populations (Boling, p. 151). The popular etymology of these place names found in Jg. 7:23-25 may be the reason for the preservation of this account, even as the saying in 8:2 may be responsible for the preservation of 8:1-3 (so with Gray, Judges, pp. 225-26; and von Rad, "Writing," p. 175.

35   One might give an alternate paraphrase of "a small amount of a superior thing is of more worth than a large

amount of an inferior thing." As Bryce has rightly pointed out, it is the qualifying elements or middle terms which create the paradox, by transforming the original meanings into their logical opposites (pp. 349-50). On a structural level, one might also observe that contrast or paradoxical sayings are only possible by the addition of descriptive elements to the basic topic-comment unit (see above, pp. 34-36).

36   Note that on a structural level, the saying exhibits chiastic form (X): gleaning Ephraim > vintage Abiezer = - + > + - . Gideon's employment of the term "Abiezer" rather than a reference to himself personally or his "tribe" of Manasseh (which would be the more usual choice to parallel Ephraim) may actually have more to do with the logical demands of the structural relationships within the saying, than with a change of sources where Abiezer is mentioned rather than the whole tribe of Manasseh. So with Moore, p. 216; contra Burney, Judges, p. 227. It might also be possible to see this traditional saying as an instance of "blason populaire," whose topic is the small, backward (?) clan of Abiezer.

37   William Kelly Simpson, ed., The Literature of Ancient Egypt: An Anthology of Stories, Instructions, and Poetry, new ed. (New Haven: Yale University Press, 1973), p. 248.

38   For other parallels to formula and paradoxical message, see Pr. 11:24; 14:20; 15:17; 16:8; 19; 17:1; 18:23; 22:7; 28:23; Ec. 4:6; 7:5; Sir. 11:11.

39   Johannes Pedersen interprets this type of paradox within his conception of the "blessing" and the power which it confers upon those who receive it. In this understanding, the blessing is the power of the soul, which "makes the soul grow and prosper, in order that it may maintain itself and do its work in the world" (Israel: Its Life and Culture [London: Oxford University Press, 1926; reprint ed., Copenhagen: S. L. Moller, 1946], 1-2: 182). Power, strength and honor are all manifestations of the blessing.Thus, one might interpret the message of this saying as a recognition that the activities of the strong, those saturated with the power of the blessing, are intrinsically more efficacious than those of the weak, who possess the power of the blessing in a lesser degree (1-2: 182-222).

40   Pr. 28:6: "Better is a poor man who walks in his integrity than a rich man who is perverse in his ways." Obviously, this sort of saying is far from being merely "observational," and embodies a faith statement based on evaluation of human behavior. The occurrence of this sort of

evaluation should be examined in the light of the inflexible "doctrine of retribution" which is often ascribed to the Book of Proverbs. A statement of this type makes it difficult to believe that the sages always viewed poverty or misfortune as the justified consequence of previous evil activities, or saw riches as a sure sign of goodness of character.

41   It is interesting that Gideon feels obligated to explain his use of the saying, lest it be misunderstood and worsen matters. Studies in psycholinguistics have demonstrated that of all possible Q and NEG constructions, the negative question is the one most likely to be misunderstood. See, for example, E. S. Howe's study, "Verb Tense, Negatives, and Other Determinants of the Intensity of Evaluative Meaning," Journal of Verbal Learning and Verbal Behavior 5 (1966) : 147-55. Without Gideon's explicit correlations, the Ephraimites might have chosen to understand the reference as uncomplimentary, since it is obvious from both the general understanding of the referents (vintage-harvest, gleaning) and that of the context events, that no "gleaning" is in fact possible unless the vintage-harvest has first taken place. Had Gideon allowed the Ephraimites to interpret his statement in this way, it would have constituted a tactless reminder that Ephraim had been left out of the initial military encounters, thus suffering a diminution in honor and material gain. Although Gideon has constructed or used a saying, and even given a subsequent interpretation which is quite flattering to the Ephraimites, it is possible that Gideon's comment that "God has given into your hand the princes of Midian" serves as a pietistic refusal to give the Ephraimites all of the credit for the executions. This stress on God's part in successful military encounters is fully consistent with the rest of the Gideon narratives (von Rad, "Writing," p. 174).

42   Hugh Blair, Lectures on Rhetoric and Belles Lettres, ed. Harold F. Harding, with a Foreward by David Potter, 2 vols. (London: T. Cadell in the Strand, 1783; reprint ed. Carbondale: Southern Illinois University Press, 1956), 1:355, 356-57.

43   Commentators have remarked on the similarity in style and function of Gideon's proverbial question with that returned earlier by his father to the outraged townsfolk of Ophrah on the occasion of Gideon's destruction of the altar of Baal in Jg. 6:31, which follows the more usual style for the rhetorical question in biblical Hebrew - that is, the double rhetorical question whose parts are introduced by "he-" and "'im," and which often concludes with a further question

introduced by "maddûaᶜ" (for a discussion of this form, see Moshe Held, "Rhetorical Questions in Ugaritic and Biblical Hebrew," Eretz-Israel 9 [1969] : 71-79). Some postulate that Gideon's familiarity with his father's cultic activities at Ophrah may account for his knowledge of traditional wisdom and the ability to turn an apt phrase in a delicate situation. So Boling, p. 151; Moore, p. 216; and C. A. Simpson, p. 35.

44   Hermisson's comments on this saying are appropriate here, although he denies that Jg. 8:2 is indeed a saying, even though it is in the form of a "better-than" saying. Such similarity, he feels, says nothing concerning the authenticity of the saying as a folk proverb (Volkssprichwort), but shows only that Israel's proverbial literature did not operate in a vacuum, and that the wisdom writers obviously had a share in the speech of the folk (p. 45). This, of course, is exactly the point - in many cases, the world view and forms of expression of the sage and the folk no doubt overlapped, and the two groups should not be considered always and everywhere mutually exclusive.

45   W.K. Simpson, p. 161.   46   Ibid., p. 263.
47   Ibid., p. 335.
48   See also Pr. 10:19; 11:12; 12:14; 16, 18, 25; 14:3, 17; 16:21, 23, 24; 17:27; 18:7, 13; etc.
49   In this respect, the present writer views Gideon as a better example of the ideals of the sages than is Joseph in the Joseph Narrative, as von Rad has so suggestively argued in "The Joseph Narrative and Ancient Wisdom," in: Problem of the Hexateuch, pp. 292-300 (reprinted in: SAIW, pp. 439-47). It is not our purpose here to claim anything as ambitious as "wisdom influence" in Gideon narratives, but merely to point out that the values exemplified by Gideon and, to a lesser degree, Joseph, were probably widely held and cannot be said to belong exclusively to a courtly wisdom circle.

50   See pages 77-78, above.
51   The designation of Zebah and Zalmunna in this passage as "kings" should probably be taken very loosely. See Gray, Judges, p. 309.
52   So with Boling, p. 154; von Rad, "Writing," p. 175; C. A. Simpson, p. 38, and others.
53   So with Boling, pp. 149ff. However, it may be best to set the action of 8:4-21 within the complex of older traditions in which the "judges" appear as local chiefs concerned with parochial tribal matters, rather than as leaders of "all Israel" (that is, a tribal confederacy) as other traditions picture

them. So with Bentzen, 2: 87-88.

54   For a discussion of blood vengeance, see Willaim Robertson Smith, Lectures on the Religion of the Semites: the Fundamental Institutions, new rev. ed. (London: Adam and Charles Black, 1914), pp. 32, 72, 272, 417ff.; Roland de Vaux, Ancient Israel: Its Life and Institutions, trans. John McHugh (New York: McGraw-Hill Book Co., 1961), pp. 11-13 and Johannes Pedersen, 2:378-80, 393-95.

55   Burney, Judges, p. 183 and Moore, p. 175.

56   Boling (p. 155) sees the negative responses of Succoth and Penuel to Gideon's request for aid in v. 5ff. as a reasonable request for proof of "some prior success to validate his military leadership." Most critics see this, however, as a violation of the amphictyonic duty to lend aid when necessary. McKenzie, p. 135 and Moore, pp. 221-24.

57   Burney, Judges, p. 234 and Moore, p. 227.

58   The names Zebaḥ ("Sacrifice") and Ṣalmunnā^c ("Protection Refused") may be word plays or inventions by the narrator for unspecified leaders in a sequel to 7:24-8:3. One need not necessarily conclude with Boling, that the names indicated "early Yahwist sympathy for Zebah and Zalmunna." Boling, p. 155 and Gray, Judges, p. 309.

59   The discrepancy between Gideon's question and the answer of the captives in v. 18 has long been noted, with the result that some have emended the text to read " 'êkāh" for "'êpōh," thus reading with the Vulgate and Syriac (Gray, p. 312). Boling translated "How about the men ...," taking the particle as one which has "deictic force." (Boling, p. 157). The present writer sees no need to emend the text or move away from the usual translation of " 'êpōh" as "where," since the interchange as it stands serves as a device to heighten the drama of Gideon's confrontation of his brothers' killers. So with Burney, Judges, p. 344 and Moore, p. 226.

60   Eissfeldt, Maschal, p. 46 and Scott, "Folk Proverbs," p. 419. Hermisson believes this to have the form (stress mine) of a true saying which may even be of popular origin, but, on the basis of content and use, classes 8:21 as a "dispute" (Streit) rather than a saying (p. 43).

61   Such style, including as it does, a certain brevity of syntax which is a common and clearly recognizable feature of sayings in every culture, has posed problems for later interpreters of the text since ancient times, showing that the saying was not always recognized as such. The LXX, Vatican Codex, and other cursive manuscripts read "hoti hôs andros hê dunamis sou," ("for according to age is the strength of a

man"). See Moore, p. 228. Both readings probably reflect interpretations which were no doubt evoked by the succinctness of the Hebrew text. While one might generally expect a "kên" or "kᵉ" to accompany the second element in a comparison, such ellipsis is by no means uncommon in "wisdom" and poetic forms (cf., Pr. 26:11 and Ezek. 16:44), and may even be expected in such fixed-phrase genres as those of traditional sayings. The need for emendation disappears once the genre of the passage has been correctly identified and understood.

62   See Is. 3:25; 28:6; 30:15; and especially Pr. 8:14, where Wisdom claims to have "gᵉbûrāh."

63   For discussion of the Hebrew concept of the nature of humanity, see Pedersen, I-2: 226ff. and Wolff, Anthropology, pp. 7-79.

64   W. G. Lambert, Babylonian Wisdom Literature (Oxford: Clarendon Press, 1960), pp. 271, 238 (cited hereafter as BWL). The second saying may seem out of place in our discussion, but it should be remembered that in ancient (as well as not-so-ancient) times, a woman was defined primarily by her relationship to a man (as kin, mate, or mother). In the saying cited, the wife's status (as a dependent or derivative of her mate) is severely downgraded because of the nature of the husband who "defines" her (A ← B). See also the Middle Assyrian text VAT 10810, lines 10-12, "Bride, (as) you treat your mother-in-law, so will women (later) treat you" for parallels to the architectural formula (BWL, p. 262, but see Lambert's later translation, preferred here, in: James Pritchard, ed., Ancient Near Eastern Texts Relating to the Old Testament, 3rd ed., with Supplement (Princeton, N.J.: Princeton University Press, 1969), p. 594 (cited hereafter as ANET).

65   Burney, Judges, p. 234. For a discussion of the concept of "honor" and its motivation in the actions of leaders, see Pedersen, 1-2:213-26.

66   Pedersen, I-2: 379.   67   Gressmann, p. 209.

68   See Burney, Judges, p. 234; Gray, Judges, p. 309; Gressmann, p. 209; Pedersen, 1-2; 379 and Wolff, p. 122. Nowhere are the changing cultural values of interpreters so apparent as in the discussion of Gideon's motivation in ordering a young boy to carry out an execution. Where earlier commentators might calmly compare this command to the custom of "blooding" a youthful participant after his or her first fox hunt, and discuss the act in terms of "manhood" or "honor," recent treatments find such terminology, as well as

the act itself, repugnant in the extreme. For the latter view, see Boling, p. 157 and Phillips P. Elliott, "The Book of Judges: Exposition," in: The Interpreter's Bible, vol. 2, ed. George A. Buttrick (New York: Abingdon Press, 1953), pp. 747-48. For the most balanced treatment, see McKenzie (pp. 135-36), who sets the action within the context of family solidarity in feud situations, and a period when acceptance of the duties and responsibilites of the tribe and family came fairly early.

69   Most commentators take Gideon's act as one which intends to humiliate the captives and honor the boy, but others mention the practice reported by Nilus of the employment of boys as executioners by the Saracens, for similar reasons, but also as a demonstration of maturity, and hence marriageability. See Burney, Judges, p. 234; Gressmann, p. 209; and W. R. Smith, p. 417. For a perspective on the relative value of Nilus' reports, see Mircea Eliade's comments in: Occultism, Witchcraft, and Cultural Fashions: Essays in Comparative Religions (Chicago: University of Chicago Press, 1976), pp. 5-8.

70   The purposeful nature of the captives' statement is clear from the MT, where the independent personal pronoun adds emphasis to the imperative, and the saying is introduced by a causal "kî."

71   See McKenzie, p. 136 and Moore, p. 227.

72   Hermisson, p. 43. One might paraphrase it with something like "You kill us yourself, if you are man enough to do it."

73   Zebah and Zalmunna may have had the "last laugh" after all, since Gideon may have used part of their booty to make the ephod of which the redactor comments "all Israel played the harlot after it there (Ophrah); and it became a snare to Gideon and his family" (v. 27).

74   One might, of course, raise the objection that the whole narrative may have no basis in historical fact, but the point here is that the interchange is portrayed in a straightforward, matter-of-fact way which leads one to conclude that similar interactions between different groups might have occurred, even if this one did not. For the purposes of our analysis, the historicity of any given passage is less important than the consideration of whether or not such an interaction might have been possible.

75   For a discussion of the problem of the sources, see Tryggve N. D. Mettinger, King and Messiah: The Civil and Sacral Legitimation of the Israelite Kings, Coniectanea Biblica (Lund: Gleerup, 1976), Part One. Given the great

diversity of scholarly opinion concerning sources and the process of compilation, the present writer agrees (dejectedly) with Peter R. Ackroyd, that "the process is almost certainly much too complicated to be unravelled from the information available to us" (The First Book of Samuel, CBC [Cambridge: Cambridge University Press, 1971], p. 5).

76   See P. Kyle McCarter, Jr., I Samuel: A New Translation with Introduction, Notes and Commentary, AB, (New York: Doubleday, 1980), pp. 5-11.

77   H. W. Hertzberg, I and II Samuel: A Commentary, trans. J. S. Bowden (Philadelphia: Westminster Press, 1964), p. 20. For other evaluations of the historicity of the narratives, see Ackroyd, pp. 12-14; Eissfeldt, Introduction, p. 281; Sellin-Fohrer, p. 226; and J. Alberto Soggin, "The Davidic-Solomonic Kingdom," in: Hayes and Miller, Israelite and Judaean History, pp. 332-33, 335.

78   Mayes, p. 314-15, 323-24.

79   Frank Moore Cross, Jr., Canaanite Myth and Hebrew Epic: Essays in the History and Religion of Israel (Cambridge: Harvard University Press, 1973), pp. 219-22; and Pedersen, 3-4, 43-46.

80   The accounts of Saul's election as king vary considerably: in the folktale of 1 Sam. 9:1-10:16, Samuel anoints Saul as king (but note the use of "nāgîd" rather than "melek"); in 1 Sam. 10:17-27, Saul is elected king through the casting of lots; and in 1 Sam. 11:1-15, the Gilgal tradition, Saul is made king after his victory over the Ammonites.

81   For a discussion of the ambiguous nature of the "sins" which caused Saul to be rejected by God and Samuel, see David M. Gunn, The Fate of King Saul: An Interpretation of a Biblical Story, JSOT Supplement Series 14 (Sheffield, England: JSOT Press, 1980), pp. 23-56.

82   It is not clear from the Hebrew whose robe was torn, but in view of Samuel's subsequent interpretation in v. 28, and the description of a similar action in 1 Kg. 11:29-32, one should probably understand the action as Samuel tearing Saul's robe in a symbolic gesture of rejection. So with Ackroyd, pp. 128-29; and William McKane, I and II Samuel: Introduction and Commentary (London: SCM Press, 1963), pp. 102-3; but contra Hertzberg, Samuel, pp. 122, 128. See also the discussion below, p. 205 and note 144; and Gunn, pp. 93-95, 153-54, on the sexual overtones of this action.

83   Gunn's work on the Saul narratives makes a convincing case for a more substantial reading of these stories in and of themselves, while also demonstrating the importance of the

"rejection" of Saul (and the institution of the monarchy) for understanding the subsequent change of attitude on the part of God toward the monarchy, with David as the freely chosen king bestowed upon the people by God. In essence, Saul is an unwitting victim of Yahweh's "jealousy" and anger at the people's rejection of divine kingship in their request for a human king. Only because the first attempt at the establishment of the monarchy has failed, thus soothing God's anger, can David become a king pleasing to the Lord, capable of being described as a "man after his own heart," God's favorite. See Gunn, pp. 65-73, 115-16, 124-128.

84   Ackroyd, p. 132; and Martin Kessler, "Narrative Technique in 1 Sam. 16, 1-13," CBQ 32 (1970) : 552. Von Rad comments that "in this story we are already listening to a late interpretation, one which introduces the Davidic dynasty into a set of concepts which was originally alien to it, namely the antecedent designation of Jahweh's elected by a prophet" (OTT, 1:309). Eissfeldt attributes this pericope to the later "Elohistic" source (Introduction, p. 272), while Artur Weiser (The Old Testament: Its Formation and Development, trans. Dorothea M. Barton [New York: Association Press, 1961]) ascribes it to that group of writings which reflect prophetic reinterpretation of history along theological lines (pp. 166-67, 170); so also Sellin-Fohrer (p. 225). John Mauchline tends toward this interpretation, although he does not discount the possibility that David may actually have been anointed at this time (1 and 1 Samuel, NCC [London: Oliphants, 1971], pp. 26, 31). Hertzberg, however, does not press the late character of the pericope, but relates it originally to a Bethlehemite tradition which came to be associated with the Gilgal complex of traditions (Samuel, p. 136).

85   von Rad, OTT, 1:309; Kessler, p. 552; and Ashley S. Rose, "The Principles of Divine Election: Wisdom in I Samuel 16," in Rhetorical Criticism: Essays in Honor of James Muilenburg, ed. Jared J. Jackson and Martin Kessler, Pittsburgh Theological Monograph Series, no. 1 (Pittsburgh: Pickwick Press, 1974), pp. 60-61.

86   Ackroyd, pp. 131-32; Hertzberg, Samuel, pp. 125, 136; Kessler, p. 546; Rose, p. 44. The major literary ties to Chapter 15 lie in the use of the verb "wayyōʼmer" to link what follows to the preceding narrative (15:36, waYHWH niḥām kî himlîk ʼet-šāʼûl ʽal-yiśrāʼēl), along with the use of the verbs "māʼas" (cf. 15:23, 26) and "hitʼabbēl" (repeated from 15:35: kî-hitʼabbēl šᵉmûʼēl ʼel-šāʼûl). The importance of the use of "mitʼabbēl" in 16:1 is heightened by its

introduction by the rhetorical ^cad-mātay.

87   Both passages contain the following motifs: the secret choice; Yahweh's direct indication of his choice at the occasion of meeting, anointing by Samuel; the dutiful son; comments on the physical appearance of the chosen one; sacrifice (9:12; 16:2); and "inversion" or paradox (in 1 Sam. 9:3-10:16, the exasperating search for the lost she-asses leads to the finding of the kingdom; in 16:1-13, the young shepherd not deemed worthy of mention becomes the shepherd of the people of Israel). For a discussion of the "shepherd" motif, see Kessler, p. 550, n. 37.

88   David as Yahweh's true choice, as the lovely and accomplished youth, the shepherd, the dutiful son, one with whom the Lord is (16:13), etc.

89   Rose, pp. 44-45, 47. The divine addresses occur in vv. 2b-3, 7, and 12b; the corresponding human responses are found in vv. 8-12a, and 13a. Verses 1-2, and 13b are characterized as introductory and concluding formulae, respectively.

90   Ibid., pp. 43, 47, 66-67. See discussion below under "Proverb Situation" and "Context Situation."

91   So with S. R. Driver, Notes on the Hebrew Text and the Topography of the Books of Samuel, 2nd ed. (Oxford: Clarendon Press, 1966), p. 133; Rudolf Kittel, ed., "Librum Samuelis," in: Biblia Hebraica, 3rd ed. (Stuttgart: Wurtembergische Bibelanstalt, 1937), p. 429; and Myles M. Bourke, ed., Textual Notes on the New American Bible (New York: P. J. Kennedy, 1970), p. 345.

92   The wisdom scholar is, of course, delighted to discover that the ancient author might conceive of Yahweh communicating with humans through proverbs and sayings. While the characterization of Yahweh as "sage" may not seem as impressive as Yahweh as divine warrior or convenant lord, the celebration of God's wisdom and desire to teach humans may be found in a number of places, and in the Psalms, this motif takes on salvific overtones (see Pss. 25; 51:6; 71:17; 73:24; 86; 94; 119:33-34; 143:10). This thought reaches its culmination in the writings of Ben Sira (cf. Sir. 17; 18:1-14; 42:18-21; 43:23), although it is Elihu who gives expression to this conception of God when he exclaims, "Behold, God is exalted in his power; who is a teacher like him?" (Job 36:22).

93   For a discussion of the Israelite conception of God, see Walther Eichrodt, Theology of the Old Testament, trans. J. A. Baker, 2 vols. (Philadelphia: Westminster Press, 1961), 1:

206-88, especially, pp. 210-14. Of course, this recognition of Yahweh's "otherness" may be comforting, as well as terrifying, as can be seen in Hosea's understanding that the one who is Wholly Other is the Holy Other as well (11:8-9):

> "How can I give you up, O Ephraim!
> > How can I hand you over, O Israel!
> How can I make you like Admah!
> > How can I treat you like Zeboiim!
> My heart recoils within me,
> > my compassion grows warm and tender.
> I will not execute my fierce anger,
> > I will not again destroy Ephraim;
> For I am God and not man ($w^e l \bar{o}$-'îš),
> > the Holy One in your midst,
> > and I will not come to destroy."

94   As Gunn has shown, the question of Saul's "sin" and guilt is a matter of interpretation, due to the ambiguity of the commands given or the exact manner in which they are to be carried out (pp. 55-56). Samuel chooses to find Saul guilty of superficial compliance; in our passage, we see a structural repetition of this move, as Yahweh chooses and reprimands Samuel for his superficial choice of Eliab. The present author is in agreement with Gunn that Yahweh's treatment of Saul and David is "less than impartial" (Gunn, p. 73).

95   Eissfeldt, Maschal, p. 46. Sellin-Fohrer refers to this saying as one of those which may "illumine religious situations" (p. 311). Old Testament scholars are no doubt hesitant to characterize this passage as a "folk proverb" (with all the implications of "origin" which that genre designation currently carries) because of its bilinear form, which is considered by so many to be a "later" wisdom form which may have developed out of the popular proverb. This presupposition, along with the stigma attached to the pericope because of its "late" date, has caused scholars to give the saying less consideration than it deserves. An example of this may be seen in Martin Kessler's otherwise insightful rhetorical study of the pericope, which makes no mention whatsoever of the fact that v. 7 exhibits striking similarities to wisdom forms (pp. 549-50). Once again, such considerations concerning origin and the suitablility of religious content to the "folk" need not deter us in our analysis.

96   Weiser, p. 40.

97   Hermisson, pp. 43-44. Presumably, by "wisdom

influence" here, Hermisson means that contact with representatives of the wisdom circle in Jerusalem influenced the forms used by the author of the pericope. This is by no means clear from his discussion, however. For a discussion of the general confusion in the discussion of "wisdom influence," see James L. Crenshaw, "Method in Determining Wisdom Influence upon 'Historical' Literature," JBL 88 (1969) : 129-42; reprinted in: SAIW, pp. 481-94.

98   See note 95 above.

99   This sentence pattern roughly corresponds to Hermisson's "zusammengesetzter Nominalsatz" (zN), which he adapted in part from the "x-yiqtol" or "maru" pattern (Hermisson, pp. 141-44, 157-59). One type of the zN form places the subject first in casus pendens, with the remainder of the sentence (either a nominal [NS] or verbal sentence [VS] acting as a predicate for the subject. For Hermisson, the NS form is the basic one found in the proverbial literature, and the zN, in that it presents an inversion which stresses the subject, actually represents a "nuance" of the nominal sentence (p. 143). For an example of a zN/x-yiqtol sentence in the Book of Proverbs, see 17:22.

100   Pr. 16:9 may be diagrammed structurally as follows:

A (N - V - O)   lēb ʾādām   yᵉḥaššēb   darkô
= B (N - V - O) wa   YHWH   yākîn   ṣaᶜadô

Other parallels to this architectural formula may be found in Pr. 11:16; 13:6; 12:23; 15:14, 18, 28; and elsewhere.

101   See Gen, 8:21; Is. 7:18; Pss. 2:4; 37:13; etc. For the attribution of human limbs and organs to Yahweh, see Gen. 3:8, 32:31; Num. 11:1; 1 Sam. 5:11; 2 Kg. 19:16; Ps. 8:4, etc.

102   Eichrodt, 1:214-15; cf. Dt. 4:15; Num. 23:19; Ps. 121:4; Is. 40:18; Ezek. 28:2, 9; etc.

103   Wolff, Anthropology, pp. 161-62. The overtones of creatureliness - that "hāʾādām" comes from and must return to "hāʲᵃdāmāh - are implicit in the use of the term here in a saying which contrasts creature with creator.

104   See Pr. 16:31; 17:28; 20:11, 29; Ec. 8:1b, 11:5; Sir. 13:25. In the Book of Job, one of the problems posed revolves around the fact that Job's friends feel forced to conclude that he is indeed guilty of something, based on the external evidence that he is being punished (cf. Job 8:4; 22:5-20, etc.). See also von Rad's discussion of knowledge and the limits of wisdom in Wisdom in Israel, pp. 53-73, 97-110.

105   In our text, "lēbāb" is preferred to the more common "lēb," no doubt for the sake of metrical balance.

106   Wolff, Anthropology, p. 43.

107   Ibid.   106   Pedersen, 1-2:102.
109   Wolff, Anthropology, pp. 44-55.
110   Most significantly, it is "in his heart" that the "fool" makes his characteristic statement, "There is no God" (Ps. 14:1).
111   See also Ps. 137; Job 28:24; etc.
112   Job, of course, is using this concept to further his own argument: if God cannot look through human eyes, "can he really understand and sympathize with man's predicament?" (Marvin Pope, Job: Introduction, Translation and Notes, AB 15, 3rd ed. (Garden City, N.Y.: Doubleday & Co., 1973), p. 80. From a New Testament perspective at least, we may assume that Job's point was well taken.
113   For similar proverbs, see also Pr. 15:3; 16:2, 33; 17:3; 20:27; 22:12. The picture of God "weighing" the heart may be developed, at least in part, from the Egyptian belief that the heart of the deceased was weighed by the god Thoth against the weight of "maᶜat" (cosmic truth and order) during judgment in the underworld after death (Scott, Way, p. 33).
114   ANET, p. 429.
115   Ibid., p. 434. See also stanza 6 of the "Babylonian Theodicy" (Lambert, BWL, p. 75).
116   Ibid., pp. 417, 423.
117   From the broader perspective of the probable late composition of this pericope, the intent of the author/redactor was probably to show the first Davidic monarch being anointed by a divine representative (von Rad, OTT, 1:309). Kenneth R. R. Gros Louis has suggested that the key to this passage, and, indeed, to all of the stories concerning David, may be found in the inner/outer contrast expressed in our traditional saying. For Gros Louis, this contrast actually refers to the differences between David the public leader and David the private individual. Whenever the desires or actions of the one overlap with those of the other, David fails to resolve the conflicts appropriately, as is so apparent in the Succession Narrative. See Kenneth R. R. Gros Louis, "The Difficulty of Ruling Well: King David of Israel," Semeia 8 (1977) : 18-20.
118   Wolff judges, on the basis of archaeological evidence from Gezer, that the average Israelite male was probably around 5 feet 6 inches (c.1.68 metres) in height (Anthropology, p. 69).
119   Pedersen, 1-2: 171.
120   Kessler, p. 548.
121   For a discussion of the nature and use of the vetitive

(*al + jussive), see Wolfgang Richter, *Recht und Ethos: Versuch einer Ortung des weisheitlichen Mahnspruches,* StANT 15 (München: Kösel-Verlag, 1966), pp. 39, 48, 71, 145, 182-83. Richter believes that this form found heavy use in didactic circles, and was directed toward concrete, specific circumstances, rather than toward abstract or timeless generalized formulation of standards for conduct. The motivations supplied for the form may be drawn from rational, historical or theological arguments. When the form is found in narrative materials, Richter feels that it represents not so much a literary device of an author, as an actual reflection of patterns of communication found in social interactions (p. 148).

122   Eliab's little-minded behavior in 1 Sam. 17:28-30 shows that he was probably a poor choice for the new leader.

123   See note 91, above.

124   *Romeo and Juliet,* act 3, sc. 2, line 73.

125   The other major character in the Book of Samuel noted for his beautiful appearance is Absalom (2 Sam. 14:25), but, in his case as well, the external criteria which might lead one to favor his claim are insufficient to take the rule from David.

126   Richter, p. 71.

127   Ezekiel attributes "counsel" to the elders rather than to the wise (Ezek. 7:26).

128   The Hebrew is a bit unusual, but the meaning - that David is in no way an "ugly duckling" - is clear. Cf. also 1 Sam. 17:42.

129   1 Sam. 17:38-39 mentions that David had difficulty in wearing Saul's armour. We may assume that this is not only because he was not used to it, but also because of some difference in size between the two. The rejection of the armour has also a symbolic significance: "The incident of the armour points up the fact that Saul's way is not David's way" (Gunn, p. 79).

130   Pr. 21:31: "The horse is made ready for the day of battle, but the victory is from the Lord."

131   See note 86, above.

132   Note that all verse numbers cited for this pericope will follow the MT, with the English RSV number given immediately following in parenthesis.

133   Folk elements may be seen in the popular etymology of "Wildgoat's Rocks," v. 3 (2); the young hero and his small band of "merry men" driven into hiding by the older, greater force; the use of a cave as the setting for the action;

biological needs as a source of amusement and momentary exposure (sic) to weakness; the torn garment; and proverbial images drawn from the natural world (dog, flea in v. 16 [14]).

134   The following locations are given as the places to which David flees: Naioth (1 Sam. 19:19); Nob (1 Sam. 21:2); Gath (1 Sam. 21:10); and Adullam (1 Sam. 22:1); etc.

135   Critics generally agree that chapters 24 and 26 represent "alternative" accounts (Ackroyd, p. 202; Bentzen, 2:93; McKane, Samuel, p. 22; Sellin-Fohrer, p. 221). Eissfeldt views the two accounts as variants within the J source (Introduction, p. 274), while Hertzberg sees them as having been greatly shaped by their transmissions in different localities (Samuel, p. 243). Weiser sets these narratives within his Group II, "Comprehensive accounts based on existing traditions" (p. 169), but understands the various duplications with the "Saul and David" cycles as "accretions from oral traditions" (ibid.). Mauchline finds "no difficulty in supposing that there may have been two occasions, in different circumstances, when David spared Saul's life," and views both narratives as reflecting different incidents despite their similarities (p. 173).

136   So with Driver, p. 204, and Mauchline, p. 173. Note that both accounts not only stress David's "magnanimity," but also his respect, whether real or feigned, for Saul as the "Lord's anointed" (1 Sam. 24:7, 9, 11 [6, 8, 10]; 1 Sam. 26:9, 11, 16, 24). The obvious climax in both pericopes occurs when Saul himself is represented as acknowledging David's position as his successor (1 Sam. 24:21-22 (20-21); 1 Sam. 26:25). So with Hertzberg, Samuel, p. 241.

137   One might comment of this ironic turn of events that "A man's mind plans his way, but the Lord directs his steps" (Pr. 16:9).

138   See above, p. 97 and note 82.

139   D. J. Wiseman reports a similar symbolic act, mentioned in the Alalakh Tablets, Level VII, where "... 'to seize (or let go) the hem of a garment' ... denotes the giving of unreserved submission to (or defection from) a person, which may imply that David's act in cutting of the 'wing' or hem of Saul's garment was an act of rebellion for which he was later repentant." See D. J. Wiseman, "Alalakh," in: Archaeology and Old Testament Study," ed. D. Winton Thomas (Oxford: Clarendon Press, 1969), p. 128. For the sexual, and hence "dynastic" significance of this act, see Gunn, pp. 94-95.

140   McKane, Samuel, pp. 148-49. So, too, Julian Lewy, in

"Les textes paléo-assyriens et l'Ancien Testament," Revue de l'Histoire des Religions 110 (1934) : 29-65. Lewy points out that in Assyrian and Babylonian culture, the hem of one's garment "represents the personality, the freedom, and the rights of a person" (p. 32). Thus, we find the image surfacing in customs having to do with marriage, payment of debts, and legal disputes, and the hem of a garment is cut off in rituals of exorcism and divorce. For this reason, David's symbolic act is a significant one which, in effect, dispossesses Saul of all he cares for, and David is properly regretful after the deed has been done, but attempts to mitigate the effect of his act by paying homage to Saul and putting a more favorable construction on his actions (pp. 31-33).

141   Mauchline, p. 25.

142   The other three traditional sayings identified as "māshāl" in the text are 1 Sam. 10:12 (1 Sam. 19:24), Ezek. 12:22, and Ezek. 18:2 (Jer. 31:29).

143   Eissfeldt, Maschal, p. 45. See also Ackroyd, p. 188; Crenshaw, "Wisdom," pp. 230-31; McKane (Samuel, p. 145), who understands this as an "aphorism" as opposed to his more paradigmatic understanding of "māshāl" as a genre; Mauchline, p. 165; Murphy, "Interpretation," p. 300; R. B. Y. Scott, "Folk Proverbs," p. 418, and Way, p. 64; Sellin-Fohrer, p. 311.

144   Budde, p. 162; H. P. Smith, p. 218; and Julius Wellhausen, Der Text der Bücher Samuelis (Göttingen: Vandenhoeck und Ruprecht, 1871), p. 130.

145   Hermisson, p. 41. Presumably, the interpretation of v. 14 as a legal declaration rests on the connection with v. 13 ("May the Lord judge between me and you ..."), which is reminiscent of Gen. 16:15b; 31:53.

146   This is no doubt the reason why some feel that 14a may be a later addition to the text. However, it has been clearly shown that this "inappropriate" or "out-of-context" appearance of a saying in contexts of use is a fairly consistent feature of proverb use, and may even function as one of the means for the identification of a saying rather than as an indication of a gloss.

147   Wisdom in the ancient world was regularly attributed to the "ancients" or the "forefathers." See Job 8:8; "The Maxims of Ptahhotep" and the "Instruction for King Merikare" (W. K. Simpson, pp. 160, 182), etc.

148   See also Pr. 18:20. Note, too, that Pr. 12:14 also conforms to the larger structure of the architectural formula:

A → B		A → B	
min + N	V N	mipp^{e}rî pî-'îs	yiśba^c ṭôb
w N	V PP	û g^{e}mûl y^{e}dê-'ādām yāšîb lô	

The two bicola here form a synonymous rather than an antithetic statement, as in 1 Sam. 24:14 (13).

149   The translation for K 4347 is taken from ANET, p. 425; the translation for Ptahhotep is taken from W. K. Simpson, p. 174.

150   McKane, Proverbs, p. 28.

151   As Job comments, although in a different context (referring to the human condition of perpetual impurity), "Who can bring a clean thing out of an unclean?" (Job 14:4). It should be noted, however, that many commentators consider this verse problematic, and Marvin Pope prefers to delete it altogether (Job, p. 106). The message (and hence the worldview which underlies it), however, is essentially the same as that under discussion here.

152   See also Mt. 7:16-18: "You will know them by their fruits. Are grapes gathered from thorns, or figs from thistles? So, every sound tree bears good fruit, but the bad tree bears evil fruit. A sound tree cannot bear evil fruit, nor can a bad tree bear good fruit."

153   Such a worldview is evident in such sayings as "The north wind brings forth rain; and a backbiting tongue, angry looks" (Pr. 25:23) and "As charcoal to hot embers and wood to fire, so is a quarrelsome man for kindling strife" (26:21).

154   So with Murphy, "Theses," pp. 194-95.

155   See Pr. 11:24; 13:7; 14:12; 16:26; 17:28; 18:17; 19:2b; 20:14, 17; etc.

156   So with Ackroyd, p. 189.

157   Such a statement shows that David's action in cutting Saul's robe is viewed as having dynastic consequences, and, as such, is less innocuous than David might have Saul - and the audience - believe.

158   The MT reads for v. 6, " ... ^{c}al 'ašer kārat 'et-kānāp 'ašer l^{e}šā'ûl." "Most commentators read with the versions and insert "hamm^{ec}îl" after "knp."

159   See 2 Sam. 1:11-16; 2 Sam. 9; 2 Sam. 19:16-30; 2 Sam. 21:1-41.

160   So with Pedersen, 3-4:56-61; and see also note 155.

161   H. P. Smith, p. 218. This is scarcely an adequate understanding of the message of the saying in its present context.

162   So McKane, Proverbs, pp. 27-29. Mauchline similarly points to the "unsuitable" use of the saying if it does apply to Saul, but recognizes that it is perfectly reasonable to assume that David is applying it to himself (p. 165), as does Hertzberg (Samuel, p. 197).

163   Such "indirection" acts as a shield for a later glossator (if there is one) as well. One might well conceive of a general reluctance to concede that David was either totally innocent or totally at fault in his encounters with Saul; the ambiguity of the saying may provide a method of resolving this ambivalence. The tradition may prefer to let events speak for themselves: David may not have been guiltless throughout his life, but he did not kill Saul, even though Saul had made attempts on his life.

164   Wisdom, of course, was well aware of the problems encountered in dealing with a monarch: "The dread wrath of a king is like the growling of a lion; he who provokes him to anger forfeits his life" (Pr. 20:2); and "A king's wrath is a messenger of death, and a wise man will appease it" (Pr. 16:14). See also Pr. 16:13 and 19:12.

165   Obviously, Saul is responding to David's strategy as though the "truth" claim in a saying were absolute, rather than relative and contextually conditioned.

166   See Chapter II, p. 60.

167   W. K. Simpson, p. 161; The Sayings of Confucius, arranged and illustrated by E. A. Cox (London: Chiswick Press, 1946), p. 60; Chinua Achebe, Arrow of God (London: Heinemann, 1964), p. 25; N. B. Sen, ed., Wit and Wisdom of Gandhi, Nehru, Tagore (New Delhi: New Book Society of India, 1968), p. 494; Donald R. Gorham, "A Proverbs Text for Clinical and Experimental Use," Psychological Reports 2 (1956): 5; Quotations from Chairman Mao Tse-Tung, ed. Stuart R. Schram with an Introduction by A. Doak Barnett (New York: Bantam Books, 1967), p. 97.

168   Robert Gordis, "Quotations in Wisdom Literature," JQR 30 (1939/40) : 123-47 (reprinted in: SAIW, pp. 235-37); Messenger, pp. 303-7. The two Anang sayings cited - although virtually unintelligible to Western readers as they stand - were used by the plaintiff and defendant respectively in a trial context to decide a case of assault with a machete. The plaintiff claimed that his former friend had attacked him during an argument, and thus he was like the smoke which

normally remains within the hut unless displaced (i.e., he would not be lodging a complaint against his friend unless something had actually happened). The defendant countered with an animal proverb which cites the habits of the common bush leopard which conceals its spots beneath a second coat of fur (much like the coats of the domestic Abyssinian and Russian Blue) when it is stalking its prey. The implication is that the plaintiff was concealing his true motives of ill will toward the defendant beneath a mask of injured friendship. The elders of the tribe, apparently feeling that it was a case of "he who quotes last, quotes best," decided in favor of the defendant.

169 W. K. Simpson, pp. 42-43; ANET, p. 489; Gordis, "Wisdom," p. 237; Lambert, pp. 281-82 (cf. ANET, p. 426); Mao, p. 123 (cf. pp. 124, 130-31); J. R. R. Tolkien, The Lord of the Rings, vol. 1: The Fellowship of the Ring (New York: Ballantine Books, 1965), p. 128.

170 Ibid. It might be noted that although Chairman Mao occasionally uses proverbs to point up a contrast between the desired state of affairs and what actually exists, his favorite use of proverbs by far is the citation of ancient wisdom as authoritative, which he uses to settle official party disputes, exhort the youth to greater diligence and perseverance, and ridicule capitalists and reactionaries (Mao, pp. 41, 43, 70, 119, 148-149).

171 So with Eichrodt, 2:147.

172 Wolff, Anthropology, p. 67.

173 Ibid., p. 68.

174 Sigmund Mowinckel, "General Oriental and Specific Israelite Elements in the Israelite Conception of the Sacral Kingdom," in: La Regalità Sacra, Studies in the History of Religions (Supplements to Numen), no. 4 (Leiden: E. J. Brill, 1959), pp. 283-90.

175 Ibid., p. 290.

176 Aubrey R. Johnson, Sacral Kingship in Ancient Israel (Cardiff, Wales: University of Wales Press, 1955), p. 15.

177 So with Ackroyd, p. 188; Hertzberg, Samuel, pp. 197-98; McKane, Samuel, p. 149; Mauchline, p. 167; Pedersen, 3-4:54-56.

178 Arvid S. Kapelrud, "King David and the Sons of Saul," in: La Regalità Sacra, p. 301.

179 So Bentzen, 2:94-95; and McKane, Samuel, p. 149.

180 Eichrodt, 1:264.

181 That is, the "act-consequence" relationship, which appears here in a slight transformation as "essence-

consequences in action."

182   This particularly is true of the treatment given to the early Omrides of Israel, especially Omri, whose brilliant and successful reign is dismissed in a mere six verses (1 Kg. 16:23-28). See A. Weiser, p. 173; and C. F. Whitley, "The Deuteronomic Presentation of the House of Omri," VT 2 (1952) : 137.

183   See John Gray, I & II Kings: A Commentary, 2nd ed., rev. (Philadelphia: Westminster Press; London: SCM Press, 1970), p. 415; J. Maxwell Miller, "The Elisha Cycle and the Accounts of the Omride Wars," JBL 85 (1966) : 443; Benjamin Mazar, "The Aramean Empire and its Relations with Israel," BA 25 (1962) : 106. For dating of the battles in 1 Kg. 20 and 22, and their possible motivations, see Gray, Kings, p. 415; William W. Hallo, "From Qarqar to Carchemish: Assyria and Israel in the Light of New Discoveries," in: The Biblical Archaeologist Reader 2, ed. Edward F. Campbell, Jr. and David Noel Freedman (Garden City, N.Y.: Doubleday & Co., Anchor Books, 1964), p. 160; and John Skinner, Kings, NCB (New York: Henry Frowde, 1904), p. 244.

184   This reordering of the chapters in question, (17, 18, 19, 21, 20, 22) reflects the order found in the LXX. However, certain literary considerations concerning the traditions in chapters 20 and 22, along with the difficulties of harmonizing the biblical accounts with the records of Shalmaneser III's battle of Qarqar and the identification of "Ben-hadad," have caused some to place the actual conflict with Aram during the reigns of the Jehu dynasty.

Aside from the historical difficulties mentioned above, it should be noted that the conflicting account of Ahab's death and the similarity of the battle account of Ramoth-Gilead in 1 Kg. 22 to that found in 2 Kg. 3 have led Miller and others to seriously question the identification of the "king of Israel" in 1 Kg. 20; 22 with Ahab. See J. Maxwell Miller, "The Fall of the House of Ahab," VT 17 (1967) : pp. 312-13; idem, "Omride Wars," pp. 444-47, 450; and Whitley, "Omri," pp. 144-48. The evaluation of Ahab's identification with the "king of Israel" as secondary is followed by Johannes Fichtner, Das Erste Buch von den Königen, BAT, Band 12/1 (Stuttgart: Calwer Verlag, 1964), p. 297; Gray, in his revised commentary (Kings, pp. 30, 414-16); and H. Donner (p. 400).

185   Sellin-Fohrer, p. 232. Fichtner also supports the grounding in an historical event, even if Ahab is not the Israelite participant (Königen, pp. 294-97). For the purposes of our analysis, we will follow the biblical identification of

Ahab with the king of Israel of 1 Kg. 20, although this identification must be viewed as questionable on literary and historical grounds. Attempts will be made as we progress to interpret the incidence of proverb performance in the text both with respect to the probable relationship between Ahab and Hadadezer, as well as that between Jehoahaz/Joash and Ben-hadad III, son of Hazael.

186   Donner, pp. 413-14.

187   Ibid. These assessments are made on the basis of Ahab's showing of military might at Qarqar, and the depredations on Israel's strength which Hazael's continual harassment of the northern kingdom must have made during the later period in which one might set these events.

188   Gray, Kings, p. 422.

189   Hayim Tadmor, "Assyria and the West: the Ninth Century and its Aftermath," in: Unity and Diversity: Essays in the History, Literature and Religion of the Ancient Near East, ed. Hans Goedicke and J. J. M. Roberts (Baltimore: John Hopkins University Press, 1975), p. 37.

190   Eissfeldt, Maschal, p. 46. See also, Bentzen, 1:168; Crenshaw, "Wisdom," p. 230; Fichtner, Königen, p. 304; Gray, Kings, p. 423; Montgomery, p. 322; Robinson, p. 227; Scott, "Folk Proverbs," p. 420; idem. Way, p. 64; Sellin-Fohrer, p. 311; Skinner, p. 247; and Weiser, p. 40. Hermisson, on the other hand, concludes that although the saying may be of popular origin, it is not a true proverb (Sprichwort), on the basis of its form (vetitive rather than that of an Aussage) and function (a Streit or taunt before battle), p. 43.

191   Eissfeldt, Maschal, p. 50.

192   Roger Fowler, An Introduction to Transformational Syntax (New York: Barnes & Noble, 1971), pp. 72-73.

193   For a full discussion of the structure of causal oppositional (negative causational) sayings, see Alan Dundes, "Structure," p. 113.

194   Ibid. Of course, not all negative causational contrastive sayings result from chronological displacement. Some, such as "You can lead a horse to water, but you can't make him drink," result from some opposition between logical cause and effect (i.e., the cause - leading a horse to water - does not necessarily produce ($\nrightarrow$) the desired effect - making the horse drink. In theory, any binary opposition should be able to serve as the "Baukern" of a negative causational contrastive saying.

195   There is considerable debate over the best type of structural description for sentences which involve negation

(NEG), imperatives (IMP), interrogatives (Q), and adverbs and adverbial phrases (ADV, AdvP). Roger Fowler, for example, treats the basic rearrangements involved in Q's, NEGs, and IMPs "provisionally" as "moods"; that is, as expressions of a certain type of orientation on the part of the user toward the proposition of the sentence. Thus, he locates them as elements of the grammatical category AUX (auxiliary), which also contains the options of Aspect, Voice, and Tense - only the latter of which is an "obligatory" element (i.e., Tense is the only member of AUX which <u>must</u> be present in all sentences in a given language). See Fowler's discussion, pp. 72-73, as well as the work of Bent Jacobsen in: Transformational - Generative Grammar: an Introductory Survey of its Genesis and Development, North Holland Linguistic Series (Amsterdam: North Holland Publishing Company, 1977), pp. 74-112.

Adverbs, especially those of manner (MAN), and adverbial phrases present similar problems in conceptualization, since it is possible to argue with equal validity (at least in current transformational- generative grammars) that an ADV or AdvP (1) presents an orientation toward the PredP (Fowler, pp. 42-44); or (2) presents an orientation toward the sentence (S) as a whole (i.e., to the verb <u>and</u> the subject which it predicates). For a discussion of the latter view, see Robert P. Stockwell, Foundations of Syntactic Theory (Englewood Cliffs, N.J.: Prentice-Hall, 1977), pp. 42-48. Thus, in certain constructions, one may view the AdvP as a "constituent" string which is embedded in the nuclear phrase-structure of the S (Fowler, pp. 44, 123). On the other hand, there is still a good deal of discussion as to whether ADVs should be generated at the level of deep structure of the S or derived by the application of T-rules (transformational rules) to underlying phrase structure. For a discussion of this and related problems, see Jacobsen, pp. 103-5, 122-123; and Noam Chomsky, Aspects of the Theory of Syntax (Cambridge, Mass.: M.I.T. Press, 1965), pp. 102-6.

Since our "architectural formula" represents the <u>syntactic</u> interpretation of the semantic relationships found in our "Type" designation (identification or contrastive), it is appropriate to mention, at least briefly, the structural syntactic components which actualize the semantic structure (e.g., $A = B \Rightarrow A \nleftrightarrow B$) in a given syntactical concatenation ($A \nleftrightarrow B \Rightarrow VET + A + ADV$ (MAN) B). The current explanation of IMP sentences found in transformational- generative grammars (TGG) is to understand the actual imperative sentence as an embedded Nominal Phrase (NP) which serves as the object of a sentence "I command you-that-NP." This kernel sentence exists in the deep structure, since the T-rule of "deletion" ($\emptyset$) has been applied to the nuclear phrase structure. For full discussion, see Fowler, pp. 110-12; Jacobsen, pp. 311-19; and Stockwell, pp. 174-79. See also Appendix B: Figure #12 presents a full diagram of the deep structure of 1 Kg. 20:11.

196   This expansion of the admonition of a motivation is roughly equivalent to the transformational "rewrite" rule of "adjunction."

197   Pr. 3:25-26 is an example of the vetitive expanded by the adjunction of an explicit motivation, introduced by "kî":

> Do not be afraid (ʾal-tîrāʾ) of sudden panic,
> or of the wicked when it comes;
> for (kî) the Lord will be your confidence
> and will keep your foot from being caught.

198   See 1 Sam. 17:39; 25:13; Jg. 18:11; Is. 45:1, etc. Our knowledge of Israelite weaponry, especially armor, is limited. It is possible that a "hagôrāh," girdle-sash, was used to tie on a breastplate. Gray suggests that the terms may refer to "putting on one's girdle in the morning and removing it at night" (Kings, p. 423). The Lucianic recension of the LXX has apparently misread the later Hebrew "ḥiggēr" ("lame") for "ḥōgēr" ("one who girds on") and is then forced to interpolate an antithetical reading for "mᵉpatteāḥ." The Greek then reads "mê kauchasthô hô kurtos hôs hô orthos" which totally misses the point of the saying. The Targum Jonathan has properly understood the referents of the saying, but has expanded the saying to make the message clearer, reading "Let not him who is girding himself and going down into the battle boast himself as the man who has conquered and is coming up from it" (lʾ ystbḥ dmzdrn wnḥt bqrbʾ kgbrʾ dnṣḥ wslyq mnyh). See Charles Fox Burney, Notes on the Hebrew Text of the Books of Kings (Oxford: Clarendon Press, 1903), p. 233.

199   E. Kautzsch, ed., Gesenius' Hebrew Grammar, trans. Arthur E. Cowley, 2nd. English ed. (Oxford: Oxford University Press, 1910), p. 150.

200   Edmund I. Gordon, Sumerian Proverbs: Glimpses of Everyday Life in Ancient Mesopotamia, Museum Monographs (Philadelphia: University of Pennsylvania Press; The University Museum, 1959), p. 150.

201   Miriam Lichtheim, Ancient Egyptian Literature, vol. 1: The Old and Middle Kingdom (Berkeley: University of California Press, 1975), p. 60.

202   Idem, Ancient Egyptian Literature, vol. 2: The New Kingdom (Berkeley: University of California Press, 1975), p. 151. See also the "Instruction of Prince Hordedef," in ANET, p. 419.

203   Skinner, p. 244.

204   So with Theophile J. Meek, "1 Kings 20:1-11: Critical Notes," JBL 78 (1959) : 73-75; he reads:

(3) ... "Thus says Ben-hadad: 'Your silver and gold belong to me; your wives and dearest children belong to me.' " (4) The king of Israel answered, "As you say, my lord, O king, I belong to you and all that I have." (5) The messengers came again and said, "Thus says Ben-hadad: 'I send to you to say, "You must give me your silver and gold, your wives and children; (6) for if I have to send my men to you at this time tomorrow, they shall ransack your house and the houses of your courtiers, and everything that you delight in they shall lay hands on and carry off." ' " (7) Then the king of Israel summoned all the elders of the land and said, "Note now, and see how this fellow is looking for trouble; for he has sent to me for my wives and children, for my silver and gold, and should I not withhold them from him?" (8) Whereupon all the elders and all the people said to him, "Pay no heed; you must not consent." (9) So he said to the messengers of Ben-hadad, "Say to my lord the king, 'All that you first demanded of your servant I am doing, but this thing I cannot do' " (p.74).

This reading makes a good deal more sense out of Ahab's responses in v. 9, which are meaningless otherwise, since Ahab obviously did not send his gold, silver, wives and children in response to Ben-hadad's first message. However, Gray has suggested that Ahab responds to the first demand by admitting vassal status and willingness to pay tribute, but the second demand, which calls for Ahab to give up his family as hostages (perhaps to assure Israel's good faith in an alliance), and to submit to the highhanded treatment of Ben-hadad's servants, is too great an insult to be accepted (Kings, pp. 422-23). Skinner (contra Wellhausen's emendation of v. 3 to read "but thy wives and children are thine") has suggested that the contrast in demands reflects the demand first for Ahab's personal resources, and second, for the surrender of the whole city (thus explaining the elders' participation in the council), which Ahab refuses (pp. 245-46). So, too, Montgomery, p. 321 and Robinson, p. 227.

205   The image is not altogether clear. The LXX has apparently revocalized the MT "šeᶜālîm" ("handfuls") as šūᶜālîm ("for foxes") thus creating an image of ruins which

are insufficient even to provide homes for small animals. See Gray, Kings, p. 419; and Montgomery, p. 321.

206   If we set this battle with Ahab's reign, before the Battle of Qarqar in 853 B.C.E., the madnesses of allowing a long-drawn siege are even more acute. With Shalmaneser III's continued advances into western Syria-Palestine, Ahab and Hadadezer, both fine military commanders, as their performance at Qarqar shows, would have recognized the need not to waste their energy and resources fighting each other when it was clear that the future would bring conflicts with Assyria. Ben-hadad's instructions to his men on how to deal with the defenders emerging from Samaria ("If they have come out for peace, take them alive; or if they have come out for war, take them alive," v. 18) may reflect this assessment of the political realities of the ninth century (i.e., that Ben-hadad would rather not destroy his potential ally if he can obtain sufficient reassurances of his vassal's obedience), rather than simple contempt for the paltry size of Samaria's defenders (contra Gray, Kings, p. 425; and Robinson, p. 229). Ahab's clemency to Ben-hadad in vv. 30-34 may also be interpreted in this way. See B. Mazar, p. 114; and H. Tadmor, p. 39.

207   Compare, for example, the reply ("Nuts!") of Anthony McAuliffe, commander of the 101st Airborne Division (which had been trapped a number of days at Bastogne), to the German surrender demands. See John Bartlett, Bartlett's Familiar Quotations, 14th ed., rev. and enl., edited by Emily M. Beck (Boston: Little Brown & Co., 1968), p. 1042.

208   There is considerable support for the recognition of the importance of indirection in proverb performance strategy, as we have already mentioned above (see pp. 119-20). The Westcar Papyrus (P. Berlin 3033) contains two analogous examples of the use of indirection to shield proverb users from the wrath of the pharaoh (lines 6,8, and 8,1). In the first context, a slave girl replies to pharaoh's offer to replace a lost possession, "I like my pot down to the end," which W. K. Simpson interprets as "evidently a proverb with the sense that she wants the full amount of the same thing" (p. 21). In the second context, a magician replies to pharaoh's piqued inquiry as to why the magician had not appeared at court previously, "The one who comes is the one who is summoned .... I have been summoned and see, I have come" (W. K. Simpson, p. 21). For another biblical example of the use of traditional genres in a court atmosphere to ease or influence conflict situations, see Jehoash's reply to

Amaziah's challenge in 2 Kg. 14:8-10.

209   Eissfeldt, Maschal, p. 52.

210   So with Gray, Kings, pp. 423-24; and Yigael Yadin, "Some Aspects of the Strategy of Ahab and David," Biblica 36 (1955) : 332-51.

211   These folk ideas find expression in the wisdom sayings of the Old Testament as well: "The lot is cast into the lap, but the decision is wholly from the Lord" (Pr. 16:33); and "Many are the plans in the mind of a man, but it is the purpose of the Lord that will be established" (Pr. 19:21). See also Pr. 16:1, 9, etc.

212   It is not to be wondered at that our pericope presents Ahab and Benhadad understanding and making use of a common proverbial stock. Not only were the great Bronze Age cultures of Palestine probably "incubated" among the cities along the Orontes River in Syria, but the biblical record points as well to "related origins and language, and ... common traditions from time immemorial." (Mazar, p. 98). For a discussion of the cultural links between Syria and Palestine, see William G. Dever, "The Beginning of the Middle Bronze Age in Syria-Palestine," in: Magnalia Dei: The Mighty Acts of God, Festschrift G. E. Wright, ed. Frank M. Cross, W. Lemke, and P. D. Miller (Garden City, N.Y.: Doubleday & Co., 1976), pp. 3-38.

213   See page 177-78.

214   Pedersen, 1-2: 36-38; 3-4:75.

215   Ibid., 1-2: 128-29.

NOTES TO CHAPTER IV

Wisdom at Work:
Towards an Understanding of the Contextual Use
of the Traditional Saying in the Old Testament

1   See Chapter III, pp. 85-86, 93-95, 106-7, 117-18, 136.

2   See Nigel Barley, "Proverb," pp. 880-81; Ben-Amos, "Context," pp. 36-327, 43, 47; and Parker, pp. 88-91, all of whom address the problem of developing analytic categories which both do justice to ethnic genre categories and facilitate cross-cultural comparisons and analyses.

3   Robert R. Wilson, Genealogy, pp. 13-18.

4   See Bascom, "Four Functions," pp. 86-89, and 293.

5   Lichtheim, I:73.   6   ANET, p. 415.

7   Lichtheim, II: 148-49.

8   That sayings were valued and preserved is readily apparent from the fact that we find sayings from the "Instruction of Ptahhotep" quoted in the New Kingdom Installation Speech for the Vizier Rekhmire (translated in Lichtheim, 2:23), and elaborated upon in the "Instruction for King Merikare." For a discussion of the latter, see Gerhard Fecht, Der Habgierige und die Maat in der Lehres des Ptahhotep (5 und. 19. Maxime), ADAIK I (Glückstadt: J. J. Augustin, 1958). In the "Satirical Letter" found in the Papyrus Anastasi I, the scribe Hori complains of receiving a letter from one Amenemope, who quoted the sayings of Hor-dedef improperly in his letter to Hori. See ANET, p. 476.

9   The didactic literature of ancient Egypt is replete with examples of "scribal chauvinism." See, for instance, the "Satire of the Trades," (P. Sallier II = P. British Museum 10182), the praise of scribes in Papyrus Chester Beatty IV (= P. British Museum 10684), and praises of the scribe in the Papyrus Lansing (= P. British Museum 9994). The Papyrus Lansing praises the teaching of scribes with the following words: "You are wise in planning, skilled in speech; farseeing at all times; what you do succeeds .... You are one weighty of counsel who weighs his answer; since birth you have loathed coarse language .... You are a man of choice words, who is skilled in saying them; all you say is right, you abhor falsehood." Lichtheim, 2:174.

10   ANET, p. 427.   11   Lichtheim, 1:172-73.

12   Lichtheim, 1:122.

13   See also Pr. 15:7; 18:2, 6-7; 19:1; 20:3; 24:7; Sir. 3:29; 4:24; 8:8-9; 21:14-16, 26.

14   The distinctions drawn in sociolinguistics between "competence" (a native speaker's intrinsic understanding of a [language] rule system) and "performance" (the social uses to which that system is put) may be helpful here. See Chomsky, pp. 3-15 for discussion; and also, for the interrelationship between competence and performance, Basil Bernstein, "Social Class, Language and Socialization," in: Language and Social Context: Selected Readings, ed. Pier Paolo Giglioli (London: Cox & Wyman Ltd., for Penguin Books, 1972), pp. 160-65. If one expands the term "competence" to include the interpretation of the content conveyed by the rule system, as well as the rule system itself, then it is appropriate to say that successful proverb performance depends on underlying competence on the part of the Source of the speech act. For

the validity of this holistic understanding of the interaction between content expressed and medium of expression, see Joshua A. Fishman, The Sociology of Language: an Interdisciplinary Social Science Approach to Language in Society (Rowley, M. S.: Newbury House, 1972), pp. 4-5; and Pierre Guiraud, "Immanence and Transitivity of Stylistic Criteria" in Literary Style: A Symposium, ed. and trans. (in part) by Seymour Chatman (London: Oxford University Press, 1971), pp. 16-23. An added variable for successful proverb performance is the necessity of shared folk ideas which not only provide the lexical key for the understanding of the message of a saying, but which also govern the uses and methods for employing the message, since the intelligible use of highly metaphorical language depends on a common cultural and linguistic background between the Source and Receiver, (i.e., the Receiver as well as the Source must possess competence). So with Bernstein, p. 165.

15   This, of course, is the final proof that the fool does not understand the content (message) of the saying or wisdom instruction.

16   From our definition of the traditional saying as a broad functional category, we would contend that, although not all "mᵉshālîm" are traditional sayings, all of ancient Israel's traditional sayings may be considered "mᵉshālîm."

17   See above, "Proverb Collections and Proverbs in Literary Sources," pp. 54-58; 64; 72-74.

18   While it is true that the correspondents of the ancient Near East generally made use of a scribe in sending correspondence (and hence the use of a traditional saying might be attributed to the scribal "wisdom" connection), and that the letter form contains some formulaic elements such as the greeting and closing, there is no need to think that the proverb performance which occurs is mere literary ornamentation. The very intentionality of the act of letter-writing to communicate specific information ensures that the occurrence of a traditional saying is context-related and not simply a literary creation as an end in itself. We may assume that the non-formulaic components of the "letter" offer a fairly realistic picture of the types of communication current in the writers' time.

19   Marzal, pp. 1-2.

20   Ibid., pp. 15-50. Those letters whose traditional sayings are cited as "teltum" are ARM I, 5:10-13; and ARM X, 150:9-11.

21   The sayings are: "The bitch in her passing back and

forth gave birth to lame puppies"; "The fire consumes the reed and its companions pay attention"; "Under the straw the water flows"; "If one treats a soldier well, he shows respect (?) to his lord and receives an important present"; and "A lion does not cultivate; he hinders the cultivators." For discussions of the texts, see Marzal, pp. 15, 23, 27, 31.

22   Marzal, pp. 15ff. An interesting similarity to 1 Sam. 16 occurs in the correspondence from a high-born woman to Zimri-Lim, king of Mari, in which she relates a prophecy for the king concerning peace overtures from the king of Eshnunna. The god Dagan (via his prophetess) says of Eshnunna's offers, "The offers-of-reconciliation of the man of Eshnunna are only treachery. 'Under the straw the water flows.'" Marzal understands the message of this saying to be that outward appearances can be deceiving - the same nuclear message which Yahweh transmits to Samuel, in 1 Sam. 16.

23   Ibid., pp. 27-31.

24   Edward F. Campbell, Jr., "The Amarna Letters and the Amarna Period," BA 23 (1960) : 2-22. For mention of Lab'ayu, see letters EA, No. 244; EA, No. 245; EA, No. 250, where Lab'ayu is called a "rebel against the king"; EA, No 280; and EA, No. 289, where CAbdu-Heba, the ruler of Jerusalem asks pharaoh bitterly, "Or shall we do like Lab'ayu, who gave the land of Shechem to the CApiru?"

25   See above, pp. 124, for a discussion of proverb performance in EA, No. 292.

26   See Campbell, p. 19, and notes 23 and 24 above. There is no need to make the questionable identification of CApiru with "Hebrew"; rather, the CApiru of the Amarna letters are better conceived of as "individuals or groups who stood outside the acknowledged social system for one reason or another, and thus were not afforded the legal protection which the system normally guaranteed its members .... Occasionally in the Amarna letters, for example, CApiru seems to apply to anyone who challenged Egyptian authority. There is nothing to suggest that any of the CApiru of the Amarna period were recent intruders into Palestine." J. Maxwell Miller, "The Israelite Occupation of Canaan," in: Israelite and Judaean History, p. 249.

27   ANET, p. 486.   28   Campbell, pp. 19-20.

29   Such a contribution is wholly consistent with certain functionalist understandings of folklore genres. Marxist theories have long viewed folklore as a traditional weapon of the oppressed classes in their struggles against a repressive

elite. While this approach can be most limiting when applied in a single-minded, reductionistic fashion (since it obviously does not hold for all folk genres), it is certainly an insight into the understanding of the function of certain forms, such as the folk song or folktales which circulated in slave communities. The traditional saying seems especially well suited for such functions, as a modern interview with a spokesperson for the Nicaraguan Sandinista National Liberation Front, broadcast on Public Television on June 19, 1979 showed. In that interview Father Miguel D'Escoto of Nicaragua quoted an aphorism of John F. Kennedy ("Those who make peaceful change impossible make violent change inevitable") to support the position of those who oppose the Somoza government. For a discussion of Marxist theories of folklore as a weapon in social struggles, see Richard M. Dorson, "Introduction," pp. 16-20; and Yuri M. Sokolov, Russian Folklore, trans. Catherine Smith (New York: Macmillan Co., 1950), pp. 3-155.

30   The Instruction of Ptahhotep, 5,10, in W. K. Simpson, p. 161.

31   Paul Ricoeur, "Biblical Hermeneutics," Semeia 4 (1975) : 88, 125.

32   See Dundes, "Structure," p. 107; and von Rad, Wisdom, pp. 26-30.

33   The attitude or "rhetorical orientation" toward the content need not necessarily be an affirmative or positive one, although this is the type which seems to appear most frequently.

34   Sackett, pp. 143-53.

35   Taylor, Proverb, pp. 8, 20-21, 26, 37, 40-41, 53-61.

36   This is true even of "coordinate" sayings, which Dundes treats provisionally as subtypes of the identificational class.

37   See our discussion above of the different worldviews underlying the Swahili saying "Haste, haste, brings no blessing" and the English, "Haste makes waste," p. 43.

38   The same stimulus is found in proverb performance in the prophetic literature (see Appendix C), only the specific Context Situation usually involves the dichotomy between human and divine evaluations.

39   In 1 Sam. 24:14, the "Object" (O) whose behavior elicits the transmission of the traditional saying is David himself (i.e., O=X). The variation in the pattern found elsewhere probably results from the fact that this instance of proverb performance is the only one where the Source is

contending that the state of affairs in the Proverb Situation does not correspond to the Receiver's reading of the state of affairs in the Context Situation (i.e., the truth of the saying is not called into question, but rather its application to yield an understanding of the context events). Hence the intent of the Source (self-vindication) accounts for the specific types of correlations which are made.

40   The situation is a bit different in 1 Sam. 16:7, where Yahweh is the apparent Source. Obviously, one might expect God to be familiar with Israel's (and everyone else's, for that matter) proverbial stock, since "he" is the true source of all wisdom. From the perspective of the authorship of the pericope, we may also assume that the Author/Source had knowledge of the proverbial traditions of his society, since he is able to make such brilliant and persuasive use of the saying in verse 7 to achieve his own literary and theological ends.

41   Rolf Sandell, Linguistic Style and Persuasion, European Monographs in Social Psychology, no. 11 (London: Academic Press, 1977), pp. 227-35.

42   For example, in Jg. 8:2, there is the possibility of violent retaliation by the Ephraimites for the slight which they feel Gideon has dealt to them; in 8:21, the possibility of a degrading end at the hands of an untried youth is perceived by the Sources to be a worse fate than the actual execution. One may imagine that a good deal of violent discussion took place over David's succession, and this is hinted at in an oblique fashion in 1 Sam. 16:2, 4-5. Similar situations in which aggressive actions threaten the Sources are found in 1 Sam. 24 and 1 Kg. 20.

43   This also holds true for 1 Sam. 16 if one conceives of the Source as a pro-Davidic author attempting to justify David's succession in traditional ways. The disadvantage with respect to the Receiver (the anti-monarchic or pro-Saul factions) then comes from the fact that Saul was anointed before David, and his rejection could not be dimissed without some legitimating comment.

44   See note 29 above for comments on folklore genres as a weapon of the "oppressed" in social conflicts.

45   William H. Ittelson, Harold M. Proshansky, Leanne G. Rivlin and Gary H. Winkel, An Introduction to Environmental Psychology (New York: Holt, Rinehart, and Winston, Inc., 1974), pp. 86.

46   See Chapter II, pp. 52-53.

47   Sandell, pp. 66-81.   48   Ibid., pp. 295-99.

49   It should be pointed out that, although we generally

assume a basic "code commonality" between the Source and Receiver in an incident of proverb performance, there is still a good deal of room for misunderstanding or variant interpretations when a traditional saying is employed, due to its indirection. For a discussion of the sources of multiple meanings in proverb performance, see Chapter II, pp. 48-50.

50   So, too, von Rad, Wisdom, p. 27.

51   See notes 1, 2, 3, and 5 to Table 3, for the changes brought about by the inclusion of the "appraisal" in 1 Sam. 24:14 as a part of the Proverb Situation.

52   To paraphrase, the Proverb Situation would then consist of a contrastive statement, "The wicked produce wickedness (A), but (≠) my hand will not be against you (B)." The Context Situation then sets up the following correlations: "Your (Saul, Y) evaluation of my character presumes that I act wickedly toward you (C), but (≠) my actual deeds toward you are not wicked, by your own admission" (D). The strategy of David's use - reassessment of context events forced by contradictions between Topics (A,C) and comments (B,D) - remains the same whether his appraisal forms part of the analysis or not. Since contrastive correlations between Proverb and Context Situations made by the Source do occur in prophetic proverb performance (see Appendix C), we do not feel especially compelled to add the appraisal to our model of the Proverb Situation for the sake of regularity.

53   See Chapter II, above, for discussions of the work of Parker and Seitel, (pp. 50-52, 57-60).

54   The "topic-comment" structure is, of course, not folklore studies' own private terminological property, but rather symbolizes "the basic grammatical relationship of surface structure corresponding (roughly) to the fundamental Subject-Predicate relationship of deep structure" as it is conceived of in transformational-generative grammar. See Chomsky, p. 221.

55   See Appendix B for an analysis of the Topic-Comment structure of proverb performance in 1 Samuel 16.

56   See Horst D. Preuss, "Erwägungen zum theologischen Ort alttestamentlicher Weisheitsliteratur," Evangelische Theologie 30 (1970) : 393-417; Scott, Way, pp. 12-15; and others.

57   See Chapter I for a discussion of these works, and Christa Bauer-Kayatz, Einführung in die alttestamentliche Weisheit, Biblische Studien 55 (Neukirchen-Vluyn: Neukirchener Verlag des Erziehungsvereins, 1969). It is also interesting to note that the sayings which we have discussed

in contextual settings and designated as "traditional sayings" (with the exception of 1 Sam. 16:7) show a remarkable similarity in form, content, and function to the "types" of wisdom which Bauer-Kayatz designates as "Erfahrungs-weisheit" and "Sippensweisheit," which she feels represent some of the earliest wisdom traditions of Israel (Einführung, pp. 1-18).

58   George M. Mendenhall, " 'Change and Decay in All Around I See': Conquest, Covenant, and The Tenth Generation," BA 39 (1976) : 153.

59   Crenshaw, "Method," pp. 481-484.

60   For a discussion of Beispielerzählungen, see Hermisson, pp. 183-86.

Appendix A

GLOSSARY OF TERMS AND SYMBOLS

A, B, C, D:
   cover symbols for proverb referents (A,B) and contextual referents (C,D).

Adjunction:
   T-rule which adjoins one or more strings in a given (set of) P-marker(s) to one or more other strings in that (set of) P-marker(s).

ADV:
   adverb; may be viewed as on orientation to or perspective on VP or PredP.

AdvP:
   adverb phrase; its constituents are (ADV + NP).

Affective proverb performance:
   proverb performance whose purpose is to change or affect behavior; usually takes place under the following conditions: time reference is to present or future events; Receiver (Y) and Object (O) are the same person(s).

Architectural formula:
   the syntactical frame or concatenation upon which a saying is constructed.

Aussage:
   saying, usually in indicative form (but not necessarily so) with variable line length.

Ausspruch:
   see Aussage.

AUX:
   "auxiliary verb or phrase"; symbol for the deictic category of syntactic meanings which provides an orientation toward the propositional context of an S. Its constituents are Aspect, Voice, Mood, and Tense, of which only the latter is an obligatory feature of AUX.

Baukern:
   the context-free core or kernel of a saying, which consists of the relationship between the terms of the saying (A∼B).

Chronological displacement:
   opposition in a saying which is created through a reversal of normal temporal order in the referents.

223

Cognitive map:
  an internal, symbolic representation of a complete behavior or environment which facilitates later performance.
Comment:
  the logical "predicate" of a saying which consists of the second term of a saying (B) and its relationship ($\sim$) to the Topic (A).
Constituent:
  those categories or elements of categories which make up the structure of an S or phrase of an S (e.g., NP + PredP are the constituents of S, where $S \rightarrow NP + PredP$).
Context:
  the broader background in which proverb performance takes place; literally, "who says what to whom under what circumstances and for what purpose."
Context Situation:
  in a model of proverb performance, the situation which the Source correlates with the Proverb Situation.
Constrastive saying:
  a saying whose kernel (Baukern) ($\sim$) expresses an opposition between the proverb terms; $A \neq B$.
Deletion:
  T-rule whereby one or more strings are deleted from a given (set of) P-marker(s).
Derived P-markers:
  in a derivational diagram of syntax, those P-markers which are derived by the application of P-rules to phrase structure.
Derived string:
  a concatenation produced by application of P-rules.
Descriptive unit:
  a Topic(A) and its Comment ($\sim$B).
DET:
  "Determiner"; a deictic category which provides a perspective on N; its two obligatory elements are number and universality.
DS:
  Deep structure; the underlying syntactic structure of an S which conveys meaning.
Elevated style:
  a constitutive feature of the saying form; the use of a variety of stylistic devices which causes the TS to be identified and remembered.

Appendix A: Glossary of Terms and Symbols

Embedding:
the process whereby an underlying string is located as the constituent of a higher-level string.

Evaluative proverb performance:
an event of proverb performance where the purpose of the saying transmission is to render a judgment rather than to alter behavior; usually takes place under the following conditions: time reference is to past or present events; roles of Source, Object, and Receiver are filled by different persons.

Folk:
any group of people whatsoever who share at least one common factor. Older works in folklore use the term primarily to refer to dependent, rural, illiterate groups.

Folk idea:
the unstated, traditional premises which underlie the thought and action of a group, and which find expression in folklore genres.

Identificational saying:
a saying whose kernel (Baukern) ($\sim$) expresses an identification between the proverb terms: $A = B$.

Image, proverb:
the literal referents (terms, A, B, etc.) of a saying.

IMP:
Imperative; provisionally treated as a constituent of Aux (M) in some TGGs.

Indirection:
the use of mataphor and/or impersonality in a saying which acts as a protective cloak for the proverb user.

Intent:
the purpose for which the Source transmits a saying.

Interaction Situation:
in a model of proverb performance, the situation in which Source (X) transmits the saying to Receiver (Y); includes such elements as the relationship between the Source and Receiver (X $\not\!\!/$ Y), social setting, age of participants, etc.

Key:
kinetic features of proverb performance, such as tone of voice, facial expression, gestures (fist-pounding, etc).

Kernel:
the nuclear message of a saying (e.g., $A \neq B$, etc.) found in the relationship between terms ($A \sim B$), which may be transformed. See Baukern.

Kunstsprichwort:
artistic saying; usually with two lines and parallelism.

L:

Language; any natural language system.

Lehrgedicht:

wisdom poem.

M:

Mood; an optional feature of AUX, which expresses the speaker's "rhetorical orientation" toward the topic of an S. M has as its constituents indicative, possibility/certainty, emphatic/permission, obligation/necessity, etc. NEG, IMP, and Q are provisionally treated as Moods in some TGGs.

Mahnrede, Mahnung, Mahnwort:

admonition (negative or postive).

MAN:

adverb of manner.

Maxim:

a non-metaphorical saying.

Message, proverb:

the meaning of a saying which is derived from the kernel or relationship between the proverb terms, A~B.

Minimum proverb:

a saying which includes at least one topic-comment unit.

Multi-descriptive saying:

saying with more than one topic-comment unit.

N:

Noun; a lexical category symbol.

NEG:

Negative; provisionally viewed as a constituent of AUX (M) which reflects the speaker's orientation toward the propositional content of an S.

NP:

Noun phrase; NP→DET + N.

Object:

in an event of proverb performance, the one(s) whose actions, proposed or completed, elicit the transmission of a saying.

Paroemiology:

the science of proverb study.

Performance:

an interaction during which an item of folk-lore is transmitted.

Permutation (Juxtaposition):

T-rule whereby two strings which are adjacent constituents of a given (set of) P-marker(s) are rearranged.

P-marker:

phrase-marker; in a derivational syntactic diagram, the

Appendix A: Glossary of Terms and Symbols

labels assigned to constituent elements in the phrase structure (e.g., NP or VP, etc.); a labelled tree.

PP:

Prepositional phrase; consists of P (prep.) + NP.

PredP:

predicate phrase.

Proverb performance:

an interaction during which a saying is transmitted; consists of the Interaction Situation, the Proverb Situation, and the Context Situation.

Proverb performance meaning:

the message of a saying as it is conditioned by its use in a given context or event of proverb performance. Three features determine proverb performance meaning: (1) participants' evaluation of the situation; (2) participants' understanding of the message of the saying; and (3) interactional strategy of the proverb user (Source).

Proverb Situation:

in a model of proverb performance, the message of a saying (consisting of the proverb terms A, B and the relationship, $\sim$ between them), which the Source correlates with the Context Situation.

Proverb user:

the Source of the transmission of a saying.

P-rules, PSR:

phrase structure rules; a set of rules which explains the syntactic relations, semantic relations, and content common to all Ss in an L; specifically, a set of replacement rules which expand P-markers into derived (or underlying) P-markers.

PS:

Phrase structure; a representation of the syntactic constituents of an S.

Q:

Question, interrogative; provisionallly treated as a constituent of AUX (M).

QM:

Question marker

Receiver:

in an event of proverb performance, the one(s) at whom the transmission of the saying is directed; Y in the Interaction Situation.

Rede:

Speech; a "realized simple form" of the simple form "Saying."

Referent, contextual:
  Any element in the Context Situation (C,D) which the
  Source correlates with the proverb referents (A,B).
Referent, proverb:
  the literal terms of a proverb (A,B).
Relevance restrictions:
  the limitation of potential applications of a saying, owing
  to the necessity of congruence with the proverb message.
S:
  Sentence; specifically, any well-formed sentence in a
  language, L.
Saying-appraisal:
  a strategy of proverb performance wherein a saying is
  presented as a proposition, and then appraised by the
  Source or Receiver. The appraisal is usually drawn from
  the Context Situation.
Simple Form (Einfache Form):
  for literary critic Andre Jolles, the ideal or archetypal
  form of a genre. The simple form is the product of a
  particular intellectual orientation, which is actualized by a
  "verbal gesture" into a "realized simple form."
Source:
  in an event of proverb performance, the one (ones) who
  transmits (transmit) the saying (X in the Interaction
  Situation); the proverb user.
Sprichwörtlicher Redensarten:
  proverbial stock; various types of sayings which make up a
  folk group's body of traditional sayings; may include
  proverbial phrases and comparisons.
Sprichwort:
  proverb; a form of variable line length which is presumed
  to have attained currency among a given group; for Jolles,
  the proverb is a "realized simple form" of the "saying"
  simple form.
Spruch:
  saying; usually indicative (but not necessarily so) with
  variable line length; one of Jolles' "simple forms."
Spruchdichtung:
  epigrammatic poetry.
SS:
  surface structure; the superficial level of an S, consisting
  of a string of elements (morphemes and phonemes).
Strategy:
  the Source's "method" in transmitting a saying and drawing
  correlations; in proverb performance, the two favorite

strategies are (1) use of a saying to point out similarities in the Context Situation, to resolve conflicts in the light of tradition; and (2) use of a saying to point out a contrast between the Context Situation and traditional wisdom.

String:
a concatenation of symbols used to represent the syntactical structure of an S or parts of an S.

Substitution (Replacement):
T-rule whereby one or more strings of a given (set of) P-marker(s) are replaced by one or more different strings.

Supposition-qualification:
a strategy of proverb performance wherein the message of a saying is appraised and qualified by one of the following methods: (a) within the saying itself; (b) through juxtaposition of a contrasting saying; or (c) through (contextual) saying-appraisal.

T:
tense; an obligatory feature of AUX.

Term, proverb:
the literal referents of a proverb image, which must exhibit a logical relationship to one another $(A \sim B)$.

TGG:
transformational-generative grammar.

Topic:
the logical "subject" of a saying; the first element of the kernel (Baukern) - (A).

Traditional saying, TS:
a syntactically complete proposition, containing at least one topic-comment unit, which exhibits a logical relationship between its terms $(A \sim B)$, some type of "elevated style," and may be presumed to be current among the folk.

Transformations:
operations which act on derived P-markers to produce underlying P-markers; more generally, a set of processes which accounts for the diversity of superficial word-orders distinguishing the Ss of an L.

T-rules:
transformational rules; operations which produce a transformation of syntactic structure. "Elementary transformations" result from the operation of one cf the following T-rules: adjunction, deletion, permutation (juxtaposition), or substitution (replacement).

Underlying P-markers:
in a derivational diagram, the P-markers produced by the

Traditional Sayings in the Old Testament

application of T-rules to derived P-markers.

UNIV:
universality; an obligatory feature of DET.

V:
verb.

Vcop:
copulative verb.

Verbal gesture (Sprachgebärden):
process by which a simple form is actualized as a specific item (i.e., as a realized simple form).

VET:
vetitive; ʾal + jussive to express a particular negative wish or desire.

Volkssprichwort:
folk proverb, folk saying, which presumes an origin among the folk. For Eissfeldt, this genre seems to include aspects of anonymity, currency among the folk, and comprehension by the folk.

VP:
verb phrase.

Weisheitsspruch:
wisdom saying, wisdom aphorism; usually consists of two lines which exhibit parallelism and literary polish.

Z :
in the Interaction or Context Situation, a person other than the Source or Receiver with whom correlations between the Proverb and Context situation are drawn.

∼ :
"is related to."

≠ :
in the Interaction Situation, used to indicate the differences in status between Source and Receiver.

→ :
indicates causation in our proverb semantic "type" system (A→B = A causes or yields B). In TGG terminology, indicates the operation of a P-rule on P-markers.

⇒ :
"rewrite as," "yields;" used to indicate that a T-rule has been applied to alter the structure of an S.

= :
equality.

≠ :
inequality.

↛:
negative causation (A↛B = A does not cause B; A should not B; etc.).

230

Appendix B: Analysis Figures and Tables

> :
  greater than.

< :
  less than.

∅ :
  zero element; indicates the operation of the T-rule "deletion."

+ :
  indicates a concatenation.

✗ :
  chiasmus.

△ :
  dummy symbol; used to represent elementary P- or T-rules in operation but not fully represented in a derivational chart.

[SOURCE for TGG definitions: Andreas Koutsoudas, Writing Grammars: an Introduction (New York: McGraw-Hill, 1966, pp. 5-35, 351-54.]

Appendix B

ANALYSIS FIGURES AND TABLES

Table B-1:
Literary types designated as "māshāl" by Old Testament

Similitudes
    Ezek. 16:44, Gen. 10:9*, 1 Sam. 10:11
Popular Sayings
    Jer. 23:20*, 31:29*; 1 Sam. 24:13, Is. 32:6*; 1 Kg. 20:11*
Literary Aphorisms
    Pr. 10:1-22:16, 25-29; Qoh. 9:17-10:20
Taunts
    Is. 14:4, Mic. 2:4, Hab. 2:6-8, Ezek. 12:22-23, 18:2-3
Bywords
    Dt. 28:37, 1 Kg. 9:7, Jer. 24:9, Ezek. 14:8
Allegories
    Ezek. 17:1-10, 20:45-49, 24:3-14
Discourses
    Num. 23:7, 18; 24:3-24; Jb. 27:1, 29:1, Ps. 49:4, 78:2

*Not specifically designated as "māshāl" by the text.

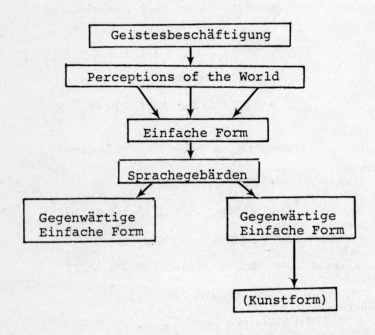

FIGURE B-1: Jolles' Conception of the Process by which a Simple Form (Einfache Form) is Actualized

Appendix B: Analysis Figures and Tables

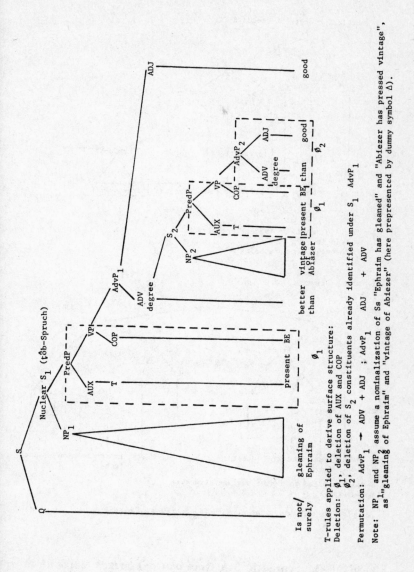

T-rules applied to derive surface structure:
Deletion: Ø₁, deletion of AUX and COP
        Ø₂, deletion of S₂ constituents already identified under S₁ AdvP₁

Permutation: AdvP₁ → ADV + ADJ ; AdvP₁ ADJ + ADV

Note: NP₁ and NP₂ assume a nominalization of Ss "Ephraim has gleaned" and "Abiezer has pressed vintage",
      as "gleaning of Ephraim" and "vintage of Abiezer" (here prepresented by dummy symbol Δ).

FIGURE B-2: Syntactic Structure of Judges 8:2 –
           haló' tôb ᶜōleᵉlôt 'eprayim mibṣîr 'abîᶜezer

233

Traditional Sayings in the Old Testament

Syntactic Structure of Judges 8:21:

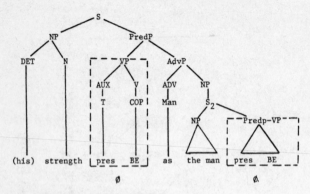

T-rules applied to derive surface structure:
Deletion (∅) of VPs
Permutation: preposing AdvP

Syntactic Structure of 1 Sam. 16:7:

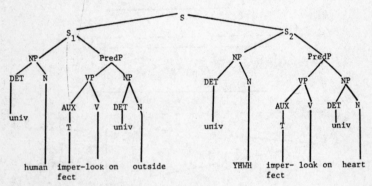

T-rules applied to derive surface structure:
Conjunction: S ⟶ S₁ + S₂

Permutation: SVO permutes normal (VS) Hebrew word order

FIGURE B-3: Syntactic Structure of (top) Judges 8:21 - kāʾîš gᵉbûrātô - and (bottom) 1 Sam. 16:7 - hāʾādām yirʾeh laᶜênayim waYHWH yirʾeh lallēbāb

Appendix B: Analysis Figures and Tables

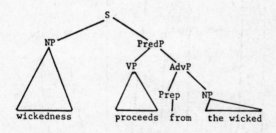

T-rules applied to derive surface structure:

Permutation: Source/agent preposed to become logical subject.

FIGURE B-4: Syntactic Structure of 1 Samuel 24:14 –
mēr^ešā^cîm yēṣē' rešā^c

235

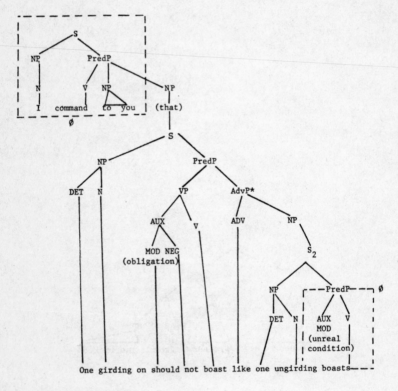

∅ = Application of T-rule "deletion"

Note: AdvP is understood here as a predication of event of VP "boast"
      Semantic structure: A ⟶ B

FIGURE B-5: Syntactic Structure of 1 Kings 20:11 -
            ʾal- yithallēl ḥōgēr kimᵉpattēaḥ

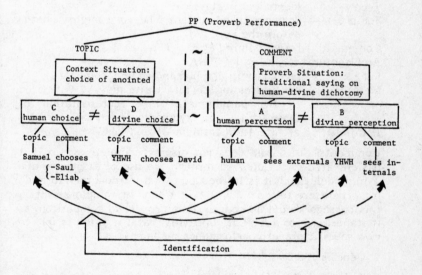

Correlations made by Source: Topic (Context Situation) is identified
    with Comment (Proverb Situation)
Strategy: Point out the identification between theoretical human/divine
    dichotomy in traditional saying and its actualization in life
    (context situation)
Intent: evaluative/affective

FIGURE B-6: Topic-Comment Structure of Proverb Performance in 1 Samuel 16:7

Excursus B: Analysis Charts for Eissfeldt's
Listing of Folk Proverbs

The following charts present an analysis of the traditional sayings listed on Table 1: "Eissfelt's Listing of Folk Proverb Outside of Wisdom Literature and Folk Proverbs Incorporated into the Book of Proverbs." The sayings presented here are those which were treated neither in Chapter III nor Appendix C. Eissfeldt's fourth category, "wisdom sayings which originated as folk proverbs," has been omitted, since analysis of these passages may be found in commentaries on the Book of Proverbs.

1. Genesis 10:9

Gen. 10:9:	"Like Nimrod, a mighty hunter before the Lord"
Type:	Identificational (A = B)
Topic:	$\emptyset$; (unspecified subject who is) a mighty hunter before the Lord (A)
Comment:	is like Nimrod (= B)
Architectural formula:	$k^e\ B = A$
Image:	legendary figure; human accomplishments
Message:	one possessing certain traits may be compared to the paradigmatic folk representation of those traits; i.e., "typological" comparison
Parallels:	architectural formula - Ezek. 16:44

Comments: This item does not display complete syntax, but has elevated style achieved through the use of assonance and T-rule "deletion." It is introduced by an introductory formula "and therefore they say." Due to the lack of complete syntax, this passage should be considered a proverbial comparison, as it stands. Due to a lack of contextual data, it is impossible to give specific proverb performance meanings.

2. Genesis 16:12

Gen. 16:12:	"A wild zebra of a man, his hand against all, and the hand of all against him"
Type:	multi-descriptive identificational (coordinate: A, (=) B)
Comment:	(is one who has) his hand against all (B_1) and the hand of all against him (B_2)
Architectural formula:	A, (=) $B_1 + B_2$
Message:	the individually free are in conflict with communal solidarity
Parallels:	architectural formula - partial, Pr. 15:20; 21:20
	image - Job 39:5-8
	(message - a rolling stone gathers no moss?)

238

Appendix B: Analysis Figures and Tables

Comments: The passage is typed here according to Eissfeldt's limitation of the item to 16:12aβ, and with this division, the passage lacks complete syntax. Contextual data suggest that this does not occur in an event of proverb performance. Elevated style is achieved through alliteration, cadence and ellipsis. As it currently stands, this should be considered a proverbial phrase, not a traditional saying.

3. Judges 14:18

Samson's reply, "If you had not plowed with my heifer, you would not have found out my riddle," made in response to the Philistine's correct answer to his riddle, probably masks a riddle, rather than a traditional saying, even though it shows a fine example of elevated style in its poetic composition. James Crenshaw has suggested that in riddle form the passage might read, "What is plowed, but not with oxen?" For a discussion of this text as a riddle, see Crenshaw, "Wisdom," pp. (242-43). It is quite probably that "to plow with (someone's) heifer" is a proverbial phrase used euphemistically to refer to intercourse. See ANET, p. 643, for use of this image.

4. 1 Samuel 10:12 (19:24)

1 Sam. 10:12: "Is Saul also among the prophets?"
Type: Context-dependent contrastive
Topic: Saul (A)
Comment: Q among prophets (B)
Architectureal formula: Q ADV A PREP B
Image: historical persons
Message: (Q) the behavior and background of a historical personage congruent with membership in a specific group

Comments: "Elevated style" is achieved here through the use of some assonance, cadence, and the use of "hagam" to intensify the question. Syntax is complete, and traditional saying is introduced as a "māshāl" in 10:12 and by an introductory formula, "and therefore they say," in 19:24. However, it is difficult to infer what the "proper" interpretation and answer to this saying is, since both contexts seem to be later attempts to explain the etiology of the "māshāl" (McKane, Proverbs, pp. 26-27). This is a good example of a traditional saying whose meaning is almost wholly dependent on the contextual information appended in a context of use.

239

5. 2 Samuel 5:8

2 Sam. 5:8:	"The blind and the lame shall not come into the house"
Type:	multi-descriptive contrastive (negative causation, A $\nrightarrow$ B)
Comment:	shall not ($\nrightarrow$) come into the house
Architectural formula:	$A_1 + A_2 \nrightarrow$ (NEG + V + PrepP)
Image:	human disability
Message:	disability prevents participation (in community life)
Parallels:	Message - Lv. 21:18

Comments: This saying shows complete syntax, and some features of elevated style achieved through the use of assonance, cadence, and reversal of verb-subject order. The context of use is obscure, due in part to some textual problems. The LXX understands "Temple" for "habbayit," and S. R. Driver connects this verse with old cultic restrictions about fitness for entering the temple (Samuel, pp. 258-61). The ostensible connection of this passage to the context is found in 2 Sam. 5:6, where the Jebusites boast that their city is so strong that even the disabled can defend it successfully, but the saying appears to have little to do with this taunt. Eissfeldt lists this item in his category of those introduced by introductory formulae (Maschal, p. 49) and Hermisson understands this passage as a prohibitive expressing the regulations in Lv. 21:18 (p.42).

6. 2 Samuel 9:8

2 Sam. 9:8 (cf. 1 Sam. 24:15; 2 Sam. 16:9):
　　　　　　"A dead dog such as I"

This is obviously not a proverb but rather a proverbial phrase. Eissfeldt lists this item in his category of those passages which "sound like a proverb" (Maschal, p. 46), but understands this as an example of the proverbial stock or idiom, but not necessarily as a true proverb. All three contexts in which this idiom appears reflect conflict situations.

7. 2 Samuel 20:18

2 Sam. 20:18:	"Let them but ask at Abel" - and thus they settled (a matter).
Type:	identificational (positive causation, A $\rightarrow$ B)
Topic:	unspecified persons of former times who sought counsel (A)

Comment: Should ask at Abel (→ B); appended appraisal
              (B$_2$: and thus they settled a matter)
Architectural formula: intensive (A→) + Prep + B
Image: human disputes; specific course of action
              recommended in connection with a specific
              locality
Message: good counsel available at a specific locality

Comments: Syntax is complete and compressed, and elevated style is achieved through alliteration, cadence, and use of infinitive absolute to intensify the verb (for use of the infinitive absolute in the Qal with inflected verbs of other conjugations, see GKC #113w). Eissfeldt lists this in his category of passages introduced by introductory formulae, since it is prefaced by "They used to say in the old time ..." (Maschal, p. 45). Hermisson, on the other hand, denies that this a saying and sees it as a law (Regel) stemming from a different intellectual orientation (Geistesbeschäftigung) than that which gives rise to a true folk proverb (p. 42).

8. 1 Kings 18:21

1 Kg. 18:21: "How long will you go limping with two different
              opinions?"

Eissfeldt classes this passage as one which "sounds like a proverb" (Maschal, p. 46), and while "limping along with two different opinions" is an extremely well-turned phrase to describe the activities of someone with divided loyalties, the context of use in which this occurs casts some doubt as to whether or not this should be considered a saying. The subsequent reference to the ritual limping dance which follows in verse 26 (even though in verse 21 "psḥ" is in the Qal, while in verse 26 it occurs in the Piel) makes this passage suspect as a folk saying, since it so well anticipates the upcoming action (contra Montgomery, p. 310). The passage may, however, contain a proverbial phrase.

Appendix C

PROVERB PERFORMANCE
IN THE OLD TESTAMENT PROPHETIC BOOKS

It has long been recognized that the prophets of ancient Israel were by no means unfamiliar with the wisdom traditions of the Old Testament (Fichtner, Isaiah, pp. 429-38; Lindblom, pp. 192-204). While it is often difficult to delineate the precise relationship of a given prophet to wisdom and its representatives, there is no question that the prophets made use of the familiar language of the traditional saying to serve their own interactional ends. Because of the typical prophetic propensity for the adaptation of existing forms (such as the "rîb" and others) to meet their needs, an inquiry into the contextual use of the traditional saying in the prophetic literature must be both more flexible and more circumspect in the identification of traditional sayings. It is quite possible that given "sayings" quoted in the prophetic literature are limitations of traditional sayings - that is, the prophet may have made use of typical proverbial architectural formulae and images to couch his own particular message in the garb of traditional language. For this reason, one might not be able to designate a passage as a traditional saying where it seems likely that the author is modeling his message on proverbial frames, although the imitation serves the function of a traditional saying as it is used in context. Similarly, it may be that in many cases, a prophet has made use of a legitimate, current traditional saying, but has so altered the form to suit contextual need that it is no longer immediately recognizable as a traditional saying (i.e., it does not fulfill our posited criteria for the identification and designation of a passage as a traditional saying). To summarize the major methodological problem in a study of prophetic proverb performance, then, we might say that, because of the fluidity of the prophetic use of literary genres, not all of the sayings which bear the form of a traditional saying can be considered to be a genuine (i.e., current) traditional saying, and not all of the genuine traditional sayings in the prophetic corpus may appear in their normal saying form. However, by switching our focus from the form to the function of the traditional

242

saying, it is possible to analyze this particular prophetic use of traditional language.

From what we know of the way in which contextual proverb use "works" (e.g., through indirection, saying-appraisal, etc.), it is readily apparent that the traditional saying is an ideal form for prophetic use in interactions. If we characterize the stimulus which elicits the response of proverb performance as "conflict situations," then we have an immediate "match" between the non-prophetic and prophetic life setting (Sitz im Leben) of proverb performance. Of all the types of literature found in the Old Testament, the prophetic corpus is the one which most systematically articulates the tensions within the society of ancient Israel; indeed, were it not for this tension and conflict, the prophets themselves, as well as their words, would not have been necessary. It has been shown that the greater the conflict with which a person is confronted, the more apt he or she becomes to fall back on internalized systems of categorization and problem-solving. Since the traditional saying deals with exactly these kinds of content, it is natural that the prophets would make use of this genre when pressed. The familiar features of proverb use - indirection to shield the Source, "elevated style" to arrest the attention of the Receiver, the use of traditional arguments to regulate ambiguous situations - are well-suited to the interactional needs of the prophet. Through the use of the traditional saying, a prophet achieves a number of ends simultaneously, which we might systematize as follows.

1. The use of traditional language (formula, image) allows the appearance of conformity to the cultural status quo, even though the actual content (message conveyed by the kernel) may be highly critical of the society. The aspect of code commonality also aids in the prophets' persuasive intent.

2. The use of traditional language creates desirable subjective responses in the Receivers in that (a) the Receiver is momentarily comfortable with the unpleasant message because it is cast in familiar terms; (b) it induces a feeling of pleasure (appreciation of the style of the traditional saying) and satisfaction when contextual correlations are unraveled; and (c) it calls up an aura of traditional authority as it evokes familiar associations which surround the Receivers' understanding of the proverb referents.

3. The use of traditional language augments the authority of the prophetic speech by (a) linking the message to the authority of tradition; and (b) linking the message to the

authority or experiential validity found in the logical relationships which make up the proverb message (e.g., the series of rhetorical questions in Amos 3 links Amos' message - the reason for his compulsion to prophesy - to the verifiable relationships observed in the natural world).

With these considerations of strategy and intent in mind, let us turn to a few brief examples of "prophetic proverb performance."

Ezekiel 16:44

Ezek. 16:44: "Like mother, (like) daughter"
Type: identificational (positive causation, $A \leftarrow B$)
Topic: (her) daughter (A)
Comment: is like the mother ($\leftarrow B$)
Architectural formula: $k^e B = A$
Image: human family
Message: heredity and parental example determine the behavior and nature of the offspring
Parallels: architectural formula - Jg. 8:21

I. Interaction Situation.

The Source (X) is Yahweh, covenant lord, speaking through the prophet Ezekiel. The Receiver (Y) is Jerusalem, which also symbolizes the entire kingdom. The behavior of the inhabitants of Jerusalem is the Object which elicited the use of the traditional saying (O = Y).

II. Proverb Situation.

The achitectural formula of the saying is a very simple one which is often used to express basic comparisons and identifications. The image, that of a mother-daughter relationship, is one that is not only familiar from daily life (and hence, verifiable), but also one which is evocative of the relationships of Yahweh as loving husband (and/or father) of wayward Israel (here specified as Jerusalem). The message of the decisive role of parents in the formation of the character (and hence, subsequent actions) of a child is one which is common to the world's proverbial lore ("The hand that rocks the cradle rules the world," etc.). The folk ideas embodied here center around the importance of the family as a determinant of the character and behavior of its younger members, and there may also be some nuances on instrinsic misogyny.

III. Context Situation.

The contextual correlations of this traditional saying are made explicit in the text itself:

Have you not committed lewdness in addition to all your abominations? Behold, every one who uses proverbs will use this proverb about you, "Like mother, like daughter." You are the daughter of your mother, who loathed her husband and children; and you are the sister of your sisters who loathed their husbands and their children. Your mother was a Hittite, and your father an Amorite. And your elder sister is Samaria, who lived with her daughters to the north of you; and your younger sister who lived to the South of you, is Sodom with her daughters. Yet you were not content to walk in their ways, or do according to their abominations; within a very little time you were more corrupt than they in all your ways.

Ezek. 16:43b-47

We may set up our contextual model as in Figure C-1. The contextual correlations of Y = A,C is a negative one, and although the time reference is to the past (Jerusalem's past apostasies), the intent is both evaluative (Jerusalem has behaved like a Canaanite city, thus betraying her origins) and affective (unless things change, Jerusalem will suffer the fate of her foreign mother and sisters). The Source correlates the Proverb Situation and the Context Situation in an identificational way; that is, the state of affairs obtaining in the saying is felt to represent the state of affairs in the context $(A \sim B = C \sim D)$. The folk ideas at work in the Context Situation have strong covenantal and theological overtones. Yahweh, even now, after Jerusalem has broken faith repeatedly, still addresses her in familial terms, via his prophet, which emphasizes his abiding relationship with her in the covenant (see Ezek. 16:6-14). Because of the covenant relationship, Yahweh will continue to love and judge Jerusalem (16:42-43a). The contextual use of this saying is evocative of the imagery of familial love found in Hosea; the underlying sentiment reflects the poignant feeling of rejection attributed to God by the prophets. It is interesting, too, that the contextual use of this saying preserves the memory of Jerusalem's Canaanite origins.

Jeremiah 31:29

Jer. 31:29:   "The fathers have eaten sour grapes, and the children's teeth are set on edge"

Type: multi-descriptive identification (positive causation, $A \to B$)

245

Traditional Sayings in the Old Testament

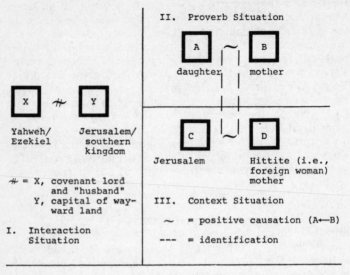

FIGURE C-1: Proverb Performance in Ezekiel 16:44

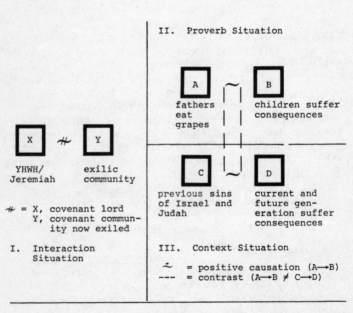

FIGURE C-2: Proverb Performance in Jeremiah 31:29

Appendix C: Proverb Performance in Prophetic Books

Topic(s):   Topic A: fathers; Topic B: children
Comment(s):   Comment A: have eaten sour grapes; Comment B: pucker
Architectural formula: A (N + V + O) → B (N + V + O)
Image: parents and offspring; properties of agricultural product
Message: activities of parents affect offspring; "retribution"

I. Interaction Situation.

The Source (X) is Yahweh, speaking through the prophet Jeremiah; the Receiver(s) are Israel and Judah. The Object whose behavior has elicited the transmission of the saying is Yahweh (O = X): although God has judged and torn down the kingdoms in the past, in the future, his dealings will be different.

II. Proverb Situation.

Elevated style occurs in this traditional saying in the reversal of normal syntactical order, the use of assonance, deliberate cadence, and formulaic word pairs. The architectural formula is a standard one, as are the proverb referents which make use of familiar images drawn from human society and the natural world. The message of the saying encapsulates the folk idea of collective responsibility and retribution for sins of the parents on subsequent offspring.

III. Context Situation.

The correlational use of the saying in 31:29 is fairly explicit from the pericope:

> Behold, the days are coming, says the Lord, when I will sow the house of Israel and the house of Judah with the seed of man and the seed of beast. And it shall come to pass that as I have watched over them to pluck up and break down, to overthrow, destroy, and bring evil, so I will watch over them to build and to plant, says the Lord. In those days, they shall no longer say: "The fathers have eaten sour grapes, and the children's teeth are set on edge." But every one shall die for his own sin; each man who eats sour grapes, his teeth shall be set on edge.
>
> Jer. 31:27-30

The contextual correlates refer to the coming days in which Yahweh will both forgive the past sins of Israel and Judah (31:34), and in restoring them from exile, will create a new convenant in which each person will be intimately related to the covenant lord on a personal level. The specific model might be filled in as in Figure C-2.

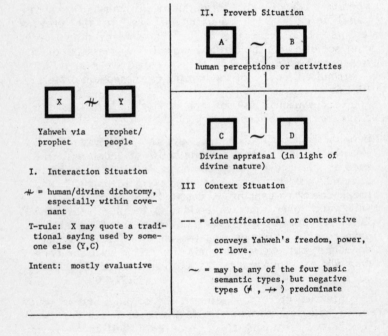

FIGURE C-3: Model of Prophetic Proverb Performance

Appendix C: Proverb Performance in Prophetic Books

The contextual correlation equates the father of Topic A with the past sinful activities of Israel and Judah which resulted in exile (Y = A,C). While this correspondence between Receiver and contextual referents is a <u>negative</u> one, Yahweh will not mete out the punishment earned by the forefathers on the subsequent generations. The traditional saying is used to say that the expected state of affairs (retribution for the sins of the ancestors) does not "match up" with God's future plans. The intent of the use of the traditional saying is affective, accomplished through pointing out the contrast between the Proverb Situation and the Context Situation: Israel and Judah must not act as if the "old rules" embodied in the saying are still in operation. Rather, they must remain open to Yahweh's ever-surprising graciousness. The Holy Lord himself will break apart the rigid correspondences of a calculating system of retribution. The use of the saying here is powerful indeed, since its meaning in context conveys the comforting and astounding message of Yahweh's dynamic freedom to love and respond to the people, regardless of past apostasies or conceptions of retribution.

Table C-1 summarizes the contextual information for all of the prophetic passages which Eissfeldt designated as proverbial (Maschal, p. 45-46). It should be noted that, because of the rhetorical or oracular nature of many prophetic utterances, it is difficult to fill in our model of proverb performance without straining some of the correspondences. Consequently, when the Receiver (Y) of the transmission of the traditional saying appears to be some unspecified audience which the prophet addresses, we have glossed this simply as "covenant community." An asterisk (*) marks those entries judged by this writer as the most likely candidates for instances of genuine proverb performance (purposeful transmission in a social interaction of an item which might have been current).

It is immediately apparent from the data that a few patterns of proverb use do emerge in the prophetic materials. Traditional sayings occurring in Ezekiel, with the exception of 16:44, are all correlated with their contexts in a contrastive way - that is, the Source affirms that the situation in the Proverb Situation is <u>not</u> identical to the situation in the context (A~B ≠ C~D). The relation ($\not\leftrightarrow$) of the Source (YHWH via the prophet) and Receiver (prophet/covenant community) is one which reflects the divine/human dichotomy; this is the reason that the Proverb and Context Situation <u>do</u> <u>not</u> "match." The Proverb Situation represents the community's reading of the general situation, whereas the Context Situation presents God's perspective on the situation and hence, serves an evaluative function (which hopefully redirects the Receiver's, i.e., becomes affective, if affirmed). In every case, (except 16:44) the proverb performances work to emphasize the difference between God's vision and that of the covenant community, and in every case, God's actions or assertions in the Context Situation are not what the community expects.

The proverbial passages in Jeremiah also seem to show certain patterns. The Source tends to make a positive or identificational correlation between the Proverb Situation and the Context Situation (i.e., $A \sim B = C \sim D$), and the intent is primarily evaluative, in terms of reference to a general content. Although it is difficult to specify Receivers in most of the passages, the relationship (H) between the Source (Yahweh through the prophet) and Receiver seems to focus on whether or not the Receivers have a proper understanding of God's nature and plans. Once again, proverb performance highlights the differences between what the people believe to be the situation and what Yahweh knows to be the case. The messages found in the relationship between topic and comment ($\sim$) of the sayings are mostly negative.

The function of proverb performance in First and Second Isaiah is mainly evaluative, with the first Isaiah making positive identifications ($A \sim B = C \sim D$), and Deutero-Isaiah drawing contrasts between the Proverb and Context Situations ($A \sim B \neq C \sim D$). For both, the relationship between Source and Receiver (H) is the tension between human and divine perspectives. The messages in context, however, are quite different - no doubt a function of the different historical circumstances under which the proverb performance took place. Isaiah of Jerusalem speaks of God's impending punishment of the apostate community and the majesty of Yahweh over against that of his human "tools," with Chapter 36-37 presenting a genuine example of proverb performance. Deutero-Isaiah uses traditional sayings to make a different point; he speaks a word of consolation to those who have already been punished and stresses the new redemptive action which God will institute. In this latter respect, Deutero-Isaiah's purpose in using a traditional saying corresponds to Ezekiel's affective uses (33:10 and 37:11) in the late oracles of Restoration, after the destruction of Jerusalem. It is interesting indeed that in a period of profound religious and social upheaval in the covenant community, each prophet marshals the traditional saying as an active weapon in the war against despair, drawing the same types of correspondences and transmitting the same message of ultimate redemption.

It is noteworthy, too, that much of the puposeful transmission of traditional sayings in the prophetic literature makes use of the "quotation" strategy. The Source (usually God through the medium of his prophet) often quotes a saying which reflects the response or attitude of the Receiver, the covenant community. This "position" of the Receiver, articulated in the traditional saying, is then appraised by God or his prophet. This may seem like a rather round-about way to further the end of Yahweh for his people, even though it represents a standard type of proverb performance strategy. We would suggest that, in the prophetic literature, the strategy or supposition (of the Receiver, quoted by the Source) - qualification (by the Source) takes on an added dimension in these interactions. By casting the attitudes of the Receiver in the form of a saying, the Source makes explicit the folk ideas which are actually functional for the covenant community at that time ("The way of the Lord is not just," etc.). By doing this, the Source presents a radically new Gestalt to the Receivers, one which bears little resemblance to the popular piety and hypocrisy which the prophets attacked. The shock and chagrin of the audience upon hearing their most deeply hidden and self-centered attitudes articulated in the form of a traditional saying - a powerful expression which carried great authority - and then ridiculed and denied by God through the prophet, must have had very great impact. Here is a type of indirection which shields not the Source, but the Receiver from direct confrontation with the awful truth - the truth of the community's misperceptions. This is presented in the appraisal, and must have descended upon the Receivers, still enmeshed in the implications of the traditional saying's content, with all of the force which language can wield. The covenant lord of Israel also appears as a "proverb user" par excellence in the prophetic corpus.

In summary, we may outline a representative model for all instances of "prophetic" proverb performance where Yahweh and his prophet are involved.

Traditional Sayings in the Old Testament

PROPHETIC PASSAGE	SOURCE X	RECEIVER Y	#	PROVERB SITUATION A	~	B	CORRELATION	CONTEXT SITUATION C	~	D	INTENT
Ezekiel 9.9	God quoting human proverb user	Ezekiel/ Israel	human/ divine tension	Lord has forsaken land	+	Lord does not see	≠	God still involved	+	will punish	E
12:22	God	ditto	Y's disbelief in X	days go by	—/→	visions unfulfilled	≠	days are here	→	visions fulfilled	E
16:44	God quoting human proverb user	Jerusalem	broken covenant	daughter	←	like mother	=	Jerusalem	←	foreign "mother"	E/A
18:2	God	Ezekiel/ Israel	human/ divine tension	father's activities	→	children's misfortune	→	Irael's previous activities	→	later communities to suffer consequences	E
18:25 (cf18:29; 33:17,20)	God quoting human proverb user	Ezekiel/ Israel	ditto	way of the Lord	≠	not just	≠	way of Israel	≠	is not just	E
33:10	ditto	ditto	ditto	transgression upon us	→	people waste away	≠	transgressions of people	—/→	not fatal (if they repent)	A
37:11	God quoting "bones" of Israel	ditto	ditto	bones dried up	+	hope gone	≠	bones raised up	+	restoration	A
Jeremiah 8:20	Jer. quoting people	pensée on people of Judah	prophet to audience or self	harvest over; summer past	+	no salvation	(=)	(drought?)			E
8:22	Jeremiah	pensée; people?	ditto	Q balm (physician)	= BE	in Gilead	=	health of people	≠	restored	E
12:13	God via prophet	(covenant community?)	(broken covenant?)	sown wheat/ tired out by activity	—/→	reap thorns/ profit no	=	productivity of people	—/→	no profit	E
13:12*	God via prophet	prophet/ then people	judgment	every jar	→	filled with wine	=	inhabitants of the land	→	made drunk and destroyed	E
13:23*	God via prophet	ditto	knowledge of God's plan	Ethiopian/ leopard Q	=	can't change	=	wickedness of Jerusalem	—/→	can't change	E
23:28*	ditto	Jeremiah & false prophets	ditto	straw	≠	wheat	=	false prophets	≠	true prophets (Jer.)	E/A
51:58 (cf.Hab. 2:13)	ditto	exilic community/ Babylon	ditto	people/ nations	—/→	labor for nothing/ weary only for fire	=	Babylon	—/→	will not prevail	E
Isaiah 10:15	God via prophet	Judah/ Assyria	human/ divine dichotomy	Q axe/saw	>	its user/ its user	=	Q tool, king of Assyria	>	God who wields tool	E
22:13	God/proph- et quoting revelers in Jerusalem	revelers to one another	knowledge of God's plan	people enjoying themselves	→	death comes	=	unrepentent people of Jerusalem	→	God will punish them	E
37:3* (cf66:9)	Hezekiah via messenger	Isaiah	knowledge of God's plan	children come to birth	≠	no strength to deliver	=	time to repel Assyria	≠	no strength to do so	E/A
Deutero- Isaiah Is.40:27	prophet	people	ditto	way is hid from God	+	right disregarded by God	≠	God, as creator, sees all (v.28)	+	gives strength to followers (vv.29-31)	E
49:14	God quoting Zion (divine appraisal)	Zion	human/ divine dichotomy	saying: God has forsaken	+	God has forgotten	≠	appraisal: mother forget	+	mother might forget; God will not	E
Hosea 8:7*	God via prophet	Israel	broken covenant	sow wind	—/→	reap whirlwind	=	Israel's foreign alliances	—/→	don't bring strength against God's judgment	E
Zephani- ah 1:12*	God quoting drunkards	people	ditto	Lord	—/→	won't do good or ill	≠	Lord	→	will punish	E

Notes: E = evaluative intent; E/A = evaluative-affective intent; A = affective intent.
   * may be genuine proverb performance (i.e., taking place in social interaction).
   ~ = relationship between proverb terms and contextual terms.

TABLE C-1: Prophetic Proverb Performance

BIBLIOGRAPHY

A. Reference Works

Bourke, Myles M., ed.
   Textual Notes on the New American Bible. New York: Kennedy, 1970.
Brown, Francis; Driver, S. R.; Briggs, Charles A.
   A Hebrew and English Lexicon of the Old Testament. Oxford: Clarendon, 1907.
Driver, Samuel Rolles.
   Notes on the Hebrew Text and Topography of the Books of Samuel. 2nd edn. rev. and enl. Oxford: Clarendon, 1966.
Jastrow, Marcus.
   A Dictionary of the Targumem, the Talmud Babli and Jerushalmi, and the Midrashic Literature. 2 vols, New York: Pardes, 1950.
Kautzsch, E., ed.; Cowley, Arthur E., transl.
   Gesenius' Hebrew Grammar. 2nd English edn. Oxford: O.U.P., 1910.
Kittel, Rudolf, ed.
   Biblia Hebraica. 3rd edn. Stuttgart: Württembergische Bibelanstalt, 1937.
- "Librum Samuelis." In: Biblia Hebraica, pp. 405-500.
Žaba, Žbynek.
   Les Maximes de Ptahhotep. Prague: L'Academie Tchecoslovaque des Sciences, 1956.

B. Other Works

Abrahams, Roger.
   "Introductory Remarks to a Rhetorical Theory of Folklore." JAF 81 (1968): 143-158.
- "A Rhetoric of Everyday Life: Traditional Conversational Genres." SAF 32 (1968): 44-59.
- "The Complex Relations of Simple Forms." Genre 2 (1969): 104-128.
- "Such Matters as Every Man Should Know and Descant Upon." Prov 15 (1970): 425-27.
- "Proverbs and Proverbial Expressions." In: Dorson, ed., Folklore and Folklife, 1972, pp. 117-128.

- "Toward an Enactment-Centered Theory of Folklore." In: Bascom, ed., Frontiers of Folklore, 1977, pp. 79-120.

Achebe, Chinua.
Arrow of God. London: Heinemann, 1964.
- Things Fall Apart. London: Heinemann, 1958.

Ackroyd, Peter R.
The First Book of Samuel. CBC. Cambridge: C.U.P., 1971.
- "Kings, I and II." IDB/S.

Albright, William Foxwell.
"A Votive Stele Erected by Ben-hadad I of Damascus to the God Melcarth." BASOR 87 (1942): 23-29.
- "An Archaic Hebrew Proverb in an Amarna Letter from Central Palestine." BASOR 89 (1943): 29-32.

Alster, Bendt.
The Instruction of Suruppak. Mesopotamia: Copenhagen Studies in Assyriology, 2. Copenhagen: Akademisk, 1974.
- Studies in Sumerian Proverbs. Mesopotamia: Copenhagen Studies in Assyriology, 3. Copenhagen: Akademisk, 1975.

Ammons, R. B., and Ammons, C. H.
"Use and Evaluation of Proverbs Test: Partial Summary Through March, 1976." Perceptual and Motor Skills 47 (1978): 1044-46.

Astour, Michael C.
"Amphictyony." IDB/S.

Audet, Jean Paul
"Origines comparées de la double tradition de la loi et de la sagesse dans le Proche-Orient ancien." Acten Internationalen Orientalistenkongresses (Moscow) no. 1 (1962), pp. 352-57.

Baalawy, Suleiman Omar Said.
Hadithi za Bibi Maahira. Nairobi, Kenya: Evans Bros., 1969.

Barley, Nigel.
"A Structural Approach to the Proverb and the Maxim." Prov 20 (1972): 737-50.
- "The Proverb and Related Problems of Genre Definition." Prov 23 (1974): 880-884.

Bartlett, John.
Bartlett's Familiar Quotations. 14th edn. rev. and enl. Ed. Emily M. Beck. Boston: Little, Brown, 1968.

Bascom, William R.
"Folklore and Anthropology." JAF 66 (1953): 283-90.
- "Four Functions of Folklore." JAF 67 (1954): 333-49. Repr. in: Dundes, ed., The Study of Folklore, pp. 279-98.
- ed. Frontiers of Folklore. American Association for the Advancement of Science. Selected Symposium, no. 5. Boulder, Co.: Westview Press, 1977.

Bibliography

- "Frontiers of Folklore: an Introduction." In: Bascom, ed., Frontiers of Folklore, 1977, pp. 1-16.

Bauer-Kayatz, Christa.
Einführung an die alttestamentliche Weisheit. BS 55. Neukirchen-Vluyn: Neukirchener, 1969.
- Studien zu Proverbien 1-9. WMANT 22. Neukirchen-Vluyn: Neukirchener, 1966.

Bauman, Richard.
"Settlement Patterns on the Frontiers of Folklore." In: Bascom, ed., Frontiers of Folklore, 1977, pp. 121-31.

Beardslee, William A.
"Uses of the Proverb in the Synoptic Gospels." Interpr 24:61-76.

Ben-Amos, Dan.
"Toward a Definition of Folklore in Context." JAF 84 (1971): 3-16.
- The Context of Folklore: Implications and Prospects." In: Bascom, ed., Frontiers of Folklore, 1977, pp.36-53.

Bentzen, Aage.
Introduction to the Old Testament. 2 vols. Copenhagen: Gad, 1948.

Bernstein, Basil.
"Social Class, Language and Socialization." In: Language and Social Context: Selected Readings, pp.157-58. Ed. Pier Paolo Goglioli. London: Cox & Wyman; Penguin, 1972.

Blair, Hugh.
Lectures on Rhetoric and Belles Lettres. Ed. Harold F. Harding with Forward by David Potters. 2 vols. London, 1783; reprint edn., Carbondale: Southern Illinois Univ., 1965.

Boling, Robert G.
Judges: Introduction, Translation and Commentary. AB. Garden City, N.Y.: Doubleday, 1975.

Bright, John.
A History of Israel. Philadelphia: Westminster; London: SCM, 1959.

Bruner, Jerome S.; Goodnow, Jacqueline J.; and Austin, George A.
"Categories and Cognition." In Culture and Cognition: Rules, Maps, and Plans, pp. 168-190. Ed. James P. Spradley. San Francisco: Chandler, 1972.

Bryce, Glendon E.
"'Better' - Proverbs: An Historical and Structural Study." SBL Seminar Papers, 108, 2 (1972): 343-54.

Budde, Karl.
Die Bücher Samuel. KHCAT 8. Tübingen: Mohr, 1902.

Burney, Charles Fox.
The Book of Judges with Introduction and Notes. London: Rivingtons, 1918.
- Notes on the Hebrew Text of the Books of Kings. Oxford: Clarendon, 1903.

Campbell, Edward F., Jr.
"The Amarna Letters and the Amarna Period." BA 23 (1960): 2-22.

Chomsky, Noam.
Aspects of the Theory of Syntax. Cambridge, Mass.: M.I.T., 1965.

Confucius.
The Sayings of Confucius. Arranged and illustr. by E. A. Cox. London: Chiswick, 1946.

Cooper, Lane.
The Rhetoric of Aristotle: an Expanded Translation with Supplementary Examples for Students of Composition and Public Speaking. New York: Appleton-Century, 1932.

Crenshaw, James L.
"Method in Determining Wisdom Influence upon 'historical' Literature." JBL 88 (1969): 129-42. Repr. in: SAIW.
- "Wisdom." In: Old Testament Form Criticism, pp. 225-64. Ed. John H. Hayes. San Antonio, Tx.: Trinity Univ., 1974.
- ed. Studies in Ancient Israelite Wisdom selected with a Prolegomenon by James L. Crenshaw. New York: Ktav, 1976.
- "Prolegomenon." In: SAIW, 1976, pp. 1-60.

Cross, Frank Moore, Jr.
"A New Qumran Biblical Fragment." BASOR 132 (1953): 15-25.
- Canaanite Myth and Hebrew Epic: Essays in the History and Religion of Israel. Cambridge: Harvard Univ., 1973.

Della Vida, G. Levi.
"Some Notes on the Stele of Ben-hadad." BASOR 90 (1943): 30-34.

Dever, William G.
"The Beginning of the Middle Bronze Age in Syria-Palestine." In: Magnalia Dei: The Mighty Acts of God [Festschrift G. E. Wright], pp 3-38. Ed. Frank M. Cross, Jr., W. Lemke, and P. D. Miller. Garden City, N.Y.: Doubleday, 1976.
- "The Middle Bronze I Period in Syria and Palestine." In: Near Eastern Archaeology in the Twentieth Century [Festschrift Nelson Glueck], pp. 132-63. Ed. James A. Sanders. Garden City, N.Y.: Doubleday, 1970.

Bibliography

Donner, Herbert.
  "The Separate States of Israel and Judah." In: Hayes and Miller, eds., Israelite and Judaean History, 1977, pp. 381-434.

Dorson, Richard M.
  ed. Folklore and Folklife: an Introduction. Chicago: Univ. of Chicago, 1972.
- "Introduction: Concepts of Folklore and Folklore Studies." In: Dorson, ed., Folklore and Folklife, 1972, pp. 1-50.
- "The Use of Printed Sources." In: Dorson, ed., Folklore and Folklife, 1972, pp.465-478.

Dundes, Alan.
  "Trends in Content Analysis." MF 12 (1962): 37-42.
- "Text and Context." SFQ 28 (1964): 251-65.
- ed. The Study of Folklore. Englewood Cliffs, N. J.: Prentice Hall, 1965.
- "The Study of Folklore in Literature and Culture: Identification and Interpretation." JAF 78 (1965): 136-42.
- "Folk Ideas as Units of Worldview." JAF 84 (1971): 93-103.
- ed. Analytic Essays in Folklore. Studies in Folklore, no.2. The Hague: Mouton, 1975.
- "On the Structure of the Proverb." In: Dundes, ed., Analytic Essays in Folklore, 1975, pp. 103-18.
- "Who Are the Folk." In: Bascom, ed., Frontiers of Folklore, 1977, pp.17-35.

Dundes, Alan, and Arewa, Ojo.
  "Proverbs and the Ethnography of Speaking Folklore." AA 66 (1964): 70-85. Repr. in: Dundes, ed., Analytic Essays in Folklore, 1975, pp. 35-49.

Eastman, Carol M.
  "The Proverbs in Modern Written Swahili Literature: an Aid to Proverb Elicitation." In: African Folklore, pp. 193-210. Ed. Richard M. Dorson. Garden City, N.Y.: Doubleday Anchor, 1972.

Ehrmann, Jacques, ed.
  Structuralism. Garden City, N.Y.: Doubleday Anchor, 1970.

Eichrodt, Walther.
  Theology of the Old Testament. Transl. J. A. Baker. 2 vols. Philadelphia: Westminster; London: SCM, 1961.

Eissfeldt, Otto.
  Der Maschal im Alten Testament. BZAW 24. Giessen: Töpelmann, 1913.
- The Old Testament: An Introduction. Transl. Peter R. Ackroyd. Oxford: Blackwell, 1965; repr. edn., New York: Harper & Row, 1976.

Elat, M.
The Campaigns of Shalmaneser III against Aram and Israel." IEJ 25 (1975): 25-35.

Eliade, Mircea.
Occultism, Witchcraft, and Cultural Fashions: Essays in Comparative Religions. Chicago: Univ. of Chicago, 1976.

Elliott, Phillips P.
"The Book of Judges: Exposition." IB 2: 688-826.

Fecht, Gerhard.
Der Habgierige und die Maat in der Lehre des Ptahhotep (5. und 19 Maxime). ADAIK 1. Glückstadt: Augustin, 1958.

Fichtner, Johannes.
- "Isaiah Among the Wise." Transl. Brian W. Kovacs. [Orig. pub.: ThZ 74 (1949): 75-80.] Repr. in: SAIW, pp. 429-38.
- Das Erste Buch von den Königen. BAT 12/1. Stuttgart: Calwer, 1964.

Firth, Raymond.
"Proverbs in Native Life with Special Reference to Those of the Maori." FL 37 (1926): 134-53, 254-70.

Fishman, Joshua A.
The Sociology of Language: an Interdisciplinary Social Science Approach to Language in Society. Rowley, M.A.: Newbury House, 1972.

Fohrer, Georg.
Introduction to the Old Testament. Transl. David E. Green, Nashville: Abingdon, 1968; London: S.P.C.K., 1970.

Forster, Eleanor.
"The Proverb and the Superstition Defined." Ph.D. diss., Univ. of Pennsylvania, 1968.

Fowler, Roger.
An Introduction to Transformational Syntax. New York: Barnes & Noble, 1971.

Gerstenberger, Erhard.
Wesen und Herkunft des sogenannten 'apodiktischen Rechts' im Alten Testament. WMANT 20. Neukirchen-Vluyn: Neukirchener, 1965.
- "Zur alttestamentlichen Weisheit." Verkündigung und Forschung 14 (1969): 28-44.

Giglioli, Pier Paolo, ed.
Language and Social Context: Selected Readings. London: Cox & Wyman, Penguin, 1972.

Gordis, Robert.
"Quotations in Wisdom Literature." JQR 30 (1939/40): 123-47. Repr. in: SAIW, pp. 220-44.
- "Quotations in Biblical, Oriental, and Rabbinic Literature."

HUCA 22 (1949): 157-219. Repr. in: Poets, Prophets and Sages: Essays in Biblical Interpretation, pp. 104-59. Ed. Robert Gordis. Bloomington: Indiana Univ., 1971.

Gordon, Edmund I.
Sumerian Proverbs: Glimpses of Everyday Life in Ancient Mesopotamia. Philadelphia: Univ. of Pennsylvania, The Univ. Museum, 1959.

Gorham, Donald R.
"A Proverbs Test for Clinical and Experimental Use." Psychological Reports 2 (1956): 1-12.

Gottwald, Norman K.
The Tribes of Yahweh: A Sociology of the Religion of Liberated Israel 1250-1050 B.C.E. Mary Knoll, NY: Orbis, 1979.

Gray, John.
I & II Kings: A Commentary. 2nd edn. rev. Philadelphia: Westminster; London: SCM, 1970.
- Joshua, Judges and Ruth. NCB. London: Thomas Nelson, 1967.

Gros Louis, Kenneth R. R.
"The Difficulty of Ruling Well: King David of Israel." Semeia 8 (1977): 15-33.

Guiraud, Pierre.
"Immanence and Transitivity of Stylistic Criteria. In: Literary Style: A Symposium, pp. 16-23. Ed. and transl. (in part) by Seymour Chatman. London: O.U.P., 1971.

Gressmann, Hugo.
Die Anfänge Israels (von 2. Mose bis Richter und Ruth). SAT I/2. Göttingen: Vandenhoeck & Ruprecht, 1922.

Gunn, David M.
The Fate of King Saul: An Interpretation of a Biblical Story. JSOTS 14. Sheffield: JSOT, 1980.

Haag, Herbert.
"Gideon - Jerubaal-Abimelek." ZAW 79 (1967): 305-14.

Hallo, William W.
"From Qarqar to Carchemish: Assyria and Israel in the Light of New Discoveries." In: The Biblical Archaeologist Reader, 2: 152-88. Ed. Edward F. Campbell, Jr. and David Noel Freedman. Garden City, NY: Doubleday Anchor, 1964.

Hallowell, A. Irving.
"Myth, Culture, and Personality." AA 49 (1947): 544-56.

Hayes, John H.; and Miller, J. Maxwell, eds.
Israelite and Judaean History. Philadelphia: Westminster; London: SCM, 1977.

Held, Moshe.
"Rhetorical Questions in Ugaritic and Biblical Hebrew."

Eretz-Israel 9 (1969): 71-79.
Hempel, Johannes.
Die Althebräische Literatur und ihr Hellenistisches-Jüdisches Nachleben. Handbuch der Literaturwissenschaft. Wildpork-Potsdam: Akademische Athenaion, 1930.
Hermisson, Hans-Jürgen.
Studien zur israelitischen Spruchweisheit. WMANT 28. Neukirchen-Vluyn: Neukirchener, 1968.
Hernadi, Paul.
Beyond Genre: New Directions in Literary Classification. Ithaca, NY: Cornell Univ., 1972.
Hertzberg, Hans Wilhelm.
Die Bücher Joshua, Richter, Ruth. ATD 9. Göttingen: Vandenhoeck & Ruprecht, 1953.
- I & II Samuel: A Commentary. Transl. J. S. Bowden. Philadelphia: Westminster; London: SCM, 1964. [Orig. pub.: Die Samuelbücher, ATD 10, 2nd edn. 1960.]
Herzog, George.
Jabo Proverbs from Liberia. London: O.U.P., 1936.
Heywood, John.
The Proverbs of John Heywood: Being the "Proverbes" of that Author Printed 1546. Ed. with Notes and Intro. by Julian Sharman. London: George Bell, 1874.
Hoffman, Daniel.
"Folklore in Literature: A Symposium." JAF 70 (1957): 1-24.
Holbek, Bengt.
"Proverb Style." Prov 15 (1970): 470-72.
Howe, E. S.
"Verb Tense, Negatives, and Other Determinants of the Intensity of Evaluative Meaning." Journal of Verbal Learning and Verbal Bahavior 5 (1966): 147-55.
Hussein, Ebrahim N.
Kinjeketile. East Africa: O.U.P., 1971.
Ittelson, William H.; Proshansky, Harold M.; Rivlin, Leanne G.; and Winkel, Gary H.
An Introduction to Environmental Psychology. New York: Holt, Rinehart, & Winston, 1974.
Jacobsen, Bent.
Transformational-Generative Grammar: An Introductory Survey of its Genesis and Development. North-Holland Linguistic Series. Amsterdam: North-Holland Publishing, 1977.
Jason, Heda.
"A Multidimensional Approach to Oral Literature." CA 10 (1969): 413-26.

Bibliography

- "Proverbs in Society. The Problem of Meaning and Function." Prov 17 (1971): 617-23.
Jepsen, Alfred.
  "Israel und Damaskus." AfO 14 (1942): 153-72.
- "Zur Melgart-Stele Barhadads." AfO 16 (1952-53): 315-17.
Johnson, Aubrey R.
  Sacral Kingship in Ancient Israel. Cardiff, Wales: Univ. of Wales, 1955.
Jolles, André.
  Einfache Formen. 3rd edn. Tübingen: Niemeyer, 1965.
Kapelrud, Arvid S.
  "King David and the Sons of Saul." In: La Regalitá Sacra, pp. 294-301. Studies in the History of Religions, Suppl. to Numen, 4. Leiden: Brill, 1959.
Kessler, Martin.
  "Narrative Technique in 1 Sm. 16, 1-13." CBQ 32 (1970): 543-54.
Kimmerle, Marjorie M.
  "A Method of Collecting and Classifying Folk Sayings." WF 6 (1947): 351-66.
Kirshenblatt-Gimblett.
  "Toward a Theory of Proverb Meaning." Prov 22 (1973): 821-27.
Koutsoudas, Andreas.
  Writing Transformational Grammars: an Introduction. New York: McGraw-Hill, 1966.
Krappe, Alexander H.
  The Science of Folklore. London: Methuen, 1930.
Kuusi, Matti.
  "Ein Vorschlag für die Terminologie der parömiologischen Strukturanalyse." Prov 5 (1966): 97-104.
- "Toward an International Type-System of Proverbs." FFC 211 (1972): 5-41.
Lambert, William G.
  Babylonian Wisdom Literature. Oxford: Clarendon, 1960.
Levin, Samuel R.
  The Semantics of Metaphor. Baltimore: Johns Hopkins Univ., 1977.
Lewy, Julius.
  "Les textes paléo-assyrians et l'Ancien Testament." RHR 110 (1934): 29-65.
Lichtheim, Miriam.
  Ancient Egyptian Literature. Vol. 1: The Old and Middle Kingdom. Vol. 2. The New Kingdom. Berkeley: Univ. of California, 1975.

Lindblom, Johannes.
  "Wisdom in the Old Testament Prophets." VTS 3 (1960): 192-204.
McCarter, Jr., P. Kyle.
  I Samuel: A New Translation with Introduction, Notes and Commentary. AB. New York: Doubleday, 1980.
McKane, William.
  I & II Samuel: Introduction and Commentary. London: SCM, 1963.
- Proverbs: A New Approach. Philadelphia: Westminster; London: SCM, 1970.
McKenzie, John L.
  The World of the Judges. Englewood Cliffs, N.J.: Prentice-Hall, 1966.
Malamat, Abraham.
  "The Aramaeans." In: Peoples of Old Testament Times, pp. 134-55. Ed. D. J. Wiseman. Oxford: Clarendon, 1973.
Malinowski, Bronislaw.
  Myth in Primitive Society. London: Kegan Paul Trench & Trubner, 1926.
Mao Tse-Tung.
  Quotations from Chairman Mao Tse-Tung. Ed. Stuart R. Schram with Intro. by Doak Barnett. New York: Bantam, 1967.
Marzal, Angel.
  Gleanings from the Wisdom of Mari. Studia Pohl, 11. Rome: Biblical Institute, 1976.
Mauchline, John.
  Samuel. NCB. London: Oliphants, 1971.
Mayes, A. D. H.
  "The Period of the Judges and the Rise of the Monarchy." In: Hayes and Miller, eds., Israelite and Judaean History, 1977, pp. 285-331.
Mazar, Benjamin.
  "The Aramean Empire and its Relations with Israel." BA 25 (1962): 98-120.
Meek, Theophile J.
  "1 Kings 20:1-10: Critical Notes." JBL 78 (1959): 73-75.
Mendenhall, George M.
  "'Change and Decay in All Around I See': Conquest, Covenant, and the Tenth Generation." BA 39 (1976): 152-58.
- "Tribe." IDB/S.
Messenger, John C., Jr.
  "The Role of Proverbs in a Nigerian Judicial System." SJA 15 (1959): 64-73. Repr. in: Dundes, ed., The Study of Folklore, pp. 299-307.

Bibliography

Mettinger, Tryggve N. D.
- King and Messiah: The Civil and Sacral Legitimation of the Israelite Kings. Coniectanea Biblica. Lund: Gleerup, 1976.

Mieder, Wolfgang.
- "The Essence of Literary Proverb Study." Prov 23 (1974): 888-94.

Miller, J. Maxwell.
- "The Elisha Cycle and the Accounts of the Omride Wars." JBL 85 (1966): 441-54.

Miller, J. Maxwell.
"The Fall of the House of Ahab." VT 17 (1967): 307-24.
- "The Israelite Occupation of Canaan." In: Hayes and Miller, eds., Israelite and Judean History, 1977, pp. 213-84.

Milner, Geroge B.
"Quadripartite Structures." Prov 14 (1969): 379-83.
- "What is a Proverb." New Society 332:29-48.

Montgomery, James A.
A Critical and Exegetical Commentary on the Books of Kings. ICC 10. Edinburgh: T. & T. Clark, 1951.

Moore, George Foot.
A Critical and Exegetical Commentary on Judges. ICC 7. New York: Charles Scribner's Sons; Edinburgh: T. & T. Clark, 1895.

Morgenstern, Julian.
"Chronological Data of the Dynasty of Omri." JBL 59 (1940): 385-96.

Mowinckel, Sigmund.
"General Oriental and Specific Israelite Elements in the Israelite Conception of the Sacral Kingdom." In: La Regalitá Sacra, pp. 283-93. Studies in the History of Religions, Suppl. to Numen, 4. Leiden: Brill, 1959.

Murphy, Roland E.
"Israel and Moab in the Ninth Century B.C." CBQ 15 (1953): 409-17.
- "Form Criticism and Wisdom Literature." CBQ 31 (1969): 475-83.
- "The Interpretation of Old Testament Wisdom Literature." Interpr 23 (1969): 289-301.
- "Wisdom Thesis." In Papin Festschrift: Wisdom and Knowledge, 2: 187-200. Ed. J. Armenti. 2 vols. Philadelphia: Villanova Univ., 1976.

Oesterley, William O. E., and Robinson, Theodore H.
An Introduction to the Books of the Old Testament. London: Macmillan, 1934.

Parker, Carolyn Ann.
"Aspects of a Theory of Proverbs: Contexts and Messages

in Swahili." Ph.D. diss., Univ. of Washington, 1973.

Peacham, Henry.
The Garden of Eloquence. A Facsimile Reproduction with An Introduction by William G. Crane. London: 1593; repr. edn., Gainesville, Fl.: Scholars' Facsimiles & Reprints, 1954.

Pedersen, Johannes.
Israel: Its Life and Culture. 4 vols. London: O.U.P., 1926; repr. edn., Copenhagen: Møller, 1946.

Permyakov, Grigory.
Izbrannłje poslovitsł i pogovorki narodov vostoka [Selected proverbs and sayings of the people of the East]. Moskva, 1968.

Pitts, Arthur W.
"John Donne's Use of Proverbs in His Poetry." Ph.D. diss., Louisiana State Univ., 1966.

Pope, Marvin H.
Job: Introduction, Translation, and Notes. 3rd edn. AB 15. Garden City, N.Y.: Doubleday, 1973.

Preuss, Horst D.
"Erwägungen zum theologischen Ort alttestamentlicher Weisheitsliteratur." Evangelische Theologie 30 (1970): 393-417.

Pritchard, James B., ed.
Ancient Near Eastern Texts Relating to the Old Testament. 3rd edn., with Supplement. Princeton, N.J.: Princeton Univ., 1969.

Rad, Gerhard von.
The Problem of the Hexateuch and Other Essays. Transl. E. W. Trueman Dicken. New York: McGraw-Hill; Edinburgh: Oliver & Boyd, 1966.

- "The Beginnings of Historical Writing in Ancient Israel." In: The Problem of the Hexateuch, pp. 166-204. [Orig. pub. in: Archiv für Kulturgeschichte 32 (Weimar 1944).]

- "The Deuteronomic Theology of History in I and II Kings." In: The Problem of the Hexateuch, pp. 205-21. [Orig. pub. in: Deuteronomium-Studien, FRLANT, n.s. 40 (Göttingen, 1947).]

- "Job XXXVIII and Ancient Egyptian Wisdom." In: The Problem of the Hexateuch, pp. 281-91. Repr. in: SAIW, pp. 267-77. [Orig. pub. in: VTS 3, 1955.]

- Old Testament Theology. Transl. D. M. G. Stalker. 2 vols. New York: Harper & Row; Edinburgh: Oliver & Boyd, 1965. [Orig. pub.: Theologie des Alten Testaments, München, 1957.]

- Wisdom in Israel. Transl. James D. Martin. Nashville:

Abingdon; London: SCM, 1974. [Orig. pub.: Weisheit in Israel, Neukirchen-Vluyn, 1970.]

Richter, Wolfgang.
Recht und Ethos: Versuch einer Ortung des weisheitlichen Mahnspruches. StANT 15. München: Kösel, 1966.

Ricoeur, Paul.
"Biblical Hermeneutics." Semeia 4 (1975): 29-145.

Robinson, Joseph.
The First Book of Kings: A Commentary. Cambridge: C.U.P., 1972.

Rooth, Anna B.
"Domestic Animals & Wild Animals as Symbols and Referents in the Proverbs." Prov 11 (1968): 286-88.

Rose, Ashley S.
"The Principles of Divine Election: Wisdom in 1 Samuel, 16." In: Rhetorical Criticism: Essays in Honor of James Muilenberg, pp. 43-67. Ed. Jared J. Jackson and Martin Kessler. Pittsburgh Theological Monograph Series, 1. Pittsburgh: Pickwick, 1974.

Sackett, S. J.
"Poetry and Folklore: Some Points of Affinity." JAF 77 (1964): 143-53.

Sandell, Rolf.
Linguistic Style and Persuasion. European Monographs in Social Psychology, 11. London: Academic, 1977.

Schmidt, Johannes.
Studien zur Stilistik der alttestamentlichen Spruchliteratur. Alttestamentliche Abhandlungen. Münster: Aschendorffschen, 1936.

Scott, Robert B. Y.
"Folk Proverbs of the Ancient Near East." Transactions of the Royal Society of Canada 55 (1961): 47-56. Repr. in: SAIW, pp. 417-26.
- Proverbs, Ecclesiastes. AB 18. Garden City, N.Y.: Doubleday, 1965.
- The Way of Wisdom in the Old Testament. New York: McMillan, 1971.
- "Wise and Foolish, Righteous and Wicked." VTS 23 (1972): 146-165.

Seitel, Peter.
"Proverbs: A social Use of Metaphor." Genre 2 (1969): 143-61. Repr. in: Folklore Genres, pp. 125-43. Ed. Dan Ben-Amos. Austin: Univ. of Texas, 1976.
- "Proverbs and the Structure of Metaphor Among the Haya of Tanzania." Ph.D. diss. Univ. of Pennsylvania, 1972.

Sen, N. B., ed.
    Wit and Wisdom of Gandhi, Nehru, Tagore. New Delhi:
    New Book Society of India, 1968.
Shakespeare, William.
    Romeo and Juliet. Ed. John E. Hankins. The Pelican
    Shakespeare. Baltimore, Md.: Penguin, 1971.
Simpson, Cuthbert A.
    Composition of the Book of Judges. Oxford: Blackwell,
    1958.
Simpson, William Kelly, ed.
    The Literature of Ancient Egypt: An Anthology of Stories,
    Instructions, and Poetry. New edn. New Haven: Yale Univ.,
    1973.
Skinner, John.
    Kings. NCB. New York: Henry Frowde, 1904.
Skladny, Udo.
    Die ältesten Spruchsammlungen in Israel. Göttingen:
    Vandenhoeck & Ruprecht, 1962.
Smith, Henry P.
    A Critical and Exegetical Commentary on the Books of
    Samuel. ICC 8. New York: Charles Scribner's Sons, 1904;
    Edinburgh: T. & T. Clark, 1899.
Smith, William Robertson.
    Lectures on the Religion of the Semites: the Fundamental
    Institutions. New rev. edn. London: A. & C. Black, 1914.
Soggin, J. Alberto.
    "The Davidic-Solomonic Kingdom." In: Hayes and Miller,
    eds., Israelite and Judean History, 1977, pp. 332-80.
Sokolov, Yuri M.
    Russian Folklore. Transl. Catherine Smith. New York:
    Macmillan, 1950.
Stockwell, Robert P.
    Foundations of Syntactic Theory. Englewood Cliffs, N.J.:
    Prentice-Hall, 1977.
Szikszai, S.
    "Kings, I and II." IDB.
Tadmor, Hayim.
    "Assyria and the West: the Ninth Century and its
    Aftermath." In: Unity and Diversity: Essays in the History,
    Literature, and Religion of the Ancient Near East, pp.
    36-48. Ed. Hans Goedicke and J. J. M. Roberts. Baltimore:
    John Hopkins Univ., 1975.
Taylor, Archer.
    "Problems in the Study of Proverbs." JAF 47 (1934): 1-21.
-   The Proverb and an Index to the Proverb. 2nd edn.

Copenhagen and Hatboro, Pa.: Rosenkilde & Bagger, 1962.
- The Study of Proverbs." Prov 1 (1965): 3-11.

Terrien, Samuel.
"Amos and Wisdom." In Israel's Prophetic Heritage, pp. 108-15. Ed. Bernhard W. Anderson and Walter Harrelson. New York: Harper & Row, 1962. Repr. in: SAIW, pp. 448-55.

Thiele, Edwin R.
The Mysterious Numbers of the Hebrew Kings: A Reconstruction of the Chronology of the Kingdoms of Israel and Judah. Chicago: Univ. of Chicago Press, 1951.

Tolkien, J. R. R.
The Lord of the Rings. Vol 1: The Fellowship of the Rings. New York: Ballantine, 1965.

Tsevat, Matitiahu
"Samuel, I and II." IDB/S.

de Vaux, Roland.
Ancient Israel: Its Life and Institutions. Transl. John McHugh. New York: McGraw-Hill; London: Darton, Longman & Todd, 1961.

Weiser, Artur.
The Old Testament: Its Formation and Development. Transl. Dorothea M. Barton. New York: Association; London: Darton, Longman & Todd, 1961. [Orig. pub.: Einleitung in das Alte Testament, 4th edn., Göttingen, 1957.]

Wellhausen, Julius.
Der Text der Bücher Samuelis. Göttingen: Vandenhoeck & Ruprecht, 1871.

Westermann, Claus.
"Weisheit im Sprichwort." In: Schalom: Studien zu Glaube und Geschichte Israels [Festschrift Alfred Jepsen], pp. 73-85. Ed. Karl-Heinz Bernhardt. Stuttgart: Calwer, 1971.

Wevers, J. W.
"Weapons and Implements of War." IDB.

Whiting, Bartlett Jere.
"The Origin of the Proverb." Harvard Univ. Studies and Notes in Philology and Literature 13 (1931): 47-81.
- "The Nature of the Proverb." Harvard Univ. Studies and Notes in Philology and Literature 14 (1932): 273-307.
- Proverbs in the Earlier English Drama. Harvard Studies in Comparative Literature, 14. Cambridge, Mass.: Harvard Univ., 1938.
- "Proverbs and Proverbial Sayings: an Introduction." In: The Frank C. Brown Collection of North Carolina Folklore, I: 329-591. Ed. Newman Ivey White. 7 vols. Durham, N.C.: Duke Univ., 1957-64.

Whitley, C. F.
  "The Deuteronomic Presentation of the House of Omri." VT
  2 (1952): 137-52.
- "The Sources of the Gideon Stories." VT 7 (1957): 157-64.
Whybray, R. N.
  The Intellectual Tradition in the Old Testament. BZAW
  135. Berlin: Töpelmann, 1974.
Wilson, Robert R.
  Genealogy and History in the Biblical World. Yale Near
  Eastern Research No. 7. New Haven: Yale Univ., 1977.
Wiseman, D. J.
  "Alalakh." In: Archaeology and the Old Testament, pp.
  119-35. Ed. D. Winton Thomas. Oxford: Clarendon, 1967.
Wolff, Hans Walter.
  Amos the Prophet: The Man and His Background. Transl.
  Foster R. McCurley with Intro. by John Reumann.
  Philadelphia: Fortress, 1973.
- Anthropology of the Old Testament. Transl. Margaret Kohl.
  Philadelphia: Fortress; London: SCM, 1974.
Yadin, Yigael.
  "Some Aspects of the Strategy of Ahab and David." Biblica
  36 (1955): 332-51.
Zimmermann, Frank.
  "Reconstructions in Judges 7:25-8:25." JBL 71 (1952):
  111-14.

LIST OF ABBREVIATIONS

AA	American Anthropologist
AAAS	American Association for the Advancement of Science
AB	Anchor Bible
ADAIK	Abhandlungen des Deutschen Archäologischen Instituts Kairo
AfO	Archiv für Orientforschung
ANET	Ancient Near Eastern Texts Relating to the Old Testament, 3rd edn., ed. James Pritchard
ARM	Archives Royales de Mari, I-X
ATA	Alttestamentliche Abhandlungen
ATD	Das Alte Testament Deutsch
BA	Biblical Archaeologist
BASOR	Bulletin of the American Schools of Oriental Research

Abbreviations

BAT	Die Botschaft des Alten Testaments
BS	Biblische Studien
BWL	Babylonian Wisdom Literature, William Lambert
BZAW	Beihefte zur Zeitschrift für die Alttestamentliche Wissenschaft
CA	Current Anthropology
CAH	Cambridge Ancient History, 3rd edn.
CB	Century Bible
CBC	Cambridge Bible Commentary
CBQ	Catholic Biblical Quarterly
FFC	Folklore Fellows Communications
FL	Folklore
FRLANT	Forschungen zur Religion und Literatur des Alten und Neuen Testament
GKC	Gesenius' Hebrew Grammar, 2nd English edn.
HUCA	Hebrew Union College Annual
IB	Interpreter's Bible
ICC	International Critical Commentary
IDB	Interpreter's Dictionary of the Bible
IDB/S	Interpreter's Dictionary of the Bible, Supplementary Volume
IEJ	Israel Exploration Journal
Interpr	Interpretation
JAF	Journal of American Folklore
JBL	Journal of Biblical Literature
JQR	Jewish Quarterly Review
JSOTS	Journal for the Study of the Old Testament, Supplements
KHCAT	Kurzer Hand-Commentar zum Alten Testment
MF	Midwest Folklore
NCB	New Century Bible
Prov	Proverbium
RHR	Revue de l'Histoire des Religions
SAIW	Studies in Ancient Israelite Wisdom, ed. James Crenshaw
SFQ	Southern Folklore Quarterly
SJA	Southwestern Journal of Anthropology
StANT	Studien zum Alten und Neuen Testament
ThLZ	Theologische Literaturzeitung
VT	Vetus Testamentum
VTS	Vetus Testamentum, Supplements
WF	Western Folklore
WMANT	Wissenschaftliche Monographien zum Alten und Neuen Testament
ZAW	Zeitschrift für die Alttestamentliche Wissenschaft

INDEX OF NON-BIBLICAL SAYINGS

Index of Non-Biblical Sayings

INDEX OF BIBLICAL PASSAGES

272

Index of Biblical Passages

Traditional Sayings in the Old Testament

2 KINGS		PROVERBS	
1	127	1-9	161
4:29	132	1:6	28
9:1	132	1:2-6	143
14:8	214n208	12:14	205n148
		3:25f	212n197
JOB	23	4:17	114
2:6	125	6:18,25	101
8:4	201n104	8:14	195n62
9:22,24	115	10:2	114
10:4	102f	10:4	144
12:11	185n158	10:15	19,82
12:12	60	10:23	113,144
12:12f	122	10:24	115
12:20	60	11:2	7,19
14:4	206n151	11:3	115
15:10	60	11:4,14	66
22:5-20	201n104	11:5,6	115
32:1-3	62,185n160	11:16,22	19
32:1-6,7-8	60	11:23,27	115
32:8	63	12:5	113
32:9	184n158	12:9	66
34	60-2	12:11	66,82
34:3	60,184n158	12:14	113,116
36:22	199n92	12:15	144
38:3	132	12:20	114
39:5-8	238	12:23	103
40:7	132	13:2	113
		13:3	86
PSALMS		13:5	114,116
2:7	125	13:6	103
21:2	101	13:8	19
25:17	101	13:12	101
27:8	101	13:23,24	19
33	103	14:3	144
33:13-15	101	14:4	19,82
23:18-19	102	14:7	144f
37:13	102	14:14	115
44:21	102	14:20	19
49:4	231,table B-1	14:30	101
90:12	101	14:32	115
110	125	15:1	86
121:4	101	15:2	66,144
139:23	102	15:5	144
141:4	114	15:11	102f

INDEX OF ANCIENT NEAR EASTERN TEXTS

INDEX OF AUTHORS

Index of Authors